Moral Education for a Secular Society

SUNY SERIES IN PHILOSOPHY OF EDUCATION
PHILIP L. SMITH EDITOR

.

MORAL EDUCATION
——————— for a ———————
SECULAR SOCIETY

The Development of *Morale Laïque* in Nineteenth Century France

Phyllis Stock-Morton

STATE UNIVERSITY OF NEW YORK PRESS

Published by
State University of New York Press, Albany

© 1988 State University of New York

For information, address State University of New York
Press, State University Plaza, Albany, N.Y., 12246

Library of Congress Cataloging in Publication Data

Stock-Morton, Phyllis, 1930-
          Moral education for a secular society: the development of morale
laïque in nineteenth century France / Phyllis Stock-Morton.
     p. cm.
     Bibliography: p.
     Includes index.
     ISBN 0-88706-737-9. ISBN 0-88706-738-7 (pbk.)
     1. Education—France—History—19th century. 2. Church and
education—France—History—19th century. 3. Moral education—
France—History—19th century. 4. Secularism—France—
History—19th century. 5. Laicism—France—History—19th century.
I. Title.
LA691.7.S76 1988
370'.944—dc19
87-22324
CIP

10 9 8 7 6 5 4 3 2 1

To Scott,
mon cher collègue

"Voilà l'originalité de la France. C'est le seul pays qui ait cherché à fonder une morale en dehors de la religion et de la métaphysique...

Ferdinand Buisson

Contents

Part IV
The Theory and Practice of Morale Laïque
123

Preface

This book began as, and continues to be primarily, an intellectual history of the development of *morale laïque* throughout the nineteenth century. However, it soon became clear that there were other people, whose voices would have to be heard beside the main figures: first of all, the lesser theorists, who turned the various stages into slogans to gain popular support; second, the vociferous opponents, religious and otherwise, whose arguments were the occasion for explanations and defense by the supporters; and third, the educators themselves, toiling in the vineyard to turn theory into practice. Without this additional cast of characters it would be difficult to show how the teaching of a secular morality in the French school system, or University as a whole, turned out the way it did. Therefore the seemingly disproportionate space given to minor thinkers.

In the years since embarking on this work, I have received aid and encouragement from a number of sources. Franklin Le Van Baumer, Robert R. Palmer, Ronald Geiger and the late Louis Greenberg read and commented on an early draft. Doris Goldstein not only read the manuscript, but provided invaluable advice and support at crucial stages. The American Philosophical Society provided a grant that enabled me to complete the material on Victor Cousin. The Intellectual History Seminar of the Institute for Research in History in New York provided a critique of one difficult chapter. And my husband, W. Scott Morton, with his unfailing ear for language, helped me arrive at more felicitous phrases than I might otherwise have found.

However, the book reflects in every case my own decisions, and I am therefore responsible for its failings.

Introduction

In company with the rest of the Western world, France has in modern times experienced progressive secularization in virtually every area of life. One of the most typically French developments in this direction has been the elaboration of a body of secular ethics. Various types of secular morality played complex roles in French intellectual life during the nineteenth century. D.G. Charlton discussed them in the context of intellectual history in his *Secular Religions in France;* in *Histoire de l'idée laïque au dix-neuvième siècle,* Georges Weill traced the general secularizing strain in the political and social life of France; Louis Capéran, in a series of volumes, *Histoire de la laïcité républicaine,* described the chaotic course of secularization under the Third Republic. Recently, general theories of secularization have associated it with "modernization," or with industrialization in general.

More complex theories by social scientists tend to account for the great differences in the course of secularization throughout the Western nations by concentrating on national patterns and their relation with the predominant religions. David Martin, in *A General Theory of Secularization,* for instance, differentiates among American, British, Russian, Calvinist, Lutheran and two Latin patterns, one of which is the French.

In the last, which involves an autocratic religion united with an autocratic state, the Revolution takes place, not against outside oppressors, but as a civil war; it involves the pitting of an irreconcilable secular ideology against that of an irreconcilable religious monopoly. In this situation, Martin notes, erosion of institutional religion tends to lead to erosion of belief as well; and an ethos of secularism, gradually gaining a mass following, confronts an ethos of religion identified with traditional elites.

This study is limited to a narrower topic. The term *morale laïque* belongs properly to the French Third Republic, and refers to the ethics taught in the public schools. However, its intellectual development spans more than a century; it is interwoven with changing social and political conditions that sometimes fostered, sometimes impeded it. The aim is to trace the development of the ethical theory—a theory of secular morality to be incorporated into the educational system of France, replacing the religious ethics based on, and closely tied to, the Catholic religion—while taking into account the non-

1

intellectual factors that both modified and favored it.

There has been a tendency among historians of the Third Republic to derogate the laic laws as merely efforts of a newly-dominant class to insure its domination for the future. It is certain that the ideology of education always represents the effort of the particular society to perpetuate itself. But the same point is made concerning the Reformation; yet few historians who make it would insist that Reformers' educational ideas were not worth investigating. Epiphenomenon or not, secularization takes place in the minds of human beings, and follows a slow development like any other major change. What is interesting about *morale laïque* is its persistence as an ideal, usually of the opposition, for a long time before the society it reflected actually came into being in France in the Third Republic. Thus it was not merely an educational program conceived by a group of bourgeois politicians to preserve the power of their group, although it was that also. It was an ongoing theme of French intellectual life, aspects of which were at every stage considered too radical by the establishment of the time, and only marginally recognized by the "official ideology".

The debates concerning a secular morality for educational purposes in nineteenth century France took place within the context of three historical traditions basic to every French thinker's understanding of the society. The oldest of these was the struggle between Church and State. By the seventeenth century the battle had been resolved in favor of the monarchy. The Church accepted royal absolutism in exchange for religious monopoly. Among its privileges was that of overwhelming influence on all education, and complete control of primary education. The Church felt its welfare to be so bound up with the monarchy that, as an institution, it opposed the Revolution and remained a center of opposition to every step in the democratization of French life for a century afterward. The predominance of the Church in education was to be reasserted in every period of political reaction (Restoration, Second Empire) and fought in every period of political liberalization (July Monarchy, Third Republic). As a symbol of the Old Regime living on in post-revolutionary France, the Church, and gradually the theology which it embodied, became anathema to progressive thinkers.

This brand of anti-clericalism did not, of course, begin with the revolution. It harked back to a second tradition, that of the Enlightenment. Drawing upon the skepticism born out of the religious wars, intellectuals began in the late seventeenth century to consider the negative and divisive effects of religious intolerance. Enlightened thinkers saw the Church as a regressive and oppressive force in French life; they labored to elaborate theories of the good society without benefit of clergy. Thus, nineteenth-century thinkers had a broad spectrum of ethical thought independent of religion to refer to in their own flight from a morality tied to Catholicism.

The third tradition was the teaching of morality as part of the school curriculum. Because of the position of the Church in education under the Old Regime, moral instruction had always been subsumed under the heading of religious training. The advent of the Revolution did not eliminate formal ethical training from the schools. Instead, the revolutionaries rang a change on the tradition by advocating the teaching of a civic or "republican" morality, rather than a religious morality. Writings on the subject of education during the Revolution clearly called for the schools to counteract the former influence of the Church in society and to prepare the students for citizenship in the new republic.

The development of *morale laïque* in the nineteenth century required the adaptation of these traditions to the changing social and political life of France. The profound shock of the Revolution had created "two Frances," which must somehow be brought together to operate as one society. The leading intellectuals who wrestled with this problem were united in their conviction that France could not return to the conditions of the Old Regime. But they shied away from radical attacks on the old verities, such as those made by the *philosophes,* which seemed in retrospect to have undermined all social order. While there was still a strong current of anti-clericalism in the society, religious ideals were making new headway in sections of the middle and upper classes in the early part of the century. Throughout the century the majority of Frenchmen of these classes rejected radical destruction of the old in favor of moderate reconstruction—from the *juste milieu* to the opportunistic republic.

However, the nineteenth century also marked the appearance on the political scene of those "laboring classes" who had made their debut in the Revolution. They became ominously evident in 1830, 1848, and 1871. How were they to be incorporated into the mainstream of political life, if at all? As the idea of universal suffrage gradually gained ground, so did the idea of universal education for good citizenship. As scholars have recently documented more and more fully, the lower classes, both peasant and working, were from the early part of the century increasingly alienated from the Church. How, then, were they to learn those moral precepts which would insure order in the society?

Only the secular state could step into the breach and educate the masses. On the one hand this would avoid delivering the minds of the young into the hands of the Church; on the other, it would provide an opportunity to inculcate into the people the values of the new society.

The French had always distinguished between *éducation,* or character-training, and *instruction,* or training of the intellect. Throughout the nineteenth century in France one sees a gradual secularization of *éducation* in the schools run by the state, following the elaboration of a secular morality conceived for this purpose. There were certain real problems involved in this process. What should be the new bases of the moral values of the society, originally founded on religious concepts? How far from religious concepts should moral theory move? And, once a secular moral theory had been achieved, how was it to be incorporated into education? At what levels of education could a secular morality be effective?

The intellectuals concerned with the working out of these problems were members of the educated elite. They may be divided into two groups. The first and largest were usually educators themselves, often graduates of the Ecole Normale Supérieure, bourgeois, and politically liberal for their time. As members of the educational establishment, they had a sense of their limitations and were therefore relatively moderate in their solutions. The second group was usually outside the establishment and tended to be more radical, for their time, than the first, both in their politics and in their formulation of secular morality.

The arguments for a strictly secular morality in education during the nineteenth century were based on the presumption that every citizen of a free society should know his rights and duties, and that the school system was the logical institution through which the state could insure that he learned them. By the end of the century, these arguments could be summed up as follows: all modern developments had taken place through a process of freeing thought and institutions from the Church and theological concepts. Therefore, education, even moral education, must be established on a secular basis. The Church was a regressive force; its morality as well as its politics were based on authoritarian principles. The ethics of a free man in a republic should be based on reason and conscience.

Furthermore, if tied to theology, moral teaching would be divisive in a state where freedom of religion was a principle, since all would not follow the same theology. And even in the case where all were nominally Catholic, a morality based on theology would lose its force in an age of declining religious belief. Only an ethic independent of religion, based on reason and conscience, was common to all men. But most important of all, such a common moral philosophy, taught to all children in free and obligatory primary schools, would unify a badly divided French society, insuring survival of the Republic.

Although the kernel of the case for *morale laïque* was a restatement of arguments already presented in the Enlightenment, the final version of the theory was the fruit of a century-long development based on the interaction of social and political conditions with philosophical trends. In fact, *morale laïque*, while developed intellectually, may be useful for its social and even political implications concerning French society. It was intended by its proponents as a tool for social control, through the formation of *honnêtes hommes* and good citizens. At the same time it was often conceived as a weapon against the traditional educator of society, the Church, which represented the forces of political reaction. The fact that the strictly moral ends sought by the reformers differed little, if at all, from those sought by the clergy should not obscure the importance of the differences in philosophical means employed by the two sides for obtaining these ends. The expounders of *morale laïque* considered their moral theory appropriate to a society of bourgeois liberalism, and that of the Church to a hierarchical monarchy. That *morale laïque* never went beyond the bounds of bourgeois liberalism is itself a significant indicator of the nature of French society at the time.

The efforts of French intellectuals to elaborate an official secular morality as an effective basis for social integration are unique, because of France's peculiar situation vis-a-vis the Church. Throughout the nineteenth century, the impetus for a practical, secular moral teaching in the schools remained strong, based as it was on a felt need for French moral unity. Their experience may be of interest in an age still marked by declining religious belief and rising social disorder.

PART I

The Enlightenment Secular Tradition

Introduction

The Revolutionary period, and the ideas that informed it, were the seedbed of all nineteenth century thought. All public personalities took their place in French society and politics according to what aspect of the Revolution, and therefore what type of Enlightenment thought, they supported.[1] Anticlericalism, whether moderate or radical, was one of the ideas inherited from that period. Universal education was another. And these had come together during the 1790s in plans for secular schools teaching a lay, or "republican" morality.

When Napoleon had come and gone, only those who opposed the Revolution altogether supported a strong role for the Church in society. But radicalism had a bad name. The supporters of liberalization in France bided their time until the Revolution of 1830, which they insisted was not a revolution at all, but only a change in the person of the king. In their moderate way, under the leadership of François Guizot and Victor Cousin, the "juste milieu" began the attempt to sidestep (certainly not confront!) the control of the Church in education, particularly in the area considered most important to citizenship in a liberalizing nation—the ethical training of the upper class.

There is reason to believe that they recognized the growing secularism of much of the upper and middle classes, and sought to provide a substitute moral philosophy to replace the religious. It is certainly clear that they were content to leave the lower classes, incapable of philosophy, in the arms of the Church.

The Enlightenment

FRENCH Enlightenment thought was basic to the development of secular morality in the nineteenth century; there is hardly a concept in that development that was not at least touched on by the *philosophes*. What follows is not an attempt to survey completely the ethical thought of that period,[1] but only to isolate those elements that were emphasized in the century to come.

They may be divided under three headings: (1) the arguments for and elaboration of a natural religion or morality, including the concepts of natural law and individual conscience; (2) the arguments for and elaboration of a social ethic; and (3) the arguments for the use of public education for moral training. References to all three are scattered throughout the works of the *philosophes*, many of whom showed little consistency and a great deal of confusion in the expression of their moral thought. They quoted one another, sometimes contradicted or modified their own former statements; they were ambivalent, in terms of both the bases and the aims of moral conduct. But they created a "climate of opinion" which led, first, away from the Church monopoly on morality, and then, toward a morality based on theories of social interaction. It would therefore be useful to summarize the statements of Enlightenment thinkers on morality which contributed to the nineteenth century development of *morale laïque* under the above-mentioned headings. While it may be argued that the main impetus for these statements was an animus against the Church, they form a relatively coherent body of ideas on morality which were later used by those engaged in trying to replace the Church as the arbiter of ethics.

Natural Religion

The emergence of the concept of natural religion, independent of Catholic theology, resulted from a weakening of the hold of the religious view of the world over the Western mind. This process began with the scientific revolution; it was heightened by the theological arguments of the Reformation. In France, however, the skeptical tendencies underlying the Enlightenment were mainly the result of reflection on the chaotic religious wars. Religious skepticism was the intellectual handmaiden of *politique*. Just as the latter led to theories of government independent of the Church, so the former led to theories of enlightenment independent of the Church.

The Christian view of "enlightenment" was that it was a gift of God, both through revelation and through man's God given reason. Even the nominalists of the late medieval period, while maintaining that the truths of religion were not explicable by reason, agreed that they must be accepted by faith. However, the defense of religious truth had led to social and political disorder. Morality, in particular, seemed to belong to neither side in the wars of religion. Thus, thoughtful observers, like Michel de Montaigne, turned from the idea that religion produced morality in human affairs. In his *l'Apologie de Raimond Sebond,* he noted that believers as well as their opponents tailored their actions to events, and even used religion as an excuse to gratify their passions. Truth seemed to change with time and place, to depend more on traditions than on firm objective principles.

Montaigne inaugurated the skeptical tradition by questioning the strict relationship between religion and morality. In the next century, during a similar period of religious chaos engendered by the revocation of the Edict of Nantes, Pierre Bayle picked up the argument of Montaigne, affirming, in his *Pensées diverses sur la comète,* that Christians were not necessarily good persons. Their motivations, like those of unbelievers, conformed more to their natural passions, their habits, their likes and dislikes, than to their beliefs; one's actions did not conform to one's creed. The supposition that a person who did not believe in a rewarding and punishing God could not live a good life was false to Bayle, as was the supposition that a good person lived morally. Believers could not be said to be more virtuous than atheists. In fact, Bayle postulated that a society of atheists would resemble pagan antiquity, where there were many moral persons.[2] In such a society reason alone, without any knowledge of God, could persuade one that some actions were good because they were useful and reasonable. Reason would be supported by reward and punishment, by the glory or infamy society attached to various actions.

Montaigne had noted that human beings tended to create God, about whom they could know nothing, in their own image. Bayle's skepticism was supported by the rise of Bible criticism and speculations on the origins and development of religious belief. Bernard Bovier de Fontenelle posited a gradual development of man's religious sense in his *Histoire des oracles* and *Origine des fables*. Religion, he wrote, arose out of man's need to explain the world about him. It was only later, as priests used oracles and superstitious fables, grafting symbolic meanings on them to control the people, that religion took on a moral character. Bayle's *Dictionnaire historique et critique* illustrated the latter point by critical examination of Bible stories. The tales on which moral teachings were based, he argued, were historically weak to begin with; as for their symbolic value for morals, it was added long after they were written. Bayle also delighted in pointing out the obviously immoral material in the Bible. Although he carefully covered himself with nominalist pleas to submit reason to faith,[3] his ironic treatment of religious material advanced the cause of skepticism by constant reiteration of the points that one was not necessarily moral because he was religious, and that a moral society was possible without belief in God. His *Dictionnaire* became the bible of the Enlightenment.

Before the eighteenth century, however, skepticism and the idea of a morality based on reason alone were confined to a small number of intellectuals. It was Montesquieu who first raised the question of the relationship between religion and morality in a literary work of widespread publication. His *Lettres Persanes* of 1821, a satirical correspondence between two Persians concerning the manners and morals of French versus Persian society, was a best-seller. It provided a foretaste of the widespread interest in other societies which grew apace in the eighteenth century; it also foreshadowed the relativism concerning religion which was to be more fully developed in *L'Esprit des lois*. Montesquieu also suggested, in Letter #83, that justice was a relationship which was always the same, whoever viewed it. He concluded that, even if there were no God, we should always love justice; that even without religion, we would be bound by the constraints of equity.

But it was Voltaire more than anyone else who, taking up Bayle's tone of ironic skepticism, shaped the *philosophes'* program of secularization. He continued the tradition of Bible criticism, pointing out contradictions in Scripture and dwelling on the immorality of Old Testament stories. In his *Dictionnaire philosophique,* he also supported the possibility of a good society of atheists. In his article on Fraud, he used a Confucian to argue that ordinary people could be taught sound morals without the aid of superstitious fables, on the basis of reason alone. Wherever it was not corrupted by prejudices induced by a religion of fear, reason would be valid, he insisted in the article called Atheist. Even before religion appeared, he wrote in Common Sense, humans possessed all the concepts necessary to the good life. Although he himself supported theism, he always claimed that a simple, uneducated person could derive ideas of God from observation of nature, without theology.

Diderot also supported the idea of a morality independent of religion. Disdainful of any metaphysical or philosophical basis for ethics in his *Encyclopédie* article on Pyrrhonism, he maintained that morality was not transcendent, but was to be found in human nature. In his article entitled Irreligious, he noted that the distinction which must be drawn between irreligion and immorality implied a similar distinction between religion and morality.

But it was Voltaire, with his hatred of the church's influence in French society, who constantly extended and popularized the thesis that had been only briefly stated by Bayle and Montesquieu—that morality, being universal, was not the property of any single religion, but was a natural endowment of humanity that rendered theology superfluous. This position, variously interpreted, was basic to Enlightenment moral thought. It was even used by the Jesuits in their quarrel with the Jansenists, and was based on natural law. To orthodox Catholic thinkers, natural law existed both in the structure of the universe and in the minds of men; it was a reflection of the essential rationality and justice of God. But enlightened men of the cloth were willing to state that morality existed in itself, even independent of God. Some theologians believed that humans had an innate sense of right and wrong. Basically, the position of the church was that natural law, and therefore any natural justice or morality innate in humanity, had its origin in God and His divine plan. Therefore, the Church, repository of God's revealed wisdom, was necessary to the moral life. But even with this modification, enlightened churchmen contributed considerably to the developing view that morality existed independent of organized religion.[4]

Voltaire, of course, always maintained that one could know nothing about God or the soul; therefore, theology was superstition. However, one could see the natural law working in the universe, and also the moral law working in society. In his *Poème sur la loi naturelle,* he asserted that a universal morality, consisting of a God-given concept of justice enshrined in individual conscience, existed before any religion. All religions partook of it, but it was independent of any of them, including Christianity. The problem was, did the moral sense come from nature or from nurture? Voltaire, an enthusiastic follower of Locke's psychology, had to admit the influence, even the necessity, of moral training; but he insisted that there was, to begin with, a kind of moral instinct which was nurtured and developed by proper upbringing. Its source was divine. As he explained in the *Epitre à Uranie,* the natural religion was written on the heart by the hand of God.

This was the first contribution of the Enlightenment to the development of a secular morality—the idea of a natural religion (or morality, which the *philosophes* considered the only important part of religion) inherent in all men. Diderot supported this view in *De la suffisance de la religion naturelle,* where he also viewed it as God-given. For most of the eighteenth century, and particularly for those *philosophes* most influential in the following century, deism was a necessary aspect of moral thought. The rewards and punishments of a future life were somewhat more in dispute. Voltaire treated the idea with some skepticism in his *Chinese Catechism,* while admitting that it might have pragmatic value for the moral life. However, in his articles on Religion and Soul, he asserted that the belief in an immortal soul was not necessary and could not be supported rationally, as could the belief in God. His natural religion was experienced in the form, not of fear, but of conscience.

This concept Voltaire shared with Rousseau, or at least with Rousseau's Savoyard Vicar, who stated:

> In following my method consistently, I do not draw these rules from the
> principles of a high philosophy, but find them in the bottom of my heart,
> written by nature in ineffaceable characters. . . . All that I feel to be good is
> good, all that I feel to be bad is bad: conscience is the best of all casuists; and
> it is only when one bargains with her that one has recourse to the subtleties of
> reasoning.[5]

The Vicar argued for the innateness of morality and offered examples of natural indignation at the sight of injustice. Agreeing that all people had the same ideas of justice and honesty, he nevertheless insisted that the moral sense was not so much a rational judgment as an emotional feeling.[6] The Vicar also referred to "la religion naturelle" which included belief in a just God, who prescribed justice for human beings and who judged our actions in a future life. But even the Vicar admitted the necessity for education, thereby indicating a problem similar to Voltaire's concerning nature and nurture.[7]

This problem was solved in the other works of Rousseau, which did not support the concept of an innate moral sense adequate for ethics. All the rest of *Emile* emphasized the importance of education. "The natural man was all for himself," Rousseau declared, and the job of moral education was to denaturize man.[8] Conscience existed, but could not be developed without reason.[9] This position was also stated in the second discourse, where humanity in the state of nature was pictured as amoral, and right was the right of the strongest. Even when humans developed intelligence, each placed his own well-being above that of all others. The only moral sentiment Rousseau recognized was pity. It was when small societies began to form—when nurture was added to nature—that morality began to appear.[10] Thus, when Rousseau stated in *Emile* that our first duties were toward ourselves, he was viewing the natural child as immoral. The first sentiment of justice, he insisted, did not come from what we felt obliged to do, but from what we felt was owed to us.[11] Rousseau was one of the first to assert that our rights, as we perceived them, were the basis of our duties, which we by logical reason perceived as being owed to others.

Diderot also expressed a similar proposition on the evolution of moral relations among humans. In his *Dialogue between the Sage and the Proselyte,* the sage asked what were the duties of man. The answer: to make himself happy, from which derived the necessity to contribute to the happiness of others, or in other terms, to be virtuous. Diderot presumed that the right to personal happiness, combined with the natural identity of all human beings, made every person's rights the duties of his neighbors. Refuting Helvétius' supposition that justice presupposed established laws, he argued that interest could lead only to the identity of wills, if each individual conceived that it was just to do for all that which all agreed to do for him.[12] Thus, justice was pictured as a kind of balance between rights and duties, based on the fact that everyone had rights.

There was clearly some confusion in the minds of the *philosophes* on the subject of natural religion and the extent to which morality was innate. Exposure to different cultures quickened the Enlightenment tendency to try to find a common basis for all moral behavior. Where the Church found it in theology, the *philosophes* attempted to find it in human nature, either as a God-given conscience, or, in Rousseau, as a natural sense of pity for one's fellow creatures, which innate sense could be developed through the use of reason. Justice between individuals existed as a natural relationship similar to a physical relationship. For Voltaire and Diderot, the difficulty was their adherence to Lockean psychology, which eliminated innate ideas. Thus, the role of nurture, or education in morality, grew larger as the century progressed.

Social Ethics

One solution to the problem of morality without religion was to view it not at the level of the individual, but at the level of society as a whole. If justice was the assumption that one person's rights were another person's duties, then not only was reason necessary, but also organization in a society which assumed that all had equal rights. Rousseau defined society as a body of men dedicated to their mutual preservation, which created laws to regulate their relationships. These laws were the rules of justice; and the source of justice was the rights of each individual.[13] Enlightenment thinkers assumed that, just as there were unvarying laws regulating the physical universe, so there must be laws operating in social life as well, which one could discover through reason. Rousseau assumed no morality before the species became engaged in social life. No society, no justice.[14]

Diderot noted that the limits of our natural inclinations were marked by the rules of justice. That is, by the common interest of men united in society, and by the constant object of that union. In his *Encyclopédie* article on Interest, he even alluded to the concept of social debt, which was later developed in the nineteenth century—that one born into society received advantages which he must repay by service; that one had to fulfill his duties to follow the laws, to preserve the dignity of others. The organization of society was the basis of morality. The physiocrats also stressed the mutual interdependence of individuals in society as the basis for norms of conduct, and saw obligations as deriving from the rights of individual persons.[15]

The problem here was, what was the source of and justification for justice in society? Was it a relationship among individuals, worked out empirically, in which the justification was the happiness of society in general? Or was there an ideal relationship among human beings, a justice existing prior to men's discovery of it, as Montesquieu had implied? The utilitarians—Helvétius, d'Holbach, Condillac, etc.—supported the first view. Self-interest, based on pleasure and pain, was the basis for banding together in society in the first place; after that, the good was the happiness of the greatest number. Helvétius said that rectitude in a particular society was the practice of actions useful to that society.[16] The relations among men which would produce this end were regulated by laws agreed upon by the members of a society in their own self-interest. Thus, virtue in a society was merely the effect of the wisdom of its laws, and of the daily experience which proved their usefulness. Justice in this sense was the contribution of each man toward the happiness of the society he lived in.[17]

However, other *philosophes* saw justice as a universal concept, necessarily arrived at through reason and experience, and insisted that since people were everywhere the same, the same basic ideas of justice would arise among them. For Voltaire and Diderot, this solution seemed not to conflict with their gradual conversion toward sensationalist materialism. Neither one could accept as adequate a narrow physical basis for morality. Both insisted that human beings had developed a moral nature on top of their physical one.[18] The difficulty was that although both men supported a social morality, they were limited by their own highly developed individualism in their thinking on what a society was.

General Will

It was Rousseau who solved this problem in his *Contrat social*. He did not see conscience, even combined with reason, as sufficient to overcome natural egoism.[19] The individual's pursuit of his own self-interest could only be vitiated by being transcended—not in a religious, but in a social sense. Thus, he posited the concept of the general will. Diderot had referred to something similar in his article in the *Encyclopédie* on Natural Rights. Noting the chaos in a society where each person would follow his own will, he called upon reason to adjudicate. However, this could not be the reason of any individual; it must be a general reason, which would arrive at a solution in accord with the general good. The general good was known to reason from the experience of human society. Thus, to Diderot the general will, or general reason, was synonymous with natural law.

For Rousseau, on the other hand, it was the will of the collective organism, society, and it flowed from the social contract, a human act.[20] In this way, Rousseau raised the problem of morality to the social level without transcending the individual. In his own *Encyclopédie* article, he wrote:

> The political body is thus a moral being which has a will; and that general will, which tends always toward the conservation and well-being of the whole and of each part, and which is the source of the laws, is for all the members of the State, in relation to them and to it, the rule of justice and injustice.[21]

This was Rousseau's first elaboration of the general will, in 1755.

In the *Contrat social*, Rousseau synthesized the moral thought of the Enlightenment in three ways: along with the natural law adherents he retained the idea of an objective justice; with the deists, he stated the necessity of belief in a God who rewards and punishes; and yet he preached along with the utilitarians a social morality totally human in its establishment. "What is good and conforms to the social order is such by the nature of things and independent of human conventions," he wrote.

> All justice comes from God, he alone is the source; but if we knew how to receive it from so high, we would have no need for government or for laws. Without doubt, there is a universal justice emanating from reason alone; but this justice, to be admitted among us, must be reciprocal. . . . Conventions and laws are needed to unite rights and duties and to restore justice to its object.[22]

Thus, although universal, God-given justice existed, it was not always available to man through his reason, and must be approximated by human conventions. In fact, in the first draft of the *Contrat*, Rousseau expressed the belief that we gained our notions of justice, not from our own reason, but from the society which already surrounded us, which disposed us to morality by laws already made. In the human world, anyway, "law [that is, an act of the general will] is anterior to justice, and not justice to the law."[23]

However, one did not, as the utilitarians insisted, concur in the common good from self-interest.[24] Rousseau always saw the interests of the individual as antithetical to those of the society as a whole. Thus, although he admitted the existence of an ideal justice, he did not see it as inherent in human nature or in any natural society that human beings could form. That is why a new moral being had to be created by the social contract. Rousseau's view of the contract was, first, that it was a convention, an agreement to associate in the most complete manner, with each member of the association forming an indivisible part of the whole; and second, that this whole was a new "moral being," greater than the sum of its parts, and directed by the general will.

It was easier to say what the general will was not than what it was. It was not the will of God, or at least no one could know that it was, because Rousseau did not believe that one could know ideal justice; it was not the voice of the majority, for the general will was indivisible; it was not necessarily even the unanimous vote of the people, who could also err in practice. However, if the people were sufficiently informed, if there were not partial associations which could represent partial or private wills within the general association, the deliberations of the people would always yield the general interest, which would be good.[25] Thus, Rousseau implied that ideal justice, which could not be attained by the reason of the individual, could be attained by the unified will of the totally associated society. The aim of political union was the unification of the wills of all its members into a general will.

It is well known that Rousseau's concept of the general will was influential in the thinking of Immanuel Kant; Kant, in turn, provided the basis for the overwhelming portion of French moral thought in the nineteenth century. His formulation of the categorical imperative was the corollary of Rousseau's general will: act so that the maxim of thy will can always at the same time be valid as a principle of universal legislation. At the same time, Kant adopted the Savoyard Vicar's view of conscience, an indispensable element in the thinking of future generations. In Kant, as in Rousseau, conscience was grounded in free will; at the same time, it was somewhat like the general will, a human connection with the universal, with will as universal reason.[26]

In practice, however (and Rousseau was more concerned with practice than Kant), for a society to arrive at the general will required that the people be properly informed. Rousseau was convinced that the multitude was usually unenlightened as to what was good for it. "The general will is always right, but the judgment which guides it is not always enlightened. . . . " Thus, leadership was required. "It is necessary to oblige some to conform their wills to reason; it is necessary to teach another to know what he wants. . . . From this is born the need for a Legislator." The Legislator was needed because, as Rousseau had already pointed out, the law preceded justice in the shaping of popular morality. The Legislator, like the social contract itself, was merely an ideal in Rousseau's thought, and even he was uncomfortable with the idea. As he admitted, "one needs gods to give laws to humans." The Legislator would undertake the task of denaturing the natural man and making him part of the new moral being which was society, through a code of law; to guard against corruption, he would have no executive powers. Only after this original code was established would humans be able to attain the general will and legislate for themselves.[27]

Just as Rousseau did not trust the natural man to found the good society, he did not trust the associates of the social contract not to slip back into their natural state. The morality of the people would have to be guarded by a civil religion which would make them love their duties. The dogmas of such a religion would be only those which were useful to society—"sentiments of sociability without which it is impossible to be a good citizen or faithful subject"—rather than actual dogmas. Rousseau summed them up as belief in the existence of a powerful and omniscient God; in the immortality of the soul, with rewards and punishments for good and evil; and in the sanctity of the social contract and the laws. All other religious beliefs would be purely personal.[28]

What was involved here was the role of education in the development of a moral society, a subject on which the *philosophes* discoursed at length. It was generally agreed that "enlightenment" was necessary for all; and there was much discussion of the role of the lawgiver, whether the enlightened despot guided by the *philosophes,* as with Voltaire and Diderot, or the shadowy Legislator of Rousseau, d'Holbach, Mably and Helvétius. "The virtues and the happiness of a people are the effect not of the sanctity of its religion; but of the wisdom of its laws."[29] The idea of a secular moral catechism was also general. For some, the mere education of the intellect was viewed as necessarily contributing to the progress and happiness of society.[30]

The sensationalists presumed that all men would be truly equal if given the same education. But the role of education in forming good citizens was most important. Diderot's *Encyclopédie* article Législator stated that the state should, through education, inspire community spirit and love of country as well as public and private virtue. Rousseau's legacy to educational theory is usually thought of in terms of *Emile* and the development of the natural child. However, Emile's education was controlled by a tutor who was, in many ways, the parallel of the Legislator of the *Contrat;* he knew the results he wished to obtain. In the opening pages of the book, Rousseau spoke of the necessity for social institutions to change the natural man to fit him into the social order. There is evidence that Rousseau intended to add to a new edition of *Emile* a section on the relationship of public and private education; unfortunately, the projected new edition was lost.[31] In his *Considérations sur le gouvernement de Pologne,* he suggested an equal education for all, with emphasis on team sports and student government, with the aim of producing patriotic and cooperative citizens. It would be conducted by the state, and not by priests.[32]

The preoccupation with public education for citizenship was not confined to the small circle of *philosophes.* There were other reasons in the eighteenth century for public control of education. The power of the Church, and particularly of the Jesuits, in French society made those who supported the monarchy against the Church cast a cold eye on clerical control of education.

After the publication of *Emile* in 1762 had stirred debate, La Chalotais published a polemic in which he made the following points: that education should be by and for the state; that it should be organized to prepare for given functions in society; that morality should be taught independent of religion; and that only laymen should be teachers. The divine law might belong to the Church, he wrote, but the moral law belonged to the state. It did not depend upon revelation, because it existed before it was revealed.[33]

The king was advised by Turgot that national education should be directed in the public interest by a national council. Since manners and customs constituted the strongest bond in a nation, childhood instruction in social duties should be a national concern.[34] Thus, the link between education—particularly moral education—and politics was made before 1789. It was the men of the Revolution who attempted the first concrete application of that link.

The Secular Approach to Moral Education

BEFORE the Revolution, there was no system of public education in France. Largely under local and clerical auspices, existing primary schools were uniform only in terms of religion. (Protestant schools had been closed down with the revocation of the Edict of Nantes; some had reopened clandestinely.) The daily routine in all schools included prayers, and usually attendance at mass. Royal decrees of 1694, 1698 and 1724 on compulsory attendance at school were generally ignored, so most French children did not attend at all.[1] Many of those who did attended schools of the religious orders—Jesuit, Frères des écoles chrétiennes, Oratorian. Enlightenment discussions on education centered on the problem that the primary goal of religious education was a religious person, rather than an enlightened one. In the *cahiers de doléance,* however, a majority seemed satisfied with religious control of education, although some sought joint civil and religious surveillance of the schools.[2] Only 137 out of 522 general *cahiers* advocated state intervention in education.[3] Nevertheless, some *cahiers* of all three estates showed an interest in public education—those of the first and second as a way of forming moral citizens, those of the third as a way to raise the intellectual level in preparation for a rational egalitarian society. Most significant of all, the majority of the third estate *cahiers* dealing with the problem, along with some of those of the second estate, called for public education separate from the Church and under control of the state, with a corps of lay teachers.[4]

From the early stages of the Revolution, there was a concern that the schools support the changes taking place in the society. The Constituent Assembly decreed on December 21, 1789 that assemblies in each department oversee public education, including moral and political teaching.[5] The Constitution of 1791 provided for a common public education for all citizens, free in its elementary stage. Departmental administrators were ordered to see that historical, political and moral instruction was inspired by the Declaration of Rights and the Constitution. They were to give a "civic education conforming to the spirit of the Revolution and no longer a purely religious education."[6] On January 8 of that year, the rector of the University of Paris had publicly sworn to uphold the work of the Constituent Assembly and had been told by its president, "Teach your students that they have rights to preserve, duties to fulfill. . . . Teach them above all to respect . . . morality, law, religion."[7] Thus, religion was not immediately separated from morality by revolutionary leaders. Religion was still to be taught in the schools, but moral instruction for citizenship was to be added.

Revolutionary Education Projects

Numerous projects on education were submitted to the Assembly during 1791. Finally, Talleyrand was charged by that body to prepare a report on the subject, which was presented on September 19. Although it recommended teaching religion, it presented the teaching of morality as a utilitarian function of the school in a society where everybody must know his rights and duties. Therefore, the Declaration of Rights and the Constitution should become "a new catechism for childhood," which students would learn to defend and perfect. As for morality, "which is the primary need of all constitutions," it was necessary "not only that one engrave it on all hearts by means of sentiment and conscience, but that one teach it as a veritable science whose principles are demonstrable to the reason of all persons and of all ages." Talleyrand's support of universal morality separate from religion was buttressed by the argument that, although people might be divided in various other ways, they could be united on the ground of ethics. Therefore, morality must be taught as a subject in itself. "How can one not see in effect that, leaving out of account all systems, all opinions, and considering human beings only in their relations with other humans, one can teach them what is good, what is just. . . . "[8]

Unfortunately, the main effect of the Constituent Assembly on the schools was chaos, since the financial support of existing education disappeared with the Civic Constitution of the Clergy, and the new government was incapable of replacing the old schools with new ones. Nevertheless, the new Legislative Assembly provided for a Committee of Public Instruction of 22 members.[9] Its outstanding participant was Condorcet, a *philosophe* associated with the sensationalist school, who considered education the crux of the progress he confidently expected would result from the new order. He too had pondered the relationship of religious instruction to public education. In his *Mémoire sur l'instruction publique,* he noted the difficulty of either including or excluding religious education in the schools—the attitude of the parents. He concluded, however, that religious education should be left to the parents themselves, and that the state must "render the teaching of *morale* rigorously independent of these opinions." Above all, education should not be left to the religious orders. Condorcet opposed any "body of doctrine which must be taught exclusively," because this would be submitting future generations to the beliefs of the past. Rather, each generation should be more enlightened than the last, more capable of self-government and reason.[10]

On April 20-21, 1792, Condorcet presented to the Assembly a report and project on education, in the name of the Committee. Speaking of the purposes of education, he laid emphasis on the moral ends to be served—an emphasis which appears in almost identical language in every educational project of the revolutionary period. "To offer to all the individuals of the human species the means to provide for their needs, to assure their well-being, to know and exercize their rights, and to fulfill their duties."[11] In the elementary school, the students should learn:

> . . . the development of primary moral ideas and those rules of conduct which derive therefrom; then they should learn those principles of social order understandable to children. The Declaration and the Constitution should be taught, not as having been ordained by heaven, but as having developed out of basic principles dictated by nature and by reason, whose eternal truth you have learned to recognize in your early years.[12]

In a note to the 1793 edition of this report, Condorcet expressed his belief in a natural moral sentiment, which could be developed by the application of reason to moral rules: " . . . and one will have no need to teach or prove the precepts, but only to point them out, because they will be found in advance in the minds of the children." In another note, he urged the application of the method of the physical sciences to the moral sciences and philosophy.[13]

Condorcet seemed to believe that there was, as some *philosophes* had argued, a natural religion or morality, which was to be understood through reason and developed by fortifying certain moral tendencies innate in human beings. In the report, he spoke of "natural justice, the essential rights of man, of which the laws are only the development or the applications." Thus, the principles of morality taught in the schools of France would be "those which, founded on our natural sentiments and on reason, pertain equally to all." It would be a morality completely separated from the principles of any religion; and no religion would be taught in the schools. Condorcet gave two reasons for this. First, the Constitution recognized freedom of religion, so public institutions could not favor one over others. And second, morality based on reason alone would survive any change of beliefs which might take place in the course of life.

In a note added to the 1793 edition, he emphasized that the elements of religion useful to morality were those which were common to all religions—belief in a supreme being and its corollaries. There was no utility in teaching the mythology of a particular religion; nor could the public power be the judge of the truth of a religion. Therefore, the development of morality could be accomplished in the schools only through the development of reason and individual conscience.[14]

Nor should the clergy serve as teachers. Condorcet's memoir of 1793, *Sur la nécessité de l'instruction publique,* emphasized the need for education to preserve people from the snares of the clergy. "It would then be a betrayal of the people not to give them, in a moral instruction independent of any particular religion, a sure protection against this danger which menaces its liberty and its happiness."[15] It is clear that Condorcet thought of moral education in the schools as the teaching of a morality of citizenship.[16] However, he did not envisage a state-controlled educational system, but rather administration by local bodies on the elementary level, and by a society of learned men on the upper levels; this would preserve that independence of ideas he felt was essential to progress.[17]

The proposed law included moral education at every level: "the first moral teachings" in the primary schools; "the development of the most important points of morality and social science" at the secondary level; and, in higher education, "metaphysics and theory of moral sentiments, natural law, people's law and social science, public law and legislation, economics, politics and history."[18] Not only the children would be exposed to the principles of morality beneficial to society. On Sundays the teacher would deliver public lectures for adults for the purposes, among others, of developing the principles of morality and natural law, of teaching the Constitution and the laws necessary to all good citizens. Books would be written for different ages and sexes to teach the rights and duties necessary to man in society. Condorcet also suggested periodic national celebrations, which would teach the people to cherish the rights and duties they had learned.[19]

Condorcet's report, and the accompanying project, was a summation of enlightened thinking on moral education. It presumed a natural morality based on deism, which existed as a part of the order of the universe and therefore was available to human reason; this was supported by an innate moral sense in man which could be fortified by reason and training. Reason would indicate that morality was useful to society; indeed, this usefulness was a prime factor in the necessity for moral training in the schools. The further development of moral knowledge and the sciences connected with it, such as law and political economy, would lead to the progress of the society and the greater happiness of humanity. Condorcet's work in the field of education was also basic to all later projects on education propounded during the revolutionary period. The teaching of a universal morality, its connection with the welfare of society, the public lectures and celebrations—all appear in later presentations, and may be presumed to be the common coin of enlightened thought on education at the time.

The discussions of the Legislative Assembly on education were halted by the outbreak of the war. Condorcet's project, in slightly altered form, was introduced again on December 12, 1792, by François Lanthenas. By this time, the anticlerical climate had become more pronounced, and there was applause from the Girondin benches at the passage excluding the clergy from teaching. In the debate which followed, Jacob Dupont de l'Indre confessed himself an atheist and opposed any religious training for children at all. "Do you think, then, citizens and legislators, to found and consolidate the French republic with altars other than those of the nation, with emblems or religious symbols other than those of the trees of Liberty?"[20]

There also developed a split in the ranks of the Education Committee between those who saw education as primarily a process of character-building for the benefit of society, and those who insisted upon an encyclopedic education of the intellect as well. Pierre-Toussaint Durant-Maillane, a Rousseauist, insisted that all that was necessary was to teach the people to be good citizens: "The French people, in order to be happy, have no need for the sciences except for those which lead them to virtue." He spoke against the elitism of the learned and for the simple *honnête homme*. All that was necessary for a virtuous republican was reading, writing, and "the understanding of the principles of natural, civic or political morality." the latter could be embodied in a "common book which would be treated as a national catechism, for the usage not only of children but also of their fathers."[21]

The writing of such texts, and their adoption for use in the schools by departmental juries, proceeded apace, and resulted in republican ABC's, republican moral catechisms, republican gospels and epistles, republican commandments, and even republican grammars, which attacked the old order—its kings, priests, superstitions, etc.[22] Almost all speakers on education before the convention justified the separation between morality and religion on the bases of unifying the nation and excluding the priests from the schools. "The primary condition of public education is to teach only truth. Therefore the law on the exclusion of priests," declaimed one speaker.[23]

Most speakers felt that the schools should provide both *instruction,* which developed the mind, and *éducation,* which developed the character. Bertrand Barère called for the replacement in the Constitution of the first term by the second, but it was deemed unnecessary. Charles-Gilbert Romme, presenting his project on December 20, after interruption of the education debates by the trial of the king, declared: "Let us from now on associate instruction and education: the one will be the guide and the other the torch of the social life."[24]

The supposition upon which this role of the school was based was stated by Danton, when demanding that education be obligatory: that children belonged primarily to the Republic rather than to their parents, and that they should be nursed by the Republic in the schools of the nation.[25]

As the convention proceeded to organize the cult of the Republic, it was this cult which was called for as a replacement for religious training in the schools. Morality in education gradually came to mean a civic religion, with regular readings of the Declaration of Rights, civic chants and patriotic fervor as its main components.[26] Educational projects consistently provided for these celebrations, not only in the schools, but on the numerous public holidays. Rousseau was often referred to in this regard. The nation should be to the young what Emile's tutor had been to him; education should coordinate the interests of individuals with the general interest of society.[27] At the same time, there continued to be mention of *la religion naturelle* and *la morale universelle* in all projects presented to the convention.

The early educational projects of the convention were Girondin; only ten of the 24 members of the Committee were Jacobins. By the end of 1792, the only agreement was the adoption of the first article of the Lanthenas project, establishing primary education which would teach "the knowledge absolutely necessary to all citizens." At the Jacobin club, opposition to a school system run by learned men was being expressed in terms of fear of a new social elite. Joseph Lakanal defended the concept of a Ministry of Education before the convention. But the Jacobins were gaining control throughout 1793; on July 3, a new Education Committee of six, including Robespierre, was established.[28] It was their ideas which were reflected in the various education projects presented thereafter.

The most extreme plan was that presented to the Convention by Robespierre on July 13. It proposed removing children from their parents' homes from age five to twelve (five to eleven for girls) in order to shield them from counterrevolutionary influences. They would be boarded in schools where they would receive, among other things, "instruction in universal morality, and not the teachings of any particular cult." After leaving school, the child would be free to choose a religion, "upon reflection." However, even the proponents of the plan realized how much opposition this would cause, and allowed instead for the possibility of releasing children for church instruction if their parents so wished.[29] The plan was voted down, mainly on the grounds of impracticability (the cost would be enormous) and of the rights of parents. This conflict of the rights of the state versus the parents in the moral education of children was to arise again in the century to come.

The most striking thing about the educational debates and projects of the revolutionary period was the agreement by all parties on the need for society to provide a moral education for children. Debates arose over centralization or decentralization of education, over public sponsorship beyond the primary level, over the nature of the texts to be used; but it was never questioned that moral education should be provided. There were differences of opinion on whether the rational development of the intellect was the main method to be employed, or whether the answer was the direct inculcation of a republican civic ideology. The latter method was increasingly popular, even after Thermidor. The Committee of Public Safety reported to the convention in April of 1794 that it was necessary to press for justice and virtue through public education, not only in the schools, but by the propagation of republican sentiments in public meetings, books and plays which offered "scenes of virtue and citizenship," and in public celebrations which made all Frenchmen feel like children of the common mother, the nation.[30]

On the other hand, the tendencies toward atheism inherent in the anticlerical radicalism of the time had frightened even Danton and Robespierre, and were sharply cut back even before Thermidor.[31] The result was that, in the revolutionary period in general, the Enlightenment concept of a natural morality based on deism merged with the revolutionary concept of a civic religion based on republicanism. What the two had in common was the assumption that morality could be propagated independently of religion, and that therefore, the French society of the future could function independently of the Church.

Idéologie

During the Empire, primary schools were returned to the control of the Church, which in turn rested under Napoleon's thumb. However, Napoleon also established the University, centralized under the government in Paris. At the time, it controlled only secondary and higher education but was eventually to establish control over all French education. This was Napoleon's contribution to a situation in which an "official philosophy," including ethics, could be propagated through the schools.

As the radical aspects of the Revolution subsided, the thought of the Enlightenment on morality was continued by a group referred to contemptuously by Napoleon as the idéologues.[32] The term idéologie was invented by one of their number, Destutt de Tracy, to denote the science particularly concerned with the analysis of sensations and ideas. They employed the sensationalist method of Condillac, derived from Locke's psychology, which had been used by Helvétius and d'Holbach before them. Their common publication was La Décade, dedicated to upholding the philosophy of the Enlightenment and the ideals of the Revolution. It was filled with discourses on the philosophy of Locke, Condillac, Helvétius, and their successors Condorcet, Cabanis and Destutt de Tracy. Strangely enough, they seemed to be interested also in German philosophy, particularly that of Kant.[33] Their other forum for discussion, after its founding in 1796, was the Institut National de Morale et Politique. Its six sections included: (1) the analysis of sensations and ideas, (2) *morale,* (3) social science and legislation, (4) political economy, (5) history, and (6) geography.

A typical member of the group, considered one of the most penetrating philosophers among the lecturers at the Institut, and, with Cabanis, master of French philosophy at the turn of the century, was Destutt de Tracy. In 1799 he published an article in the *Mercure* which emphasized the role of the legislator in public morality. Since he subscribed to the sensationalist doctrine of self-interest, Destutt did not believe in any innate moral sense. Therefore, education was necessary to show the individual how his interest fit into the general interest of society. The science of morality, he wrote, was only an application of the generation of ideas from sensation; that is, of ideology.

In 1799, although unhappy with Napoleon's first constitution, Destutt accepted nomination to the Senate; he devoted himself to the Council on Public Instruction. In a report to the Senate, he proposed the adoption of a curriculum favorable to the development of reason, including the study of the moral and political sciences necessary to citizenship. This aroused Napoleon's suspicion that the Institut was a center of ideological agitation; the second section and the Council of Public Instruction were both eventually dissolved.[34]

In 1801 Destutt published his *Elémens d'idéologie,* in which he discussed the role of will in morality. Will was described as a mode of the faculty of perception. Ideas of rights and duties arose from will—rights stemming from desires, duties from the means of attaining these desires. One attained his desires through a succession of exchanges which made up human society and which added to the power of human beings.[35] Destutt also noted the role of the division of labor in the process of social exchange (a factor which was to be central to the moral thought of Durkheim in the Third Republic).

Destutt saw morality as a relationship between the individual's interest in self-preservation and his connections with his neighbors. Through education and legislation, society must mold the judgment of its citizens so that they chose aright. Avoidance of punishment and social obloquy could be induced through legislation; avoidance of personal remorse, through education.[36] The human being he considered to be, not innately good or evil, but eminently modifiable. One's actions might be determined by will, but will was deter-mined by previous sensations, which could be controlled.[37] The goal of both education and legislation would be the common good. There was no universal morality; education by parents, teachers and society should instill feelings and opinions which corresponded with established institutions.[38]

Thus, the Enlightenment relationship between morality and education in France petered out into a narrow utilitarianism, based on the sensationalist dictum that there was nothing in the mind that was not first in the senses, and relying on the unproven thesis that somehow the self-interest of the individual could be identified with the general interest of society—through the increase of knowledge in social science, the wisdom of legislators, the reliability of education. The *idéologues'* main contribution to a secular morality did not consist of any original thought, but in the fact that they served as a bridge from the Enlightenment to the positivism of the nineteenth century, which was to be influential in the Third Republic.

Philosophie *in Secondary Education*

The influence of the Church in education persisted into the Restoration, with the attempt to turn the clock back to pre-Revolutionary times. However, during this period, substantial progress was made in elaborating a moral theory independent of religion. As in all periods of reaction, this effort was not accorded recognition; but it was to serve a purpose in the more liberal regime of the July Monarchy.

The believers in a morality based on philosophy rather than religion in the Restoration were inheritors of the Enlightenment tradition. In 1815 the Société d'instruction élémentaire began to organize mutual schools, which had no religious training. They published the *Journal d'éducation,* which included long discussions of *morale,* but none of religion. The personnel of the Society were adversaries of the Church—Voyer d'Argenson, Odilon Barrot, Lafayette, Lafitte. The Church strongly opposed the experiment with mutual schools, which partook too much of Enlightenment ideas. As a result of this opposition, the schools were forced to institute the same religious training as other schools.[39]

However, at the University two groups of moralists carried on the tradition of the previous century. The *idéologie* of Daunou and Destutt, still strong in the Masonic lodges and among republicans, was taught by sensationalist philosopher Pierre Laromiguière, a disciple of Condillac. The faith of Rousseau's Savoyard vicar, opposing any narrow utilitarian basis for morality, was represented by Camille Royer-Collard, who was also inspired by the Scottish moralists Thomas Reid and Dugald Stewart.[40] It was out of this second group that the moral philosophy of the next fifty years in France was to develop. And French moral thought was renewed by exposure to the theories of the greatest Enlightenment philosopher, Immanuel Kant.

The intermediary between German idealism and French moral philosophy was Victor Cousin, who interpreted Kant's moral theory in such a way that a purely philosophical *morale* could be taught in French secondary schools without reference to Catholic theology.

The importance of Cousin for the development of *morale laïque* in the nineteenth century was capital. His moral philosophy, developed during the Restoration, was taught in all the secondary schools of the state during the July

Monarchy; it survived to become the basis of the *morale laïque* taught in the Third Republic. His pupils surpassed him to pave the way for new developments in moral theory at the end of the century. But this should not obscure the fact that it was he who took the first step in explicating and establishing in the educational system a secular moral philosophy independent of the Church.

Born the son of a watchmaker, Cousin foreshadowed the traditional path of nineteenth-century intellectuals, as a graduate of the first class of the Ecole Normale Supérieure, where his early brilliance marked him for a prominent University career. Under the influence of Laromiguière, Royer-Collard and Maine de Biran, he turned to philosophical studies. The idealistic and voluntaristic psychology of the latter two refuted sensationalism for him.[41] He began to lecture at the Ecole Normale in 1812, at the Sorbonne in 1815. From 1817 to 1820, traveling in Germany and Italy, he came into contact with German idealism. This combination of French, Scottish and German philosophical influence was to result in Cousin's eclectic, "spiritualist" view of man, which he considered his contribution to French philosophy.[42]

Already, philosophical independence was associated with liberal political ideas. Cousin's lectures of 1820 in Paris drew large crowds of liberal students. In the reaction following the assassination of the Duc de Berry, heir to the throne, Cousin was dismissed from his post; but during the brief liberalization of 1827-28, he was recalled by Royer-Collard. His arrest in Germany had contributed to his radical reputation; again, his lectures were crowded.[43]

However, Cousin was not a radical, but a "doctrinaire" liberal. He believed in the Charter, which had provided France with a constitutional monarchy under limited suffrage. Like his fellow-doctrinaire, François Guizot, his preference was for a government of the educated elite. Just as he considered his philosophy to be the golden mean between sensationalism and idealism, so he considered the Charter to be the mean between absolute monarchy and democracy.[44]

For more than a decade during the July Monarchy, Cousin was to dominate French secondary education. In 1830 he was appointed to the Royal Council of Public Instruction, where he controlled all teaching of philosophy. He also became director of the Ecole Normale Supérieure, where he taught philosophy. He was later, briefly, to be Minister of Education. A series of tours through schools in Germany and Holland soon after the July revolution convinced him that moral instruction should be offered in the schools under the aegis of religion. His general findings on education were embodied in the first primary education law since the revolution, presented to the Chambers by Guizot, then Minister of Education, in 1833. It provided for state-subsidized primary schools; however, they were neither free nor obligatory, and religion was part of the curriculum. It was not in primary education that Cousin was to make his contribution to a secular moral philosophy, but on the secondary level, where he organized philosophical education and established it as a required course in the curriculum.

This was a far-reaching institutional change. In the Old Regime, philosophy had been dominated by theology in the educational system. After the revolution, it was taught in the *écoles centrales* under the headings of *idéologie* and *grammaire*. Royer-Collard had reinstated it into the curriculum for a few years during the Restoration; but from 1820 to 1830 all judges for the *agrégation* in philosophy were theologians.

The Charter of 1830 decreed freedom of religion, expressly omitting any special position for the Catholic Church. And as the Church was gradually forced to relinquish its powerful role in education, the teaching of *morale* was not ignored by the establishment, which was deeply concerned with the moral formation of its citizens. Paul Janet recalled that, to the liberals of 1830, ''the establishment of an independent philosophy curriculum was not only the consequence of the secular state; it was at the same time an instrument of propaganda for the principles of secularism.'' This step was envisaged as serving a social and political end, the unification of a society split by the revolution. The ideal, Janet recalled, was ''to create a society which rested on common and fraternal principles, without excluding the diversity of opinions and beliefs;'' and it was Cousin who ''wished to found and who founded the secular teaching of philosophy in France.''[45]

Cousin's eclectic philosophy, tied to no particular religious sect, but in conformity with all the religions of the country, became the official philosophy of the July Monarchy. It was propagated in the secondary schools through his position at the University.[46] He personally passed on all candidates for the teaching of philosophy, and presided over examinations for chairs in royal colleges. Philosophy professors throughout France were known as his ''regiment.'' He knew the record and publications of each one. Most of them called on him in Paris during the Easter recess, and were questioned about their work, as well as about their relations with the local clergy, on which Cousin placed great importance.[47]

Cousin always claimed that his philosophy was in no way inconsistent with religion, and made every effort to conciliate the Church short of total abnegation. Nevertheless, he insisted upon the independence of philosophy from theology, and sought to make it serve the moral needs of the elite.[48]

3

Victor Cousin and the Secularization of Moral Philosophy

Spiritualism

COUSIN'S philosophy was known as spiritualism (or, because of its diverse origins, as eclecticism). His first course dealing with moral philosophy, taught in 1818,[1] was to form the core of his basic work, *Du Vrai, du beau et du bien*. It was based on his study of the Scottish moral philosophers of the psychological school (Reid, Ferguson, Stewart) and on his reading of Kant.

What made Kant so useful to French moral philosophy at this time was his reversal of the relationship between theology and morality. Whereas traditional Catholic dogma held that the source of good for humanity was God, Kant insisted on a moral force in human beings, the awareness of which caused them to postulate a good God and a life hereafter. The moral imperative in each person was a connection with the noumenal world, where cause and effect were not operative. The agent of the noumenal in human beings was conscience, as in Rousseau's Savoyard Vicar. The fact that morality was inherent in human beings allowed them dignity and participation in the world of ends. Thus, one aspect of the moral imperative was: Act always so as to treat other persons as ends, not means.

Kant's noumenal world was also a world of absolute reason. Thus, the second aspect of the categorical imperative was: Act in such a way that the principle of your action might be valid as universal law. The universal law of Kant's moral theory had a genetic relationship to Rousseau's general will, which was an absolute and rational good, not dependent on particular or partial or even unanimous wills of individuals.

Kant's moral theory included the two consistent elements of French ethical thought in the nineteenth century—the innate knowledge of good and evil, centered in the individual conscience, and absolute justice as the regulating law of that conscience. Thus, the dominant themes of French ethics were opposed to pure sensationalism. Morality was restored to the individual as part of his nature, and was interpreted through subjective, rather than sensationalist, psychology.

The Kantian predicates of individual moral freedom and objective reason presumed ideal moral goals toward which human beings strive. The French theory resulting from this reading of Kant was known as spiritualism. The French departed from Kant, however, in refusing to accept his separation of the noumenal and phenomenal worlds. They emphasized the psychological aspects of human moral sense; they insisted that practical reason and individual freedom were part of the real world. They tried to draw the principles of morality from the French Revolution; and, like Rousseau, they considered that politics was the test of morality.

Cousin's spiritualism maintained the French tradition of founding metaphysics on psychology, in the manner of Maine de Biran, even of Descartes. Thus, in the third section of his work, *Du Bien,* he abandoned the method of observation and experiment for "the psychological method," which "does not invent, but verifies" what is. All men, Cousin maintained, have a sense of what is just and unjust; they esteem or blame other men according to their actions. All men also believe that they are free, or they could not attach moral value to their acts and those of others.

Here Cousin sidestepped the Kantian problem of establishing human freedom; he grounded it in subjective psychology and deemed it a psychological fact. From this basis, he proceeded to draw four inferences: (1) that there was an essential distinction, for all free and intelligent beings, between good and evil, and a feeling of obligation to conform to the good; (2) that human beings were free and intelligent, capable of comprehending this distinction and this obligation independent of any positive law; (3) that all acts not conforming to the good deserved punishment; and (4) that people recognized the justice of that punishment. Together these truths formed the basis of society, but they were anterior to society. Education developed, but did not create them. The proof was that society persisted and progressed toward greater justice.[2]

Having started with what he conceived as basic elements of human consciousness, as empirical facts, Cousin proceeded to discuss the objects of that consciousness as independent and eternal truths. *Morale* had its axioms, like other sciences: human consciousness of good and evil, of personal liberty and obligation to fulfill the good. But "before the facts exists the right [droit], and that idea alone, if it is real, suffices . . . to save human dignity." The idea of the right was a "universal idea" and as such it was absolute. Thus, Cousin based man's dignity, his moral consciousness, in an idea which was beyond man, though felt by him, and was explicated by his reason. He fixed the obligation to obey the law in the necessary distinction between good and evil, and in the logical implications of the freedom to choose between them.[3]

Part of the difficulty in the French interpretation of Kant stems from the double meanings of the two French words—*conscience,* meaning both consciousness and conscience (or moral consciousness); and *droit,* meaning both law and right, as in the "rights of man." This ambiguity allowed, in the first case, a psychological interpretation of conscience which claims to be empirical: one was conscious of right and wrong, conscious of oneself as a free being; the moral sense was a fact of consciousness. But at the same time, there was implied a normative interpretation: one's conscience decreed the obligation to perform the good, which was a universal law. The second ambiguity relates to the first. As Cousin first used the word *droit,* it partook of one aspect of Kant's categorical imperative. The law was the obligation to choose the good, that which reason understood as being a universal law. However, the use of the word in Cousin's and other French moral philosophy came to refer more to the other aspect of the categorical imperative—the rights of the person. A person, Cousin said later in this same course, unlike a thing, belonged to himself, had dignity, had liberty, and therefore responsibility. "It is because there is in me a being worthy of respect that I have the duty to respect myself and the right [droit] to be respected by you. My duty is the exact measure of my right." One's duty to oneself was not to degrade one's liberty by enslaving it to passion, not to diminish one's self-respect or one's dignity; essentially, it was to be a responsible moral person. One's duty to another person was constituted by the other's rights, the rights of a person, which were the same as one's own. The respect of the rights of others was called justice.[4]

In Cousin's course of 1819-20, cut short by the political reaction of that year, he gave a more precise account of the purely human aspects of morality, as an introduction to a survey of eighteenth century moral philosophy. Each person, he insisted, recognized himself as a force whose true nature, beyond that of things, was to be free; therein resided his dignity. Reason told him that this force of freedom was equal in other persons, and equally to be respected. "The majestic idea of mutual liberty develops that of mutual equality, and thereby the idea of the mutual and equal duty to respect that liberty." Thus, Cousin drew moral law from human nature itself; it was to preserve that nature, which was the dignity of the free person. The emphasis, however, was on the duty [devoir] rather than on the right [droit] of the moral agent. The duties of others conferred rights upon the self. And in this way, "liberty and equality in their development engender all rights and duties."[5]

Cousin's basic ideas remained constant throughout the 1848 revolution. In July of 1848 the Académie des sciences morales et politiques, of which Cousin was a member, was asked by the Cavaignac government to aid in the "defense of social principles" after the June Days. A special meeting was held; it was decided to publish a series of popular pamphlets on social issues (e.g., *La Famille, La Propriété, Les Causes de la richesse et ses inégalités*). Cousin undertook to write the one on *Justice et Charité*. It is a popular and succinct version of his moral philosophy, distilled from his other works.

"Moral and political philosophy," he wrote, linking the two, "is and ought to be a science of observation." It was also, he noted, a necessity of all societies. The first moral fact gathered by consciousness was "the dignity of the person relative to things;" that dignity resided particularly in freedom. When humans considered one another, they found each other to be equally free beings. "Unequal in every other aspect . . . they are equal only in liberty, for no single person can be freer than another." Cousin then went on to develop the idea of mutual rights and duties. "The duty I have to respect you is my right to your respect. . . . Duty and right are brothers. Their common mother is freedom."[6]

However, this was not all of morality, although it was the fundamental law of justice. Cousin never preached a completely human morality; this approach to morality on his part is singled out only because it was the basic method of later assertions by others that morality was independent of religion and even of metaphysics. In all of his moral teachings, Cousin went beyond justice, to charity—"an instinct superior to the law [loi], which is in morality what genius is in the arts." The poor man who was hungry had no right to the least part of one's worldly goods; yet one felt a duty to feed him. "Here there are duties which have no correlative rights." (Cousin noted here that the state should help workers who were unemployed, although it was false that they had a "right to work," for all rights imply the idea that one can vindicate them by force.) This instinct, to go beyond the demands of justice to the point of devotion, or even sacrifice, was to Cousin "le souffle divin," which penetrated the soul and raised it above ordinary laws; "it is God in us."[7] For Cousin, the study of the moral life led inevitably to the recognition of God and the immortal soul, and these were always a part of his teachings.

To what extent did Cousin believe that morality and religion could be separated? He certainly never admitted that morality was separate from the concepts of God and the immortal soul. But he maintained that basic philosophical principles were available to everyone, by virtue of the psychological approach. In 1848 he also published an introduction to a new edition of Rousseau's *Vicaire Savoyard,* in an attempt to counter "the poisonous doctrines of materialism and atheism."[8] Here he stripped philosophy of all technical language and tried to show that morality was part of the makeup of the common man. Each person had a soul, was free, desired to reach the infinite, loved others, distinguished between good and evil, was aware of a created order in the universe and of a moral order within the self.

There were reasons why a philosopher who was so much a part of the French establishment of the time should propagate a moral philosophy which started from a purely human basis, but which, nevertheless, led inevitably to religious concepts. One was, as we have seen, to fight materialism and atheism with a morality based on individual reason. Another was to establish, on an independent basis, the principles of the Revolution. Liberty and equality were "givens" of human nature in Cousin's moral philosophy. (In his lectures he emphasized the protection of liberty as the role of good government, which should guarantee national representation in legislation, a jury system, a national guard, and freedom of the press.[9]) Even fraternity, in the guise of charity, played a role in his theory. (But Cousin warned that charity should be used carefully, since it carried with it the danger of demeaning human dignity, on which justice was based.[10]) It has been pointed out that Cousin formulated an "official philosophy" whose purpose was the maintenance of the stability of French post-revolutionary society.[11] To the extent that the Church prevented the necessary social equilibrium, Cousin tended to insist on the independence of philosophy from religion.

His first expression of the necessity to separate the two may be found in the "Argument" preceding his translation of Plato's *Euthyphron,* written in the twenties, when political reaction and clerical power were at their height. God, being truth itself, Cousin wrote, all moral truths must relate to him. Therefore, morality and religion were united in the unity of their basic principle, both in reality and in the mind of man who conceives them. However, when religion was misconceived, "when anthropomorphism lowers theology to a drama, makes of the Eternal a God of the theater, tyrannical and passionate, who arbitrarily decides from on high what is good and what is evil," then the critical philosopher must, in the cause of saving the moral verities, establish them on their own foundation, "independent of any outside circumstance, independent even of their primitive source", thus "placing them by design on a narrower but surer ground, knowingly losing something in order not to lose all."

The reference was, of course, to Socrates; but the context was not entirely removed from nineteenth-century France. Cousin went on to emphasize, as Diderot had done before him, that "the good is not good because it pleases God, but it pleases God because it is good;" therefore, the legitimacy of moral truths was not to be sought in religion. "These truths, like all others, legitimate themselves, and have no need of other authority but that of the reason which perceives and proclaims them." And reason was its own sanction.[12] This was probably Cousin's clearest statement of the view that a morality independent of religion might be needed by society, in order to safeguard ethics in a time of religious decline.

Despite Cousin's care in dealing with religious authorities,[13] the Church saw his establishment of independent philosophical studies in secondary education as a threat. And it was by attacking this religiously neutral philosophy that the clerical party, in both Louis Veuillot's *Univers* and the Comte de Montalembert's Committee for Religious Freedom, hoped to break the monopoly of the University on French secondary education. The required course in philosophy, they maintained, was indifferent on matters of religion; such education should not be forced upon the children of the faithful. Therefore, the Church demanded, under the terms of the Charter of 1830, the right of "freedom of education."

It was Cousin and his philosophy which was the focal point of attack. In the provinces, professors of philosophy appointed by Cousin were forced from their posts by the clerical party.[14] Cousin tried to head off the attacks with a scholarly work on Pascal in 1842. Charging Pascal with denying the efficacy of human reason in belief, he pointed out that this position was opposed to the best Cartesian principles of French theology. He equated Pascal's thought with the *Essai sur l'indifférence* of Lamennais, who had now become an apostate.[15] And he accused Pascal of rejecting "what we call in philosophy *morale* or natural religion." He claimed that, before Christianity, men had learned morality by means of natural religion, aided by philosophy; every increase of secularization was thus an homage rendered to the power of natural reason, and thus to the power of philosophy.[16]

The Church's opposition to Cousin's view of natural morality was summed up by the Archbishop of Paris in his *Introduction philosophique à l'étude du christianisme*. The necessary rules of morality, he wrote, were impossible without faith in God, and were only preserved in their full integrity in the teachings of Christianity. Too great a dependence on human reason had always led to moral decline. The archbishop listed the errors of philosophers of all eras, claiming that morality was only saved by its union with Christianity. While not denying the existence of natural morality in man, he insisted that its purity was dependent upon its connection with revealed religion.[17]

Even Sainte-Beuve, who opposed the power of the clergy in education, admitted that the Catholic party had an argument.

> On the whole, professors of the University, without being hostile to religion, are not religious; the students feel it, and they leave this atmosphere, not so much nourished on irreligion, as on indifference to religion. . . . Whatever one can say for or against . . . one hardly leaves the schools of the University a Christian.[18]

Responding to an attack by the Marquis de Barthélemy, Cousin defended himself in the Chamber of Peers on May 15, 1843. There was, he maintained, no proposition taught in any philosophy class in any college of the kingdom that could directly or indirectly threaten the Catholic religion.[19]

The clerical demand for "freedom of education" immediately raised fears of a return of the Jesuits to their once-powerful role in French schools. For three years the quarrel raged in the press, and finally reached the Chambers in debates on the Villemain bill for secondary education in 1844. Cousin's position on the relationship of philosophy and religion emerged more clearly in his "grand days of oration," during April of that year before the Chamber.

Speaking of the philosophy taught in the *lycées* and *collèges,* Cousin described it as not "pure philosophy," but "philosophy in relation to society." Its aim was to form "sound vigorous minds and honest souls," by teaching the verities necessary to man and society everywhere: the spirituality of the soul, the freedom of man, the law of duty, the distinction between vice and virtue, merit and demerit, and "divine providence with its immortal promises." These truths were the property of no particular system. In fact, for this teaching to fulfill its mission to serve both religion and society, "it must not repose on the particular dogmas of any recognized cult; for otherwise it does not serve all, it serves only one; it applies to a certain segment of youth and is not made for the entire society."

True religion, he went on, united naturally with true philosophy; it lived in peace with the great spirit of the society and of the century, since it was of all centuries. The University was being attacked, he claimed, because it was "above all a great moral and political institution."[20]

Here Cousin touched upon a basic argument for the separation of philosophy and formal religion, which was to determine the development of moral philosophy in France for decades to come. It expressed a double conviction about the relationship of the Catholic Church to French society in the nineteenth century: first, that the Church no longer represented the beliefs of all Frenchmen, or even of all who were nominally Catholic; and second, that the Church had not only failed to accept the changes wrought by the revolution, but was actively working to oppose them. Therefore, concluded Cousin and many others, a philosophy, and particularly a moral philosophy which aimed at unifying France and stabilizing her society, must preserve its independence from Catholic dogma.

Even after the turbulent days of the Second Republic, when many other liberals were ready to capitulate to the Church as the guarantor of social order, Cousin did not change his views in this regard. Participating in the extra-parliamentary commission which prepared the new education law of 1850, he fought a losing battle for over four months, often reproaching Thiers for delivering the University to the clergy.[21] During the fifties, he wrote in a letter: "Philosophy and religion ought to extend a hand to one another, but each one should rest in the sphere which belongs to it."[22]

Cousin's personal view of the relationship between religion and philosophy was probably best expressed in his course of 1828:

Philosophy and religion have the same object, only, what religion expresses in the form of symbols, philosophy explains and translates into pure and rational truths. Christianity is the philosophy of the masses: philosophy is the light of lights, the authority of authorities. . . . It does not destroy faith, it enlightens and nurtures it and raises it gently from the half-light of symbol to the full light of pure thought. . . . Happy to see the masses in the arms of Christianity, it contents itself with gently extending its hand and helping them to raise themselves yet higher.[23]

Religion for the masses, philosophy for those capable of it—clearly Cousin's view was informed by a class bias. The new intellectual elite at which secondary education was aimed would be drawn largely from the upper and rising middle classes. Not that this elite was closed to those capable of attaining that intellectual level. Cousin himself had risen from the artisan class. But the products of secondary education were assumed to be the new ruling class. It was they who would be capable of the philosophic morality taught by Cousin and his "regiment." For the masses in the primary system, religion would produce the same moral results.

Thus, it is interesting that Cousin put so much emphasis on the unifying value of his philosophy in his defense before the Chamber. True, it might serve to unify those of different religious beliefs attending the secondary schools. But like the school system itself, divided between a primary system for the masses and a secondary system for the elite, moral education was to be divided. Having adopted the view that education should be controlled by the society for the purpose of unifying the state, he applied this concept only to the higher levels of education. It was a flaw his successors were to attempt to correct.

The Second Republic

The University, and indeed the intellectual establishment of France, was to remain strongly "spiritualist" almost to the end of the century, although Cousin's personal influence waned after 1845. The developments of Cousin's position led in two directions: toward an insistence on the separation of religion from education; and toward a complete denial of the necessity of religion for morality and a demand for secular morality in primary schools. The revolution of 1848 modified both of these in particular ways. The separation of the Church from education was muted, first because of the enthusiastic participation of the clergy in the early stages of the revolution, and later, because of the desire of the Party of Order to utilize the Church's influence against radical demands. At the same time, the existing demand for a secular morality was defined in much the same terms as it had been in the first republic—as a civic morality whose aim was to create good citizens of the new order.

As early as 1847 the tendency of liberal students was to identify morality with the values of the revolution, as did their popular teacher, Jules Michelet, before his course was closed down in January, 1848. The *Journal des écoles,* published by the students of the Collège de France, called for a moral and social science which would form the "spirit of education." If there was no religious faith, "there is a civic faith and it is in the virtue of that civic and national faith that the state should educate . . . with a spirit of unity." Noting that civil society was in advance of the church, and that the University was under the control of the government, it demanded a spirit of initiative and progress in education. The faith of the moment, the students insisted, was "human solidarity, love of country and of family." As for morality, "liberty confers imprescriptible rights; fraternity, sacred duties."[24]

The February revolution made possible the publication of Michelet's course with the missing lessons and a new preface. "The Revolution," wrote the historian, "must not be exterior, on the surface, it must enter and penetrate. . . . It must go to the depths of man, must act on his soul, must touch the will, so that it is a willed Revolution, a Revolution of the heart, a *moral and religious* transformation." And in one of the lessons, never given, he blamed the first revolutionaries for not having recognized that laws were insufficient without the means to make men accept them so that they would be assured for the future. "The first of these means is education, both of children and of men." Michelet called upon the students to prepare a moral crusade of fraternity, joining with the people in the common building of a new world. Educated persons must compensate for what was lacking in the schools of the people.[25]

After February the *Journal des écoles* reappeared under a new name, *l'Avant-Garde,* representing, as they put it, "diverse classes of students, in or out of school." Their manifesto stated that all religions were changing forms of the same deistic religion, which had two stages, religious and civil. "We are present today at the *second incarnation* of the Christian idea, in the civil era," they announced, "which is merely the *French Revolution and its further developments.*" The task of the century, they maintained, was social reorganization.[26]

Social reorganization through education was also the goal of the man appointed minister of public instruction in the Provisional Government. Hippolyte Carnot had been secretary-general of the Société pour l'instruction élémentaire during 1846-47; he strongly believed in education for all. His view of the task before him was, "in a word, to tie the citizen to the State through the reciprocity of duties: the State gives to each of its members the means to be what he can be, each of them gives to the State all the service of which he is capable."[27] Carnot's ideas on education were drawn from the first republic, and were those of Condorcet, taught to him by his father, Lazare Carnot.[28] Public education was to have a crucial role in the creation of citizens for the new republic. As he told the University Council, "let us form new citizens for new institutions.''

However, as a member of the Société de la morale chrétienne, Carnot did not try to abridge in any way the rights of the Church in education, as he made clear in his decree on primary education of June 30.[29]

On March 6 Carnot issued a circular to *instituteurs,* urging them to fulfill their duties to the republic by creating citizens. "A revolution must renew men."[30] Teachers were urged to prepare their communities for the elections, and to preach the idea that future national representation would include ordinary people of good sense. As he said to the Assembly on May 10, "It is [the duty of] public education to make all of France republican in spirit and in heart, as it is today in institutions."[31] Special schools were given uniforms as "soldiers of liberty." Adult education courses were opened, with volunteer lecturers from the school system. Carnot also called for the creation of manuals that could be used by the *instituteurs* to teach the rights and duties of citizens.[32]

A large number of textbooks were produced, of which three were singled out for commendation by the Haute Commission des études scientifiques et littéraires. (Among those drafted by Carnot to serve on this commission were the historian Edgar Quinet, the scientist Augustin Cournot, the philosophers Edouard de Laboulaye, Geoffrey Saint-Hilaire, and Charles Renouvier).[33] The contributions varied, from the Golden Rule to rules for good citizenship.[34] Renouvier contributed one of his own (see infra), which turned out to be too radical for the Assembly, and became the occasion for Carnot's downfall.

The teachers responded to Carnot's program with enthusiasm. In May *L'Education républicaine,* a journal of *maîtres d'études* in secondary education, declared the necessity to lift the souls of the people, by giving them the sense of their dignity, their rights and duties; after the question of work, it was the most important issue of the new republic. They called upon the primary schools to do their part:

> To uproot the masses from their eternal ignorance . . . to enlighten them concerning their rights and duties, to explain to them the true meaning of those sacred words Liberty, Equality, Fraternity . . . that is the role of primary teachers.[35]

On June 30 Carnot issued a decree concerning primary education. It stressed that more was required of the schools than teaching students to read and write:

> The duty of the state is to make sure that all are raised up to become truly worthy of that great name of Citizen which awaits them. Primary education . . . should converge most closely with moral education, and particularly with the principles of fraternity. It is there that it joins itself to religious education, which is not the province of the schools, but to which we make a sincere appeal. . . .[36]

In 1848, all spokesmen for moral education were situated somewhere within the tradition laid down by Cousin—willingness to work with the Church on the one hand, as long as the aims of the Church seemed compatible with those of the society, and on the other hand, insistence that morality was a public matter, which could be taught independently of religion.

The tradition was stated by Cousin's students in a new periodical edited by Amedée Jacques, *La Liberté de penser*.[37] Defending the philosophy taught in the secondary schools, Jacques maintained that it was above all highly moral, but that it did not rest on any particular system of beliefs which would be personal and therefore changing. "It professes to teach only that eternal philosophy of which Cicero spoke, which is hidden at the base of all systems." Going further than Cousin, however, he denied that it was the role of religion to teach morality. "Religion begins in mystery. . . . Reject a single one of its mysteries, and what becomes of morality? Furthermore, religion affirms in the name of authority, philosophy demonstrates in the name of examination." Moral philosophy, which could be one of the bases of moral and social unity, should be obligatory in the secondary schools. "The state rests on rights, on duties, on the dogmas of freedom and responsibility; it should make sure that these great fundamental truths are taught to youth."[38]

But Jacques also went further than Cousin in demanding that morality be taught in the primary schools as well, and chided Carnot for delivering this task into the hands of the clergy. However, although the position taken by his students was more strongly anti-Church than that of Cousin, its philosophy remained his own. Morality implied God and the immortal soul.[39]

No one in the University or in governing circles in 1848 went beyond spiritualism as the content of the moral education which would support the republic. The writings of Michelet, extolling the virtues of the first revolution, were filled with a verbose kind of mysticism. What was sharpened, particularly as the first flush of clerical enthusiasm for the new republic paled, was anticlericalism. In this campaign, at least with regard to education, Michelet must be ranked second to his fellow historian Quinet.

If Condorcet may be viewed as the spokesman for national education in the first revolution, Quinet commanded that role in the Second Republic. His book, *l'Enseignement du peuple,* went through five editions in 1849, and was partially summed up in his discourse of February, 1850, to the Assembly, where he pleaded for the separation of Church and State in the schools. The question of education, he insisted, was a question of moral direction. Recalling Montesquieu, he maintained that religion must accommodate itself to the political structure. It followed that, if the political revolution preceded the religious revolution, the old religion must be separated from the state. "Here the national religion is in full contradiction with the national revolution. . . . The result is that the revolution in France is neither ruled, nor governed, nor limited by any religion or sect whatsoever. . . . The French Revolution is its own origin, its own rule, its own limit.''

In such a state, where freedom of religion had been proclaimed, the clergy had lost the right to direct education. Not only should the clergy be eliminated from the schools; so should the religion which it represented, to be replaced by a secular education. ''You are creating what you call the teaching of the people, but you are forgetting one thing, which is to give it a soul. Deprived of all moral force, *the instituteur*, every moment in his teaching, must count upon his natural adversary.''

Claiming that all of the progress of the human mind in modern times had taken place in opposition to the Church, Quinet insisted that the basis of the new secular society was the love of citizens for one another, independent of their beliefs. The new life of France would rest on a social morality; thus the organization of education in general, and particularly of primary education, would be the organization of society itself. The *instituteur* should say to his students: you are all children of the same God and of the same country; take each other by the hand until death. The school system would comprise ''a secular corps charged with teaching and conserving, from generation to generation, the spirit of the secular society.''[40] Quinet's statement of the importance of a purely secular morality to a republic was prophetic, particularly as it influenced prominent educational reformers of the Third Republic— Jules Ferry, Jules Barni, Frédéric Buisson, Jules Steeg, Henri Marion among others.[41]

However, Quinet offered no new basis for teaching morality in the schools beyond the ones laid down by Cousin in his philosophy. Like the other men of 1848, he sought moral values in a generalized deism, to which was added the religion of *la patrie*. It was this very timidity which was to be blamed by a new generation of republicans for the failure of the Second Republic. In retrospect, the spiritualism and mysticism of the old republicans seemed to the new generation to have been a weakness. Young republicans tended to emphasize action and to reject any philosophy that included the supernatural, or the absolute in any way.[42] By the end of the Second Empire, this trend was to lead to a stronger emphasis on a truly independent morality.

PART II

The Debate on a Secular Moral Philosophy

Introduction

Cousin's spiritualism, particularly as applied to ethics, was a secularized form of religion. With its ties to German Idealism and the Scottish moralists, it represented merely one form of a general European tendency, in the nineteenth century, to convert religion to philosophy. However, the French, because of their particular situation vis-a-vis the Catholic Church, developed this secularization further than other countries.

First, the new philosophy became "official" and an arm of liberalization, instead of remaining confined to the academy and the intelligentsia in general. Second, through the radical tradition of the Revolution, it was shaped to be taught, not only at the secondary level, but also at the primary.

The radicalization began after the failure of the 1848 revolution; and by the 1860s, the dialogue on teaching *morale* without connection to religion in the schools had reached and far surpassed the level of that dialogue in the United States today. In fact, it had become a certainty that when the republic should again be established, a secular morality would be taught in the context of a system of universal education.

Charles Renouvier and the Radicalizing of Spiritualism

Cousin Rejected

SPIRITUALISM began to undergo changes after 1848, when Cousin's own students, disappointed with the outcome of the revolution, turned on him. One of them wrote a book in 1849, blaming Cousin and his philosophy for the failure of the Second Republic. It pinpointed the problem in two areas: Cousin's philosophy curriculum was designed to preclude original thought; and it taught only accepted ideas from the past. The book also charged that the "lama, the pasha of philosophy" had prevented any non-spiritualists from gaining influential teaching positions.[1]

Other students of Cousin opposed their master in the pages of *Liberté de penser*. Some blamed him for those writings on morality during the Second Republic in which he warned the workers against socialism,[2] as they themselves were leaning toward the new doctrine. Emile Deschanel was dismissed from the University for an article suggesting socialism as a replacement for the Catholic religion.[3] Amedée Jacques also lost his position, because of his proposal for a popular philosophy based on atheism.[4] In the same year, 1851, Etienne Vacherot, who had been close enough to Cousin to edit some of his works, and who had been director of the Ecole Normale Supérieure, was dismissed because of the third volume of his *Histoire de l'école d'Alexandrie*.[5]

Vacherot later elaborated on the relevant portions of the book in a series of articles. The Alexandrine mind, he wrote, which had tried to make Christianity acceptable to the ancient world by transforming it into a Greek philosophy, returned periodically to attempt the prolongation of a dead idea. Although a creative spirit, it nevertheless devoted itself to restoring and transforming traditional ideas, rather than to building anew. These understandable attempts to preserve the past were often made in the name of progress; but progress consisted in freeing minds from the past. And in the nineteenth century it was a matter of forming, developing, and fortifying reason so that all could practice morality in its simplicity, without symbols. This was the only solution to the problem of educating the people. "Let us create, or at least develop (for only nature creates) minds and souls through education, through science and philosophy . . . and then let us not fear to leave them alone face to face with truth."[6]

This is one of the early statements under the Empire of the need for a morality independent of religion. Moral philosophy was now moving to free itself, not only from the Church, but from religious concepts.

Many of those dismissed from the University during the Empire, some for their refusal to take the required oath to the Emperor, emigrated. Edgar Quinet was one of these. He became the leader in exile of the republican, anticlerical *universitaires* who were to establish the secular schools of the Third Republic. (See Chapter 7.) Other scholars stayed in France, teaching in private schools. That of Auguste Delacour included on its faculty Jules Barni and Frédéric Morin, both active later in the philosophical movement toward an independent morality.[7] (See Chapter 5.) Before his own later emigration, Barni participated with Morin, Vacherot and others in the philosophical review *L'Avenir,* which was closed down in February, 1865, after ten months of publication.[8]

It was in *L'Avenir* that Vacherot pursued the battle for an independent moral science. He insisted that once human nature was known through psychology, its end, its laws and duties were easily deduced, and that this was a scientific enterprise. The moral law was a corollary of human nature; moral duties were the application of that law. Such a morality needed no supernatural sanctions, since individuals bore it as an immutable law in their own beings.

Vacherot insisted that morality should be disengaged from all metaphysical speculation and founded on observation and analysis. The advantage to be gained was putting ethics at the disposal of everyone. But if some felt it necessary to include metaphysics, or even theology in moral theory, these could be tolerated, "not at the base, but at the summit of morality, where they can crown, but never found it." The real task of philosophy, however, was to construct a morality both scientific and popular.[9,10]

Continuing the emphasis on the necessary relationship between democracy and moral education which had marked the Second Republic, Vacherot wrote in *La Démocratie* that, up to this point, the moral conditions of society had been upheld by religion; but religion was based on the principle of authority through revelation. Intolerant of other points of view, opposed to freedom of thought, religion was in all respects incompatible with democracy. All aspects of a democratic society—its morality and its education as well as its industry—must be based upon science. He suggested that religion was a "transitory social fact . . . proper to the *minority* of human societies, useless and harmful in their maturity." As science progressed, religion gradually disappeared. Vacherot claimed that "there is no sensible mind which doubts that morality is a veritable science founded on facts susceptible to verification and observation."[11] In these passages, written by a spiritualist, the influence of Comte's law of the stages is clear; there is also a foreshadowing of Durkheim's sociological explication of religion as a "social fact."

Vacherot maintained that the teaching of a moral science to all, in gradual stages for each age group, with proper textbooks, was necessary to a democracy. Such an education could be undertaken by the state if it confined itself to teaching scientific morality which produced good citizens. Without such an education, the population might become divided; with it, the nation could be unified. "One cannot repeat it too often, the public school is the cradle of the *cité*," he insisted. This work of 1859 laid down the basic principles on which the educational reformers of the early Third Republic were to proceed.[12]

In 1869 Vacherot emphasized again, in *La Religion,* that Christianity was a thing of the past, and that it had "only one possible heir, science and philosophy." The transmission of these would be solved by the organization of public and private education. Again he stressed, quoting Condorcet, that it was necessary to separate the morality taught in the schools from the principles of any particular religion.[13] By 1870 Vacherot was fighting positivist and materialist views as well as religious ones in morality. In *Science et conscience* he insisted on an integral view of man, and on the freedom revealed in man's consciousness. Materialism, he said, attributed all to fatality; spiritualism, to Providence. As a good Kantian, he maintained that one must distinguish moral necessity from physical necessity, while at the same time insisting on a morality contained in conscience, independent of theological or metaphysical speculations.[14]

Another of Cousin's students whose thought turned to the independence of ethics from religion was Barni.[15] After the coup d'état, he resigned his post as professor of philosophy. Like many other *universitaires,* he took refuge in Switzerland, where he gave public lectures at the Geneva Academy. The first series was on the moral and political thought of the *philosophes,* and was published as a book in 1862. It contributed to the growing interest in Voltaire and other Enlightenment figures during the 60's.[16]

In 1864-65, Barni gave a course called "De la morale publique," which was also published as a book. He began by stating that moral freedom and moral obligation were facts of "inner experience." Thus, morality had its basis independent of all metaphysics; that is, of any system concerning God and the immortal soul. Like Vacherot, he considered religion a primitive form in the development of man's reason, which gradually came to recognize moral law without need of dogma. For morality was an ensemble of rational laws which should govern our actions. The regular exposition of these laws constituted moral science. Rights and duties had the same source.

> It is because I am a reasonable and free being, a person, in a word, that I have duties to fulfill, and it is for that reason also that I have rights, the respect of which constitutes in turn a duty for my fellow man, just as the respect of their rights is a duty for me.[17]

Barni declared that democracy depended on such a morality, since democracy declared all men equal in rights. Thus the cultivation of a morality of mutual respect of each others' rights was the means of moving toward a perfect democracy. Certain aspects of morality were controlled by law, and the citizen must have respect for the justice embodied in law. But laws could not and should not cover all aspects of life; what remained must be left to the domain of conscience. Therefore, "there is nothing more dangerous for the future of [democratic] institutions than to regard morality as a politically indifferent matter."

The maintenance of liberty, Barni insisted, depended upon its regulation by the moral law; the maintenance of equality, on mutual respect. In a democracy, a state religion was an offense against freedom of conscience; the state should remain strictly neutral in religious matters. But the state did have a duty to supply universal education, which should be free and obligatory, because this was absolutely necessary to universal suffrage.

By the time the lectures were published, in 1868, the movement known as *morale indépendante* was already influential. (See Chapter 5.) Barni stated in his introduction that he could have entitled the course "Leçons de morale indépendante"; he also referred to them as "these popular lessons in morality, these *sermons laïques*." He claimed to have followed Kant in maintaining the autonomy of morality, independent of both metaphysics and theology. "One will find nothing in this course in ethics which is not derived directly from human nature itself."

Like Vacherot, Barni did not completely break the tie between morality and metaphysics. Morality must be attached to a supreme principle which both crowned and sanctioned it. However, it was better to establish morality in all its autonomy, thereby making it impervious to all metaphysical quarrels.[18]

Barni did reveal in this introduction some doubts about the adequacy of a purely rational and psychological morality for popular consumption. Vacherot, also, had seen this weakness, and had suggested that the emotional and aesthetic replacements for religion might be found in art.[19] Barni noted that it was not enough to teach morality in a rational way, although it was essential. Some method must be found to make morality pass into everyday life—"an assiduous moral cultivation which is not only a matter of intelligence, but which develops in us the love of the good and makes of it the motivating force of our life.''

He felt that, unfortunately, this moral culture was lacking in French society; and he seemed to have been willing to accept religion as the emotional and aesthetic reinforcer of ethics, but not the Catholic religion. He referred to the church as Voltaire's *infâme,* and deplored the fact that it had not yet been crushed. On the other hand, he indicated that a religion which would truly enforce a rational morality, such as American Unitarianism, would be acceptable to him.[20] Other attempts to solve this problem were undertaken by partisans of a universal religion, which will be discussed below.

Barni was made an inspector-general of secondary education in the Government of National Defense of 1870, and continued to be active in politics and education. As a member of the Société d'instruction républicaine during the early Third Republic, he worked to ''enlighten citizens concerning their rights and duties, and to place them in a condition to govern themselves,'' through lectures on government and public morals and the publication of inexpensive books and pamphlets.[21] He also published a *Manuel républicain* to explain his views on public morality. Public education on the primary level, completely separate from the Church, was essential. ''To instruct the people is to uproot them from the hold of brutal appetites . . . to elevate them to the moral life; it is to render them worthy of the republic.''[22]

Republicans had already learned in the elections of the Second Republic to distrust the people, uneducated as they were. The connection between moral education and a successful future republic had by this time become quite clear to them. Here can be seen the beginning of the merger of moral education with political ideology which was to take place in the Third Republic.

It is clear that Cousin's students did not travel very far, philosophically, beyond their teacher's moral philosophy. To the extent that they did, they were driven by the situation of political opposition in which they found themselves during the Second Empire. As good republicans, they saw the Church as the enemy of the republic they firmly believed must win out. Since Catholicism was the only possible religion for France, they felt the need to seek a foundation for their moral philosophy outside religion.

Even Jules Simon, the student of Cousin who had best reconciled his philosophy with Catholic beliefs, and whose *Religion naturelle* (1856) clearly stated the necessary connection of morality with religious concepts, weakened at this time. In February, 1869, he spoke out for the independence of morality from religion. Admitting that he had always believed it, he nevertheless publicly abandoned the argument that morality exists because there is a perfect God who wills it:

> There is not, there cannot be a will which creates morality any more than

there can be a reason which creates an axiom. . . . To argue that good is good, not because it is good, but because there is an absolute being who wishes it to be good and who could, if he wished, make good evil, is to suppose an impossible thing. . . . No, there must be a justice as there must be a principle of contradiction. . . . I would like to see a philosopher who can manage to establish that there is a just God without parting from the idea of justice.[23]

One is drawn to the conclusion that the spiritualists still really believed in the moral philosophy of Cousin; the difference was that they had surpassed his political position. The republic, in contrast to the *monarchie censitaire,* required moral training independent of the Church for all levels of society, not only for the elite. Thus, their more radical political stance radicalized their philosophical theory, at least for a time.

Universal Religion and Universal Education

Spiritualists in the society had for some time been seeking another way out of the problem of a morality attached to Church dogma—the propagation of a "universal religion," with minimal dogma, which would unite all Frenchmen. Simon's concession to the idea of a morality independent of religious concepts was only temporary. But it must be seen in the context of a general feeling of a crisis in morality that had been building in the society with the decline of Church influence. Not only was the established church opposed to the political liberalism of the intellectuals, but it was fast losing its sway over the minds of ordinary Frenchmen.[24] Therefore, it was no longer even useful to look to the Church as a source of moral stability.

As early as 1830, M.-L. Boutteville had published a work entitled *De la Nécessité d'un nouveau culte en France,* in which he maintained that France was degenerating because she had lost her religion; that attempts to revive Catholicism, such as that of Lammenais, had failed; and that a new religion, conforming to the wisdom of all ages and all nations, should be founded. Pierre Leroux claimed that France was on the verge of becoming atheistic; the enlightened part of society was already irreligious, and the masses would soon follow. It was time to create a religion without a theocracy, which would be "the true religion, the religion of unity invoked by our forefathers" in the revolution. As they had conceived it, a "pouvoir éducateur" would take its place alongside of the executive, legislative and judicial powers. Through universal education the society could perform the mission of unifying religious education, which would include those religious beliefs held by all.[25] Leroux's idea was much like Rousseau's—a basic civic religion, which all men must believe, and complete freedom beyond that.

Some intellectuals undertook the task of trying to reform Catholicism to fit modern philosophy. One of these was François Huet. Recognizing that "moral virtues could no longer be accepted under the old form of orthodoxy,'' where they were based on supernatural and legendary conceptions, he saw the heritage of religion as devolving upon philosophy. But philosophical systems were also in a state of chaos. The answer was for religion to disengage itself from the supernaturalism of its infancy and become scientific, while philosophy developed a religious character. With sweeping eclecticism, he declared, ''the superior combination of the religions and philosophies of the past, revivified, augmented by the fertile cooperation of all the sciences, that is in our eyes the natural and necessary issue of the present revolution.'' A reformed education would reunite reason and faith, thereby reuniting the family, divided by the differing beliefs of husband and wife, and the state, divided by quarrels with the Church.[26] Huet eventually gave up on religious reform and settled for a secular morality in the schools, based on deism, and refraining from polemics against ecclesiastical dogma.[27]

By the '60's suggestions for a new religion, which would be minimal on dogma, unite the nation, and provide a basis for morality, were legion. At this point, it was noted, ''everyone agrees that we are in an epoch of transition; that means that the great ship has broken the cable which attached it to the old shore.''[28] The necessity for a new context for ethics was the subject of debate in widely diverse circles. In the article on *morale* in the *Dictionnaire des sciences philosophiques,* Adolphe Franck noted that ''morality has become the dominant preoccupation of all minds; the questions that it is charged with resolving figure in the first rank among those which today stir everyone.'' Patrice Larroque, a Kantian philosopher, undertook an examination of Christianity from a safe spot in Brussels in 1859, and found it unsuited to current needs.[29]

The following year Larroque tried to reconstruct, out of the debris, a religion which would respond ''both to the general and permanent needs of humanity and to the present needs of the moral order,'' a religion based on reason and favoring the progress of civilization. He pointed out that the decline of morality, which had begun in the upper classes with the recognition that the dogma on which morality depended was false, had now reached the lower classes. Larroque offered a general formula for the profession of faith of a new religion which included belief in God, the immortality of the soul, an objective good and evil, and the ideal of order and justice in social life. He also outlined the structure of the new religious organization, including sample ceremonies for marriages and funerals, sample prayers, and a governing council of elected leaders.[30]

Larroque moved in a circle which included intellectuals of varying opinions, grouped in a salon presided over by Charles Fauvety. A skeptic attracted by mysticism, Fauvety was preoccupied with finding a religious formula which would unite all men in a feeling of fraternity. He had failed to find his answer in Freemasonry. Another member of the salon, Henri Carle, whose goal was also a universal religion, joined with him in founding *l'Alliance*, edited by Fauvety. Carle was closer to Cousin's spiritualism than Fauvety, who then founded his own journal in 1866.

La Solidarité was devoted to "the moral world," which Fauvety claimed was as knowable as the world of nature. Relationships in both worlds were subsumed under universal solidarity. This supposed the freedom of individuals and, in the moral sense, their equality. Fauvety acknowledged his debt to Pierre Leroux as the forerunner of his concept of solidarity.[31] The periodical included approving reviews of Huet's book and those of other rationalists on religion. *La Solidarité* gave way at the end of 1868 to *La Religion laïque*, also edited by Fauvety. Neither had great success.

The Alliance religieuse universelle, guided by Carle, drew support from a larger group, including Huet, Larroque, Ferdinand Buisson, Eugène Despois, Léon Richer, Henri Martin, Victor Hugo and Barni. Carle addressed the group on the decadence of religion and the necessity of an "intellectual moral reconstruction." In the past, religion had guided the development of the masses, and philosophy, that of the elite. What was needed was a synthesis that would apply to all. He saw the work of the Alliance as comparative studies leading to such a synthesis, elucidating the changing view of God and elaborating the concept of progress. The group would also hold regular meetings for the moral education of families, experimenting with forms of religious ritual. Education would be a prime task. They must work out a "purely secular and rational teaching," and then establish schools on all levels, emphasizing the free enquiry of science and moralizing the young in the new faith.[32]

The outlines of the new faith appeared in *L'Alliance* and later in its continuation, *La Libre Conscience*, founded to promulgate "a higher development of enlightenment and of moral culture." In it, Carle called for a "natural religion" and a "natural morality" free of any revelation or priesthood.[33] The religion supported by the Alliance was based on theism and the immortality of the soul; it preached a morality of human solidarity.[34] In 1868 the periodical reported the formation of religious groups in departments in northern France, devoted to forming a new religion "in accordance with the precepts of nature . . . in accord with reason, justice and truth."[35]

By 1869 the group was preparing for a universal Congress of Freethinkers, to offset the coming Vatican Council. The motto of the congress was to be: Each is free to believe or not to believe, no one has authority over consciences.[36] In January of 1870 a central committee of the Alliance was formed, with Carle, Michelet, Quinet and Simon as honorary members.[37] A committee for the coming congress, chosen in February, vowed to demonstrate their rejection of the Roman Church.[38] But *La Libre Conscience* put out its last issue on March 26, and the congress was never held.

The proponents of universal religion during the Second Empire represented, philosophically, only variations of Cousin's attempt to establish a moral philosophy independent of the Church. Like Cousin and his disciples, they believed that morality was linked with the religious concepts of God and the immortal soul; but they agreed that the panoply of traditional theology was not necessary to morality, and could even be a detriment to it in an age of declining faith. Therefore it was necessary, either to found an ethics on a theologically independent philosophy, or to establish a religion of minimal dogma that would preserve moral concepts.

Cousin, presuming that only the educated were skeptics, and that only they would form the electorate, chose the former course, while trying to placate the Church by ceding the lower classes to its influence, and insisting that his philosophy did conform to Catholic dogma. However, the events of the short-lived Second Republic indicated to liberals, not only that the masses were becoming dechristianized, but also that universal suffrage was an inevitable part of the liberal politics of the future. Thus some intellectuals preached the role of universal religion in a mass society; Cousin's students radicalized his position by insisting on the complete independence of morality from religion. Both groups demanded universal secular education. Indeed, the moral education of the masses now seemed essential to all those who hoped for a successful republic in the future.

Neo-Kantianism

Charles Renouvier was crucial in this development because he represented the advances made since Cousin—not only in Kantian philosophy, but also in social and political stance. He actively campaigned amongst the intelligentsia for the institution of free and obligatory primary schools for all, teaching a purely secular morality. He was also important in the development of a morality based on social theory.

Born into a family of independent wealth, Renouvier was nevertheless a republican all his life, as well as a philosopher. During the July Monarchy he was a member of the *Encyclopédie* group, founded by Pierre Leroux to spread Saint-Simonian ideas. Other participants were Frédéric Le Play, Geoffrey Saint-Hilaire and Carnot. Thus, when Carnot was appointed Minister of Education in the Second Republic, Renouvier was launched into the milieu of those concerned with education. His participation took three directions. He became a contributor to *Liberté de Penser;* he wrote one of the popular manuals of *morale* called for by Carnot; and he served on a legislative committee to draft a primary education law.

The bill resulting from this committee proposed a modest three-year obligatory, free, secular education for all French children; they would be taught ''what is useful to all men, either in itself, in that it initiates them into the summary knowledge of their rights, their duties, their country, humanity, and nature, or as a universal instrument towards the utilization of all special studies.'' As for moral education, it would consist of ''universal religion . . . which is engraved indestructibly on all hearts.'' Sectarian religion, being in the domain of individual conscience, had no place in republican instruction, where it should be ''neither admitted nor combatted.''[39]

In his *Manuel républicain,* arranged as a catechism of questions and answers, Renouvier's secularism emerged more clearly. The teacher explained that religion taught one how one should conduct himself in this life in order to be worthy of eternal happiness. ''I speak to you only in the name of the Republic in which we are going to live, and of that morality that all men feel in the bottom of their hearts. I want to teach you the way to be happy on earth, and the first thing which I have to tell you is: Perfect yourself.''

The first degree of perfection was perfect justice, which was a form of equality; the second, perfect fraternity. Duty was a rule of conduct to which one felt obligated by conscience or in one's heart. Justice and fraternity were the two main duties; from them one could deduce the duty of tolerance. The counterparts of duties were rights. The freedom of each person required some restrictions because of the rights of others. The interests and dignity of each would be best conciliated with the interests and dignity of all in a republic. Although the republic could not provide equality of conditions, the duty of fraternity would lead the citizens, united in a representative assembly, to both preserve liberty and move toward equality. Thus, the liaison between politics and morality.

When the student asked why the teacher spoke only of the love of one another, and not of the love of God, the teacher answered: ''Notice . . . that I teach you here the elements of politics, and not those of religion. . . . That order which we feel in ourselves and to which the best among us conform is the same order to which God has subordinated the world.'' However, ''the time has come when the morality taught up to now by the Church in the name of Jesus Christ ought to enter into the assemblies of men who make governments and laws.'' It was the Republic, the teacher announced, which would establish the morality of Christ in the society.[40]

Although Renouvier had already surpassed Cousin in his social ideas (advocating free justice, elected judges, women's rights, divorce, higher inheritance taxes, graduated taxes, universal military service, besides the republic of universal suffrage), it is clear that at this time he was close to Cousin on moral ideas. That is, secular morality should be separate from but equal to religious morality. Its basis, however, was found in the individual, not in the relation of the individual to the order of the universe; the development of each individual toward perfection was linked to that of others in the society.[41] During the fifties, Renouvier's thought took a more Kantian turn;[42] he became preoccupied with the problem of moral freedom. He claimed that reason, reflection and freedom were indigenous to man, but were developed only through experience; therefore, morality grew with social progress.

Renouvier criticized Kant's conception of the categorical imperative as "purely intelligible, not phenomenal, without temporal conditions," and claimed that such actions did not exist. In rebuttal, he posited a kind of individual and social solidarity. (See Chapter 9.) He accused Kant of not really believing in free will, which was the ability to choose the moral law over other possibilities. The ideal of the Just, he wrote,

> envelops each person in a sphere of morally inviolable dignity, accords him, imposes upon him by need a right of self preservation, and at the same time the duty to respect others . . . the passionate development of consciousness leads to, calls out for a regulation of rights and duties of those freely associated.[43]

This work of Renouvier's was contemporaneous with the work of Pierre-Joseph Proudhon on justice (See Chapter 5), and expressed many of the same themes—personal dignity and a justice founded on equality and reciprocity. When Proudhon accused Renouvier of betraying freedom by admitting cosmic absolutism, Renouvier defended himself: "If to admit general laws in the universe is cosmic absolutism, I am guilty. But freedom itself supposes these laws and makes use of them. However, I deny a unique, eternal, total, necessary, absolute law." He in turn praised Proudhon's practical applications of freedom.[44] The two men agreed that the essential idea of justice had always existed in humanity, varying only in its applications; that the moral law implied reciprocity, and therefore equality among persons. But Renouvier felt that love of others was a necessary element in justice, even while finding the moral law sufficient in each human being. "Actually, we are forbidden to appeal to an order imposed supernaturally upon humanity; it is in consciousness that we seek the laws of conscience." There was no law, he felt, which demanded subjection of the person to *a priori* rules which none of the passions could consent to. But one could find in consciousness a law calling for coordination of the passions, to satisfy reason and the feelings that reason judges to be good, such as bonds uniting the self to others. Thus, love, reciprocal and regulated by reason, was a basis of justice. Of course, without the limitation of reason, love as a basis for morality could lead to self-abasement and slavery.[45]

Renouvier credited the followers of Kant with having founded a morality both rational and historically based. While not denying freedom, duty, conscience and justice, they had escaped from the illusion of absolute principles and avoided determinism.[46] In the second of his critical essays the following year, he again defended freedom in moral action, while admitting that it had never been logically demonstrated. As between freedom and necessity, he felt the former thesis more probable.[47]

In *Science de la morale* Renouvier went over the various demonstrations of free will, admitted they were all weak, and contented himself with viewing it, as Kant had, as a necessary postulate for moral philosophy, rather than as the empirical fact of consciousness pictured by Cousin.[48] He was also influenced by Jules Léquier,[49] who argued that one can only choose to affirm freedom, since choosing to affirm necessity is no choice.[50] Ethics constituted a science, Renouvier maintained, although not one of precise knowledge. Both ethics and political science fell into the category of *critique générale,* and could be reduced to the term *morale.*

Morality related to the individual, first, in himself and in his relations to other beings, and second, in conditions of legitimacy and perfection of the political and economic institutions of society. "We contract with our hearts in the first and vaguest feelings of the good and of justice. We feel ourselves bound by the same [sentiments] to others. That is the beginning of morality and of the universal religion of the human species." Societies, he wrote, were founded on a moral and religious contract. Even if the contract was originally between the people and God, the social fabric eventually became exclusively human and explicitly recognized. When people became free, the chain of religious tradition was broken and each man became capable of applying criticism to traditional "facts."

In applying such criticism to the traditional facts of God and immortality, Renouvier ended by accepting them. Immortality seemed to be implied in the perfectibility of man, which Renouvier supported not only on a species level, but on the level of the individual. God was implied in the notion of the Good which existed in man's consciousness.[51] Thus, although Renouvier's morality was based on the freedom of the human being, it implied God and immortality at the summit, as did that of Vacherot and other students of Cousin.

Renouvier's *Science de la morale* of 1869 was in one sense a clarification of the difference between his moral philosophy and the *morale indépendante* then in vogue. Morality, he agreed, was a science like mathematics, in that it was founded on pure concepts. When one said that morality was independent, one could only mean that it ought to be so, since historically it had always depended on metaphysical or religious doctrines. These doctrines should be eliminated, because they were based on often conflicting hypotheses. This could only be done by critical philosophy, which was not a doctrine or a system. "Criticism subordinates all unknowns to phenomena, all phenomena to consciousness, and within consciousness itself, theoretical reason to practical reason." Here is where freedom came in. "The mind that would accept morality as such and for itself ought to free itself . . . from any intervention of scientific hypothesis and religious faith in the actual domain of ethics."[52]

Renouvier postulated the individual as an isolated moral agent—reasonable, with unequal and often conflicting goals—whose choices were regulated by self-interest and reason, to the end of preserving himself physically and developing his capabilities. The association of two such moral agents would result in a *bien commun,* a combination of their individual goals. At this point duty to the self would become, in part, duty to the other. This was, however, not only a matter of reason, but of emotion. Human sympathy had its role in morality. The conclusion he drew from this was in line with contemporary moral theory; the rights of one person equalled the duties of his neighbor, and the union of the two, rights and duties, constituted justice. However, while insisting on the absolute equality of *droit* and *devoir,* Renouvier manifested a preference for those who mistakenly emphasized duty over those who mistakenly emphasized rights.[53]

Renouvier, like most French Kantians, criticized Kant for removing morality to the noumenal world, apart from practical and social ends, and for working with *a priori* concepts. He returned, as had Cousin, to psychological givens. ''The moral sense is a natural combination of sympathy and benevolence . . . and of the social tendency which is their result, with reason, which postulates the equal dignity of persons.'' Justice became generalized by extending the moral reciprocity of two persons—always in such a fashion that it could become a general law—to greater and greater numbers of people. Society was a collection of reasonable agents; ''the reasonable agent finds his law in himself and follows it freely, and that law is not in all unless it is in each, it is not universal unless it is eminently particular.''

The supreme principle of morality was individual autonomy; the moral task of the society was to work toward the freedom of the individual. Progress in a society could be measured by the amount of freedom employed and respected therein.[54]

The neo-Kantian philosophy of Renouvier, incorporating as it did the influence of social thinkers like Fourier and Proudhon, moved closer to a morality of social justice than did that of Cousin. Renouvier also attempted to speak to the problems of his day as they affected the longed-for republic— religion and education. Where religious regulations conflicted with moral and social ones, he saw no answer but complete separation of ''the moral and social domain, with its necessary dependencies, from the religious domain, left to personal choice.'' However, he raised the question of how well men could accomplish justice and order influenced only by moral ideas. The education of the will was also the education of the mind. ''In all times there should be a lively study of ethical matters; this would suppose an organized public education, an education well understood in families and in the nation.''[55]

A consideration of Renouvier's moral philosophy in its broad outlines leads to the conclusion that, despite its greater depth and subtlety, it would provide a basis for moral education in the schools hardly different from that of Cousin. Where Renouvier differed was in his desire to make his moral philosophy the foundation of popular education in the cause of the republic.

Pierre-Joseph Proudhon
and Morale Indépendante

T HE radicalization of the spiritualists had been hastened by the pressure of a group more radical than they, particularly in moral theory. Their influence on Barni has already been mentioned. Starting from a different philosophical base, the theory of *morale indépendante* was also to extend its influence into the Third Republic.

The distinction between the spiritualists, who, with variations, followed the basic philosophical lines laid down by Cousin, and the more radical *morale indépendante* group was both philosophical and social. In the metaphysical sense, the spiritualists did not depart from support for the existence of God and the immortal soul. Some, like Barni and Vacherot, and even Simon on that one recorded occasion, stated that these concepts were not necessary to the moral life; but basically, they continued to support them. The *morale indépendante* group maintained the absolute independence of ethics from any religious or metaphysical premises. This independence allowed for a morality which did not in any way transcend humanity; it comprised the first step toward a true social morality, as distinguished from the individualistic and formal ethics of Cousin.

In the course of grounding ethics in the social nature of human beings, the *morale indépendante* group, like the spiritualists, emphasized the reciprocity of rights and duties. But, further from Kant's categorical imperative than Cousin, they put consciousness of one's rights first, as Rousseau had, and derived the duties of one person from the rights of another. This enabled them to call upon the principles of the Revolution for morality, and to set the stage for the more developed social ethics of the Third Republic.

Like the spiritualists, the *morale indépendante* group had its theoretician—not an urbane scholar of repute in the academic world, but a rough-hewn, self-educated man, Pierre-Joseph Proudhon. The difference between the two thinkers roughly symbolizes the difference between the two groups. While the first were largely *universitaires,* only temporarily removed from the educational establishment during the Empire, the second included members of the society at large—journalists, Freemasons, students and workers.

Proudhon's Justice

There could hardly be two thinkers more different in life and temperament than Cousin and Proudhon. Although both rose from humble circumstance to the intellectual life, Cousin, whose father was a watchmaker, took the characteristic nineteenth-century path, through the state educational system and into the University establishment. Proudhon, son of a cooper and a cook, was forced to drop out before completing secondary school and work for a printer, reading proofs to support his family. From then on, he was self-educated. Besides the Bible and the classics he had read in school, he read in proof the works of Fourier and books of theology and linguistics. He even wrote on his own an *Essai de grammaire générale.* For a time, believing himself suited for the role of Christian apologist, he began to read anti-religious works, only to find that they sorely tried his faith.

In his application for the Suard pension, offered by the Besançon Academy to a needy scholar, Proudhon elaborated a project to establish the truths of the Christian religion through linguistics. He believed that he could discover that "primitive philosophy or religion" of which Christianity was an expression, by a comparative study of religious systems and of the formation of languages, "independent of any other revelation." His purpose, he stated, was to work for the "moral and intellectual amelioration of those whom I like to call my brothers and my companions," and to spread among them "the seeds of a doctrine which I regard as the law of the moral world."[1] In a sense unpredictable by him at that time, this was what Proudhon was to do for the rest of his life.

Once established in Paris as a scholar of the Besançon Academy, he soon put aside linguistics for economics, which seemed the key to the social misery he knew firsthand. However, when the Academy announced a competition on the subject of the Sabbath in 1838, Proudhon's entry, although a social commentary, established him as, above all, a moralist. At the time he referred to it as his "program."[2]

Proudhon based *De la célébration du dimanche* on the ancient Hebrews, and on Moses as the wise lawgiver, whose purpose in ordering the Sabbath was to create a unity of his people stronger than one of material interest. The Sabbath was the celebration of human dignity, a dignity too great to allow the degradation of society by social ranks. The fourth commandment prescribed leisure, not only for the householder, but for the servants within the household, who on that day were peers of their masters. Proudhon also claimed that the Hebraic law was an attempt to prevent both poverty and great riches. Moses was aiming at a society of solidarity, in which each person would have the right to gain his living through work, and to be equal in the apportioning of property and privileges. Therefore, property could not be considered absolute; one always received more from society than could be returned to it, so enjoyment of property was to be regulated by society.

> All inequality of birth, of age, of force or capacity, is nullified before the right to produce one's subsistence, which is expressed by the equality of conditions and of goods . . . the differences of aptitudes or facility in the worker, of quantity or quality in the execution, disappear in the social product, when all members have done what they could . . . their duty . . . in a word, the disproportion of power in individuals is neutralized by the general effort.[3]

The social problem for Proudhon was "to find a state of social equality that is neither communism, nor despotism, nor division nor anarchy, but liberty in order and independence in unity." There should exist, he declared, a science of society, based on the nature, faculties, and relationships of human beings, "a science that does not have to be *invented,* but *discovered.*"[4]

Moses spoke to the people "in the name of God, that is, in the name of truth."[5] The Sabbath was the day for the instruction of the people—in religion, politics, and morality. All jurisprudence, Proudhon claimed, consisted in a simple exposition of principles. "Justice and legality are two things as independent of our assent as mathematical truth; to be obligatory, it suffices that they be known."[6] Those chosen to lead the people, to teach them their rights and duties, to raise the young, were not masters but *instituteurs* of the people; "they command no one . . . they do not impose belief, they expose the truth." The law should be the expression of neither a single will nor of the majority will; "it is the natural relationship of things, discovered and applied by reason."[7]

Here may be found both the persistence of Rousseau's general will and the germs of Proudhon's later program for the moral life of society: human dignity and equality as the basis for morality; the right of the individual to fulfillment and the duty of society to make this possible; the negation of absolute property rights, which prevent equal opportunity; the right of the individual to acquiesce in those arrangements that concern his well-being; the objectivity of the moral law, independent of individual interests; and the importance of education in the revelation of truth, religious and political, to human beings.

Although Proudhon had clearly equated law and truth with God in this work, the clergy at Besançon prevented its sale,[8] thus inaugurating the series of official persecutions that dogged Proudhon's career as a writer. They undoubtedly sensed that Proudhon was more of a deist than a Catholic. In fact, he believed that both Moses and Jesus had professed "pure deism."[9]

The role that Proudhon had given to religion in *Dimanche* was completely negated in *La Création de l'ordre* of 1843. Here he agreed with Comte that it belonged to a past stage of human development and that at this point it was antithetic to human progress. Philosophy, the stage which followed, had now reached the level of eclecticism, which was preparatory to the elaboration of metaphysics—a term which corresponded to Comte's positivism.[10] In the same year Proudhon commented on the current battle between Church and University described in Chapter 2. What the bishops did not realize, he noted, was that if a breath of Catholicism still remained in the people, it was at the pleasure of the University. He felt it unworthy of Cousin to protest against his accusers, when he should state frankly that he was not a Catholic and that his opponents were stupid. In the following year he noted that the people were moving further away from religion. "The people conceive of virtue without the assistance of religion. Think where that will lead," he wrote.[11]

By the time he wrote *Contradictions économiques* in 1864, Proudhon had developed his thoughts on God—"an act of faith in the collective mind." Whereas an individual consciously determined his own actions, society tended to move by a kind of inner spontaneity, which it then deified. Thus, as Feuerbach said, the God that humans adored was an ideal projection of themselves. However, one could not conclude from this, as Comte had, that the collective, Humanity, was to be worshipped. The question was, was the nature that humanity had given the deity compatible with human nature? Proudhon's answer was a resounding NO. For humans to exist and perfect themselves, they must deny God. Since God was "the type and basic principle of the authoritarian and the arbitrary," he was synonymous with the state in politics and with property in economics, which was why he must be opposed in science, in labor, and in political life. In positing God, one denied oneself, imposed upon oneself an ideal that negated one's human essence. Thus Proudhon's famous statement, that ranks with his "Property is theft": "God is evil."[12]

During the 1848 revolution, Proudhon expressed some of the same ideas in his newspaper, *Le Peuple*.[13] In its successor, *Voix du peuple* he concluded: "In two words, Religion and Society are synonymous terms: Humanity is sacred to itself as if it were God." Not that humanity was God—at least not the immutable, infinite, eternal and absolute God of the philosophers. Humanity was perfectible, progressive, and changing.[14]

The only absolute in human life, Proudhon insisted, was the objective moral law within. "Thus morality has no sanction but itself; it would derogate its dignity, it would be immoral, if it took its cause and its end from elsewhere."[15] He compared morality with the truths of mathematics: that two and two made four was independent of God. In *Contradictions* he wrote that "the human race is on the verge of recognizing and affirming something that will be for it equivalent to the old notion of divinity."[16]

Throughout his works, Proudhon had been developing a view of human nature. In *Création de l'ordre* he had emphasized equality, insisting that intelligence was the same in everyone; it was modified in each by particular aptitudes, but all aptitudes were equally estimable. Apparent inequalities between persons were the result of abnormalities—improper education of the mind, physical problems, the mutilation of aptitudes by poverty.[17] In *Contradictions* he discussed the moral sense, opposing both the concept of original sin and the modern assertion that human nature was basically good. He insisted that human morality was inconsistent, because it was free; therefore one could not assume the inevitability of moral progress.[18]

In his explanation of human freedom, Proudhon blended materialism with the insistence upon human ability to surmount it. The essential condition of human existence, he wrote, was the antinomy of necessity and freedom. Although all the elements of an individual were determined, the collectivity of those elements, the person, was free. Freedom was the consciousness of necessity, but was not bound by it. The person could oppose nature, could deny his reason's understanding of it.[19] "The progress of humanity can be defined as the education of reason and of human liberty by fatality." That is, human reason, if followed, set the limits of human freedom.[20]

Humans were also social beings. Proudhon saw human sympathy as the basis of sociability. However, the addition of reflection to this simple instinct resulted in a second level of sociability, "the recognition in the other of a personality equal to our own," which he called justice. The addition of an aesthetic, ideal element created a third level, called equity, which included friendship and devotion. In his early work, Proudhon tended to base rights and duties on needs (eating, sleeping, working, family life, appreciation by others) to which each person had a right, and which others had a duty to make possible. In *Propriété* he defined justice as "the end of privilege, the abolition of slavery, equality of rights, the rule of law." Justice was not the result of law; law was an application of the just.[21]

In this early stage, Proudhon viewed the presence of morality in the individual as a product of society—"a revelation that society, the collectivity, makes to . . . the individual."[22] In *Philosophie du progrès* he described society as an organism perfecting itself bit by bit.[23] However, by the time he wrote *Justice,* he was insisting that society did not transcend individuals, but existed as a result of their reciprocity and common effort, of which it was the expression and synthesis. He denied any solution of the social problem that would completely subordinate the individual to society, as well as any solution of unlimited liberty that presumed the harmony of divergent interests.[24]

Justice dans la révolution et dans l'église was organized as an opposition between the principles of the Church and those that Proudhon believed were replacing them, those of the Revolution. The Church represented the principles of authority, transcendence and the absolute. The Revolution represented human freedom, immanence, and the progressive. To the first belonged all systems that derived justice from revelation, from society itself, or even from Kant's "great human Being." The system of the Revolution declared the immanence of justice in the human consciousness.

Proudhon's demonstration of this was psychological, but not like Cousin's: What does a person feel when faced by another person? His own dignity and that of the other. "To feel and affirm dignity, first in all that pertains to us, then in the person of the next man," that was right (*droit*). "To be ready in all circumstances to undertake the defense of that dignity with energy, and if need be against oneself," that was justice.

What all had in common was this individual dignity and their desire that it be respected. Each person's right was to demand from others the respect of human dignity in his person; each person's duty, to respect that dignity in the person of others. Basically, the two were identical. Since all were the same in reason and dignity, justice also implied equality.[25]

Dignity was individual; justice was social. As one subordinated one's own interest to what was just, one developed a social self. Therefore each person had awareness of self "as person and as Species." An injustice was resented by the injured, by the onlooker, even by the offender himself. But the source of justice was not in society, for the species could not have anything in common that was not already in the individual. Nor could justice come from religion, whose authoritarian nature negated the dignity of man, both the basis and the object of justice. "Justice is human, all human, nothing but human. . . . The theory of Practical Reason subsists by itself; it neither supposes nor requires the existence of God and the immortality of the soul."[26]

As a human faculty, justice was also not immutable, but susceptible to development. It supposed a constant readjustment as human relationships grew and changed. "We will never know the end of Right because we will never cease creating among us new relationships. We are born perfectible, we will never be perfect."[27] Justice operated in society by means of free contracts among individuals, gradually extending to contracts among groups. Because one is free, one may turn one's back on justice, but it always survives. The very fact that all invoked it, even when they violated it, proved that progress was possible.

To support humanity in the accomplishment of justice, the Church had provided Grace; Proudhon instead found this support in a purely human faculty, the Ideal. Human beings were artists, who, by virtue of their freedom, were able to create ideals, which then operated in their conscience.

Although Proudhon agreed that the just act might differ in different times, he insisted that the principle did not depend upon external factors, but always upon the reciprocity of respect among persons. Thus he emphasized the second aspect of the categorical imperative, treating persons as ends, rather than the first, which stressed universal moral rules. Like Kant, he insisted that if one possessed the notion of justice, it became automatic to practice it, as something properly one's own. The human faculty of justice was *conscience* (here, it would seem, in the sense of both consciousness and conscience). The perception of justice then, was identical to justice itself; the sanction of justice was an inner sanction.

Like Cousin, Proudhon made the distinction between acts of precept (justice) and acts of counsel (charity). It was *"de précepte"* to abstain from stealing from another; *"de conseil,"* to assist the impoverished. However, unlike Cousin, Proudhon felt that charity was compensation by the generous for the injustice of a system which impoverished others. In a truly just society, all moral acts were acts of precept, relating to recognized rights.

In economic life, justice required a system of reciprocity of services. This implied that a worker's salary would equal the value of what he produced; that there would be equivalency in all exchanges of products; and that credit would be extended without interest.[28]

Proudhon always expressed the manifestations of justice in terms like equilibrium, reciprocity, equivalency, equality, depending upon the application. He conceived of the laws of justice as universal laws, like the laws of nature. If justice had not been accomplished in the human world, it was because its cultivation had been neglected. Religion had attempted to repair the faults in human justice; but in any society where justice was dominated by another principle, such as religion, it would eventually be annulled, and the society would perish.[29]

By the time *Justice* was issued in a second edition in 1868, a group of Freemasons had founded a review to support Proudhon's idea of a morality independent of religion. Proudhon was feeling a sense of urgency about the necessity for a *philosophie populaire*: "When religions are dying . . . when the republic, everywhere the order of the day, seeks its formulation . . . the time has come to attempt, through a new propagation, the social restoration." It was not that the people themselves did not understand. "The people, by their native intuition and their respect for right are more advanced than their superiors; they are only lacking . . . the word." Putting the truth into words did not require geniuses or saints; they were written in every soul. Proudhon insisted that society needed "no authority, no priesthood, no churches."[30]

Proudhon exerted little influence on the establishment of his time. Elected to the Assembly in 1848, he shocked everyone by proposing an economic measure that threatened property. Only one deputy, the socialist working man

Jean Louis Greppo, voted for the bill. During the Second Empire Proudhon spent considerable time in jail for attacking the authorities. However, his influence was to extend into the Third Republic—not only through workers' movements, but even into the establishment, through the *morale indépendante* group. And later many Proudhonian themes were to emerge in the social theories of Léon Bourgeois and Emile Durkheim.

The Masonic Lodges

French Freemasonry was ripe for a moral philosophy like that of Proudhon, because of its growing adversary relationship with the Church. After a period of government persecution early in the Empire, this predominantly republican organization had been allowed to survive, at the cost of receiving Prince Murat as its Grand Master. Further attempts to co-opt the Order were resisted by most of the Leagues, however; and by 1862 the order was again growing. Up to this point, although often opposed to the political positions taken by the Church, French Freemasonry had been deist, strongly impregnated with Catholicism, despite the fact that the papacy had condemned Masonry with encyclicals in 1832 and 1846.[31] However, while not anti-Catholic, the Order became anti-clerical as soon as it was safe to manifest such a tendency under the Empire. In 1862, the lodge France maçonnique was founding schools and libraries in Paris to extend the moral and intellectual ideas of Freemasonry and to counter the influence of the Church.[32]

In 1865, after the Archbishop of Paris had participated in the funeral of the Grand Master of the Grand Orient, Pope Pius IX again denounced Freemasonry. The result was an increase in the number of Protestant and free-thinking Masons and a sharp increase in the rate of Catholic desertions. A profession of faith had always been part of the initiation into the Order. Proudhon's own response in 1847 had been to deny the traditional view of God in favor of "the personification of the universal equilibrium."[33] In June, 1865, less than a year after Proudhon's death, the profession of faith had been dropped from the Grand Orient's initiation. They continued to maintain as principles of the Order the existence of God, the immortal soul, and human solidarity.

In 1863 following a speech at the Renaissance lodge by Marie-Alexandre Massol, a discussion had begun in the pages of *Monde maçonnique* on whether Masonry was a universal religion. A missionary of Saint-Simonian social reform, Massol had traveled through France as a manual laborer. He had also founded schools in Egypt with Père Enfantin. After the dispersal of the group he founded *L'Observateur français* in England, returning to France in 1848 to work for *La Réforme*. He became a disciple of Proudhon, working on his *Voix du Peuple,* tutoring his children, and becoming an executor of his will.[34]

Massol became a leading figure in Masonic debates on morality. He maintained the necessity to free ethics from theology as all other areas of life had gradually been freed. What Masonry represented, he insisted, was "the idea of a *morale indépendante,* pure of all outside elements," based on the fact that a person was conscious and free. One respected oneself, and therefore demanded respect from others. "That reciprocity of respect, and the peace or the discomfort that accompanies it, constitutes conscience. . . . Such is, in its simplicity, the moral law." The inviolability of the person should be the principle, the end and the means of every institution. In thus making itself independent of religion, morality would become human.[35]

This definition of *morale* did not go unopposed, and in 1864 Massol printed and distributed 1,000 copies of a letter restating his whole theory of morality. "Good is all that favors, preserves and increases respect of the human person. Evil is all that tends to destroy or decrease this same respect. Obligation, duty is the impossibility of the mind or reason to deny that this same respect [which one demands for oneself] is demandable by others, owed to others. . . . Human dignity, elevated to its ideal state, completes the moral order."[36]

Paris Masons now began to argue over the necessity to recognize the "Grand Architect of the Universe" in their constitution. Some lodges were willing to rewrite the preamble to their constitution, removing God and the immortal soul and substituting the principle of "the inviolability of the human person." But the attempt to dispense with God and the immortal soul was not successful during the Second Empire,[37] although interest in *morale indépendante* continued.

Interest in independent morality was heightened by the civil funeral of Proudhon in December, 1864. Three thousand persons followed his casket to the burial in Passy, for which a collection had been taken. Massol was one of the three speakers, eulogizing Proudhon as "one of those who have worked hardest at building the major work of this century, the foundation of a morality exclusive of all superstition."[38]

However, at the convention of the Grand Orient in July, 1865, Massol and his group failed to move a majority. Fifty supporters gathered at a banquet afterward and welcomed the suggestion of Lazare Caubet, another disciple of Proudhon, that they publish a journal devoted to their cause.[39] It was an effort to convince the public at large of the value of *morale indépendante.* The five years of the periodical's existence were to make it a respected and influential term.

The first issue of *Morale indépendante* appeared on August 6, 1865, with Caubet as director and Massol as editor. It included articles by Henri Brisson, Frédéric Morin, Charles Renouvier, Louis Redon, and Amédée Guillemain. A letter from Vacherot promised to aid in the "great work" of making morality a matter of science and not of faith. Massol outlined his definition of *morale* and declared that the editors believed that only the complete independence of morality appeared likely to regenerate morals and to furnish the base of a truly solid education.[40] Renouvier's article on "Morale et Religion" admitted that all religions taught the same morality, which made it possible to speak of *the moral law*. But external imposition of ethics prevented people from feeling the moral law as a link with the rest of humanity. Thus religious morality failed to contribute to the solution of the problem of human relationships. He attributed morality based on the *person* to Kant.[41]

Renouvier was later to use the pages of the periodical to clear up the misunderstandings caused by this statement. He assured the readers that, although he had denied that immortality was an absolute necessity as a basis for ethics, he personally believed in it. Renouvier's gradual pulling away from identification with *morale indépendante* became clear in this second article, which questioned whether, in its efforts to separate morality from history, its followers had not ignored the law of moral solidarity.[42] Two years later his own publication, *L'Année philosophique,* was to link *morale indépendante* with Proudhonian thought rather than Kantian, and to criticize it on the ground that it started from a feeling of self-respect, rather than from a feeling of duty.[43]

There was a real difference between the Kantians and the Proudhonians on this very issue, despite the fact that both emphasized the reciprocity of rights and duties and the primacy of *conscience*. For the Kantians, the latter term meant conscience, or consciousness of duty, whereas for the Proudhonians it meant consciousness, or the awareness of rights. Clarisse Coignet, a regular contributor to *Morale indépendante,* later criticized Renouvier for using love as a basis for the moral law, (probably as a reinforcement for duty). As Proudhon had proved, she pointed out, love could not lead to justice, because it was a passion. The foundation of justice and the moral law was reason, (as a reinforcement of the logic of reciprocal rights).[44]

The writings of the main proponents of *morale indépendante* show a range of opinion that makes it difficult to define the doctrine too precisely. But Coignet's book, *La Morale indépendante,* written in 1869, is worthy of note because she herself was to write *morale* textbooks during the Third Republic.[45] She based the person's rights on human freedom, a fact accessible through reason and consciousness, in one's own experience. Freedom, "in establishing the individual on rights and obligations, establishes society on the equality of rights and the reciprocity of obligations, and makes the human being the origin, the end, and the creator of morality."

Morality, Coignet maintained, was not the condition of human rights, but the consequence of them, since human rights were anterior to society. By an extension of individual rights and the duty to observe each others' rights, one arrived at collective freedom and justice. Humans might be born physically, socially and economically unequal; but they were equal in rights. Therefore the moral person attempted to alter society in such a way as to ameliorate these distinctions. She mentioned the suppression of class privilege and monopoly, the right for all to be educated, to own property, to have access to credit. The implication was that those endowed with natural and social benefits had a duty toward those who were not. (But, unlike later solidarity theories, this duty was deduced, not from social debt, but from equality of rights.)

Like Proudhon and many supporters of *morale indépendante,* Coignet compared the "primitive fact" of individual freedom to mathematics. But the axiom of *morale,* freedom, was a living fact of our inner experience. Thus it differed from the positive sciences. However, the aid of the positive sciences would be necessary to achieve social justice—to regulate physical phenomena for human well-being, to free people from grinding manual labor, to achieve economic justice.[46]

Morale indépendante was greeted enthusiastically by much of the Paris and provincial press.[47] Individual readers also lent their support. One suggested that the periodical compose a small treatise to guide ordinary people in the development of moral truths.[48] A contest was conducted for the best moral catechism for children, which was won by a mother.[49]

In December, 1865, Père Hyacinthe began a series of six Advent sermons at Notre Dame on the subject of *morale indépendante,* which he declared a topic worthy of discussion because it was not merely a product of Freemasonry or democratic journals, but the echo of a broad stratum of thought and feelings. In the first sermon, with Cousin in conspicuous attendance, he extended the hand of friendship to all Christians, even all deists. But he accused the partisans of *morale indépendante* of being Proudhonians, and of trying to be independent, not only of particular religions, but even of that "natural religion which is the basis of all religions."[50] As the series continued, his sermons reflected the repercussions of the topic within the Church hierarchy. And at the last sermon, Msgr. Darboy provided his own summing up of the topic, including a warning to mothers to guard their children against *morale indépendante.*[51]

By mid-1866 the topic had been treated, pro and con, by a large number of periodicals, and had been the subject of a congress of social sciences.[52] Emile Deschanel had supported it in the *Journal des débats* and Edmond About in *l'Opinion nationale. Le Siècle* commented on the growing popularity of the subject in its praise of a *Manuel de morale populaire* by Leon Goudounèche. Louis-Auguste Martin, editor of *Annuaire philosophique,* offered a 500-franc prize for the best catechism of universal morality for young people, to be judged by the editors of *Morale indépendante.*[53]

In the autumn of 1867 three courses on *morale indépendante,* not necessarily approving, were being offered at the Sorbonne, by Emile Beausire, Charles Lemmonier, and Emile Caro.[54] The town of Dijon was offering a course on secular morality in their adult education program. Meanwhile discussions took place in Masonic lodges on the importance of teaching an independent morality in the schools, a project considered by some to be a matter of extreme urgency.[55]

Under the imperial laws it was impossible to organize for this purpose; but a Society for the Encouragement of Public Education was formed, and Masons propagandized for moral education as individuals. Some lodges opened their own schools for both sexes, in Marseille and Lyon.[56] Speeches at the distribution of prizes in such schools emphasized the necessity of moral training as a preparation for democracy, and the independence of morality from religious concepts.[57] At the general assembly of the Grand Orient in 1869 it was decided that Masons should patronize the free secular schools, and should concern themselves in educational affairs.

By that time the Ligue de l'enseignement had come into being, joining together all those who sought a free, secular public education. And time was running out for the Empire.

6

Workers and Secular Morality

The Ligue de l'Enseignement

As the Empire waned and the Republic began to seem a distinct possibility for the future, popular education was on the agenda being worked out in all groups of the opposition. They joined their hopes for universal education in the Ligue de l'enseignement, founded by Jean Macé. A republican and professor of history, Macé had left Paris after the coup of December 2, taking refuge in Belgium. There, early in 1865, anticlericals formed a Ligue de l'enseignement to oppose Church control of education. Macé joined in 1866. His interest in education led him back to France, where he taught in a girls' school in Beblenheim. Gradually he began to found communal libraries throughout Alsace and to write books for children.

In October of 1866 Macé launched his first appeal for formation of a French Ligue de l'enseignement in *l'Opinion nationale.* It was to be a religiously neutral organization, devoted mainly to furthering popular education.[1] The first three members were of the working class—a railroad conductor, a stonemason, and a policeman, each of whom contributed five francs. By December 15, there were 510 members; by February 15, 2101; within a year, 4792 members spread over 71 departments, including 41 French citizens abroad.[2]

In each area, local circles operated on their own. The first step was usually the founding of a communal library. A general assembly of the Ligue was planned for 1867, but the necessary permit for such a convocation was not granted by the government. Macé nevertheless circulated the constitution he proposed for the national body. Its aim would be to stimulate initiatives for the development of public education. They would found and support libraries and public courses for children and adults. Each circle would organize and conduct its own business independently. One clause stated that members "would abstain from anything that could be perceived as polemical, either political or religious."[3]

Despite this caution, the Ligue in Metz was excommunicated by the bishop, because it included Masons. This action only increased the support of Freemasonry for the Ligue. Macé, however, remained moderate. In his article, "Philosophie de la Ligue," Macé's only direct rebuttal to attacks on the organization, he wrote that all religions had their dogma, "but at the basis of all . . . is found the law of voluntary submission to the ideas of human justice and fraternity."[4]

In 1848 Macé had made his own contributions to texts on morality: *Les Vertus du républicain* and *Petit catéchisme républicain*. In the latter, liberty was defined as the right to obey one's own will, limited by that same right in others; equality, as a right, imposing the duty to consider all others equal, founded on the equality of persons before God; fraternity, as the duty of persons to love one another as children of God. "A democratic republic founded on liberty, equality, fraternity is none other than the law of God," Macé wrote. In *Les Vertus du républicain* he outlined the virtues of fraternity, the sentiment of human dignity, courage, modesty, disinterestedness, frankness, justice, and patriotism.[5]

An early subscriber to the Ligue was a Paris businessman, Emmanuel Vauchez, who resigned his position to spread the Ligue in the countryside, and to found the Paris circle. By June of 1868 it had 234 members, including a senator, 3 deputies, and the editors of *Le Siècle* and *Le National*. In 1869 (June 19) they held a general assembly, electing their founder secretary-general and Macé president. The board of directors included Massol; and headquarters were opened on the rue Saint-Honoré.[6]

The national campaign for free and obligatory instruction began in 1870, with a petition launched by the Strasbourg Ligue. By April 20, one hundred thousand names had been signed; by July 15, 350,000 names, from 83 departments. Then the Franco-Prussian war put an end to the matter for the time being. However, when the war was over, the Paris circle reorganized and drew up a petition demanding the establishment of public education with *obligation* and *gratuité*. It was sent to all branches, to be circulated for signatures. Republican newspapers strongly supported this move, printing the petitions and collecting them when signed. *Le Temps* only included obligation, not *gratuité*, in theirs. But *Le Siècle* and some other papers included *laïcité* as well. Even before this action, the clergy had come out in opposition to the petition.

Almost one and one-half million people signed the Ligue petitions, most of which were arranged so that the three demands could be voted on separately. Of the 917,267 petitions thus organized, the breakdown was: 119,251 for obligatory primary education; and 387,895 for free, obligatory and secular primary education.

What was the meaning of *laïcité* to the Ligue? Macé summed it up as follows:

> That the schools will be placed outside of any particular rite, any confessional doctrine. As for that common basis of universal religion which is imposed on all, and which from age to age enlarges the progress of the human conscience, it could certainly not be eliminated from the program of our schools. They would fail basically, if the conscience of children were not the object of the same solicitude as their intelligence and their reason.[7]

Perhaps the greatest triumph was that the Ligue de l'enseignement, violently opposed by the clergy, had managed to acquire the names of 118,819 women on their petitions.[8] Macé himself had taught in a girls' school in Alsace, and the Ligue, along with the Masons, had supported Victor Duruy's program of secondary education for women. Never had a petition been so successful in France. The Ligue came to include practically all of the adherents of *morale universelle* and *morale indépendante* as well as many spiritualists. It would later support Jules Ferry's laic laws with the slogan, ''La science à l'école, les religions aux églises.'' Becoming less neutral and more republican, it joined in 1880, the Société républicaine d'instruction.

Socialist Views

Although the Ligue had a large working-class constituency, it was led for the most part by the bourgeoisie.

The working class segment of the movement for secular education was closer to Proudhon than to the spiritualists in its thinking, at least by the late sixties. Workers had gradually been developing ideas on morality separate from religion in their own milieu. Sharing the anticlericalism of the bourgeois intellectuals, but viewing the unification of French society from a socialist viewpoint, interested members of the working class had begun to demand universal and secular education for their children during the Second Republic.

It was in this working-class milieu that the term *solidarité*, later adopted as a form of *morale laïque*, was generally used in France. Macé had been secretary of the group led by Ledru-Rollin during the Second Republic called Solidarité républicaine. Greppo, socialist and Mason, who had voted for Proudhon's project in the Assembly, had written at that time a *Catéchisme social, ou exposé succinct de la doctrine de la solidarité*. A silk-weaver of Lyon, he had organized mutual societies there and participated in the riots of

1831 and 1834. A member of Blanqui's Société des familles, he had taken part in the 1848 revolution in Lyon, and been elected to the Assembly. (Because of his origins, it was rumored that Greppo was not educated enough to write this book, and that the author was Constantine Pecqueur, a rumor not generally accepted.)[9]

Greppo depicted solidarity, rather than competition, as the natural rule of society. It should go beyond the exigencies of mutual need, to become the basis of all human relations. Society should concern itself primarily with the children—their lodging, nourishment, clothing, and instruction. There should be no question of religious training in the schools; that would be left to the "fors intérieur de chaque citoyen." But the goal of all instruction, as Greppo and the workers in general saw it, was to produce socially useful citizens. And *morale* should be taught, not only in the family and in schools, but in society as a whole, "more by example than by precept."[10]

In examining the nature of working-class support for secular education, it is useful to return to Proudhon, who saw it as an essential element in the establishment of justice in society, although not in a state-sponsored form. Proudhon's theory of education was based on labor. Instead of imparting to the young conceptions of science, technology and society, and then sending them to work, Proudhon preferred to treat them primarily as workers, who would learn to analyze the instruments and operations of their labor, as well as the interdependent nature of society, after the fact.

The education of intelligence would begin, then, with education in a series of industrial and/or agricultural operations, graduated in complexity, with subsequent analysis of the basic concepts on which each one rested—"a simultaneous education of the intelligence and the organs." The young worker would serve an apprenticeship in every special operation of an industry, and would also be provided with an overall view of the work done in all industries. Thus education and apprenticeship would be combined. The products of student labor would pay for the education, so that workers' associations, not the state, would bear the responsibility and lay down the curriculum.

The student would gain a sense of the contribution made by each job to the whole, as well as the idea of his "labor debt." It is here that the concept of solidarity, originating in working class circles, foreshadows the "official philosophy" of the same name in the Third Republic. In Proudhon's system, education would gradually reveal that one owed one's developed capabilities to society as a whole, which had developed the techniques of survival and progress one was learning to master—agriculture, technology, science, arts and letters.

Along with greater ability and understanding would come participation, in the direction and the benefits of the student's particular work unit, and later, in the operations of commerce, public works, military training and political economy. This synthesis of moral and intellectual activity would provide a consciousness of the necessity of work, of different functions in a society, and of the individual's place beside his associates in the continuation of a great human endeavor.[11]

During the Second Republic, before the publication of Proudhon's *Justice,* a group of socialist teachers had published an educational program stressing the need for moral reform. Among them were Pauline Roland, who spoke for women's rights, particularly in education, and who had tried to register to vote in 1848, and Gustave Lefrançais, a former Mason, who had left the Order because he found it too religious. Both spent time in jail under the Empire— Lefrançais for three months after the publication of this program. He joined the International after 1871.[12]

In the preface to their educational program, the teachers blamed the downfall of the July Monarchy on moral corruption, and called for education to engender moral renewal. Their declaration of principles included belief in God, humanity and its perfectibility, equality, the principles of voluntary association, popular sovereignty, republican government, the sanctity of the family, the equalization of wealth, the right of all persons to develop their physical, moral and intellectual faculties, and the right to work.[13] An entire outline of moral education for children from the cradle to age eighteen was included.

In the first three years, an indirect moral education, depending on music and the character of the teacher; from 3-6 years, in the école maternelle, the child would learn no dogma or catechism, but some history of religion, and "the morality that regulates the rights and duties . . . of human beings to one another." In the sixth to ninth year students would begin to make a contribution to society by working in fields and workshops part time. Moral education would be taught in action as much as possible, in relation to real situations. The Golden Rule would be the basic principle.

The first formal lessons in *morale* would be given to those aged nine to twelve years, structured around liberty, equality, fraternity and the rights and duties implied by them. History would be taught as both a moral and a scientific discipline. In the next three years, up to age 15, one-third of the school hours would be devoted to labor, either industrial or agricultural. Moral education would now be enriched by instruction in art and religion. On the latter, the program specified that, "in the absence of a unified and complete dogma, we can give to our children, not a religion, but religion. All our religious teaching will arise from *morale* and history understood philosophically." Any ritual observances were up to the parents. Although superstition would be attacked, there would be no effort, under any pretext, to attack the bases of faith.

From age fifteen to eighteen, the child would be seriously, philosophically instructed in the way his duties must be fulfilled, "as a person, member of a family, and citizen." Politics, which was simply morality in action, would be taught in its most elevated form, as well as political economy. Each day would include instruction in music and the arts, "in a manner by far more moral than didactic."[14] (The use of music was often cited by secular moralists as a pedagogical aid in teaching ethics.)

It has been said that Proudhon was the only leading writer of the period who expressed the thoughts of the working man, and that many workers were Proudhonians before they found their ideas expressed in his works.[16] This socialist program of education, published before *Justice,* verifies that assertion. Although Proudhon had derived his "workshop" method of education from Fourier, he applied it to an industrializing, or at least an artisanal, society, thereby making it relevant to all workers.

Nevertheless, unlike Proudhon, the socialists of mid-century were still bound, if not to Catholicism, to religious concepts. It was not until the Second Empire that French socialism freed itself of that vague religiosity* which informed its thought.[17] Even the Proudhonian and anticlerical Henri-Charles Leneveux, typographer, still included religious training as one aspect of education in 1861, in *La Propagande de l'instruction.* Leneveux had been one of the founders of the Catholic socialist Buchez's *L'Atelier,* but had later turned against Catholicism. A collaborator on *Le Siècle* toward the end of the Empire, he opposed centralized socialism and favored cooperatives.[18] His own contribution was a project for popular education, La Bibliothèque des connaissances utiles.

But Leneveux thought that religion had no place in the schools. A rational education, he wrote, should show people that the moral ideas of Christianity corresponded fully to the ideas of justice and fraternity based on conscience and reason, and were the necessary bases of all human societies. "One could

---

*A program in *morale* by a group of socialists in the Second Empire:[15]

0-3 years - instinctive development of the sentiments of liberty, equality, fraternity

3-6 years - recitation of historical and moral anecdotes

6-9 years - religious and moral notions founded on the development of republican liberty, equality, fraternity

9-12 years - religious, moral, dogmatic and sentimental notions

12-15 years - same, plus artistic studies, including design, sculpture, painting and music (harmonic composition)

age 15 on - moral and literary studies. Political instruction, including the study of administration. Philosophical studies based on history or social science. Notions of the history of law. Artistic studies (similar to the above).

say that in France civil society is more truly Christian than religious society. That new road to Christian philosophy was opened by the authors of our great Revolution."[19]

Younger republicans, reflecting on the downfall of the Second Republic, tended to blame their elders for "their religiosity, their mysticism." They preferred to commit themselves more and more to action, and less to any philosophy that included the supernatural or absolute concepts.[20] Auguste Vermorel, a Proudhonian and collaborator on *La Presse,* tried at the end of the Second Empire to revive *La Réforme,* with Prosper-Olivier Lissagaray as editor. Both were later members of the Commune. Vermorel criticized the republicans of 1848 for seeking liberty through political formulas, "when it resides in the sovereignty of individual conscience." The work of democracy, he wrote in 1869, was to proclaim the moral and social equality of all, leading to liberty in justice instead of the egoistic liberty of laisser-faire. The indispensable condition of freedom in justice would be the abolition of ignorance and misery.[21]

In the manifesto of his newspaper, *Courrier français,* in 1866, Vermorel had maintained that any politics that did not have as its direct and immediate aim the moral education and amelioration of the lot of the people (in that order) was necessarily sterile, and could in no way suit a democracy.[22] Reviewing Jules Simon's *L'Ouvrière,* he called the education of the people a question of capital importance. "What is necessary is not a religion, it is a moral law." Religion, he wrote, might be an excellent adjunct to morality in the beginning of societies; but as humanity learned to think for itself, it rejected religious despotism. "It is then that the moral law must be made precise, determined in its absolute existence, shown to be sufficient unto itself." It had been the error of recent apostles of new religions—Fourier, Saint-Simonians and neo-Catholics—to believe that moral law was necessarily linked to dogmas.[23]

Although there were few workers groups, even in the sixties, that maintained a strong opposition to all religious training, most were moving further and further away from religious concepts as a basis for ethics. They always insisted on a "rational" education for all children, claiming that it would improve public morality. At the 1867 Exposition, the metalworkers maintained that education should inspire in students the sentiments of justice, which were the best social guarantee; the tinsmiths, one of the few groups to reject religious morality altogether, advocated a kind of moral training based on the biographies of benefactors of humanity. Many workers' groups, influenced by Proudhon, opposed a state-run school system in favor of education by local communes.[24] All tended to stress the value of manual labor. In the program of socialist workers published in *La Démocratie* in 1869, one article demanded "complete secular education, obligatory for all, at the expense of the nation."[25] (This newspaper carried a regular column, "Chroniques irreligieuses." It supported mutual aid societies of freethinkers among students and workers.)

The advanced ideas of some workers on education probably reflected the fact that those interested in the subject tended to be, not those in big factories, but those in small workshops—construction workers, typographers, metal-workers—who were artisans.[26] However, the teaching of morality was on the much broader agenda of the International Socialist Congress of September, 1867, in Lausanne. Tolain, bronzeworker and one of the founders of the French section, spoke against seeking the bases of morality in any *a priori* conception outside of humanity itself. (A Proudhonian, Tolain was called "the chef moral de la classe ouvrière." He was active in mutual societies and wrote workers' news for Vermorel's *Courrier français*.[27]) André Murat, mechanic and follower of Massol, spoke for *morale indépendante*, inviting the International to become collaborators of the movement.[28]

In Marseille, the Ligue de l'enseignement, backed by the Masonic lodges, actually become linked to a section of the International. The Masonic lodges in Paris, particularly those of the Scottish rite, had sections of workers who discussed social and political questions. Freemasonry and the Ligue were both active in helping to systematize the thoughts of the workers on education.[29] By the end of the Second Empire the workers in the cities were overtly hostile to religious education, on the grounds that it was unscientific and that it created divisions in society. The elite of the working class were almost all Freemasons.[30]

The group around Macé had strong ties to the working class. A direct connection was Massol himself, spokesman of *morale indépendante*, whose years as a traveling metalworker before the 1848 revolution, as well as his stint on Proudhon's *Voix du peuple*, had developed his ability to relate to the needs and desires of the workers.[31] Charles Sauvestre, another Mason, published articles on education in *La Presse*, which had a large working-class readership. Leneveux did the same in *Le National*. The works of François-Vincent Raspail, the doctor of the poor, whose views on education were close to those of Proudhon, were widely read by workers.[32]

In 1869, when the Société d'enseignement was founded in Paris, aiming to provide an education for both sexes that would foster moral and intellectual self-discipline "outside any dogmatic conceptions," the socialist Lefrançais served on the committee along with Massol and Boutteville. "We had resolved to found, in cooperative form, the only thing permitted to us—a society for independent education, having as its goal the provision of an education for the children of its members outside of any religious conception." Boutteville, who had lost his position as philosophy professor at the Lycée Sainte-Barbe for his abovementioned book, was to be in charge of the school. More than a hundred members of the society raised a tenth of the capital necessary, then sought official registration. No notary in Paris would agree to handle the registration required by law; the society was illegal because no religious instruction was to be offered at the school, and the administrative council included three women. All efforts to form a legal association were in vain; money raised was returned to the parents.[33]

Workers were also involved in freethinking student associations during the late Empire. French students, returning from an international student conference at Liège, inspired by a group called Solidaires belges, founded an association called Agis comme tu penses. Its by-laws read, in part:

> Considering that it is necessary to separate progressive and scientific morality from the superannuated dogmas that reason condemns and that feelings should censure . . . that to give the child a faith and a science which negate one another is to oppose his feelings to his reason. . . . The undersigned regard it as a duty to break in fact with these doctrines, which they reject in principle; they pledge never to receive any sacrament of any religion. . . . They organize under this name: Act as you think, an association that takes science as its law, solidarity as its condition, justice as its aim.

Clemenceau was one of those who joined this association and recruited workers as members.[34]

Students and workers also were associated in the more militant Masonic lodges, and at public lectures. (Young *normaliens* were also reading Proudhon during the Empire.[35]) A law permitting public meetings was passed in 1868, setting off a number of lecture series in Paris. The first, in October of that year, was on the topic of female labor. Although many series were for bourgeois audiences, other working-class lectures on social issues followed. Entretiens et Lectures, founded by Lissagaray and Albert Leroy in the rue de la Paix, drew such speakers as Eugène Pelletan, Elysée Reclus, Henri Brisson, Charles Floquet, and Jules Vallès.[36] The Société libre d'économie politique organized meetings at La Redoute. A series organized by liberal Catholics at Pré-aux-clercs was often taken over by atheist audiences.[37]

As the Empire moved to its close, speakers at these lectures, like Jules Simon, were often booed by the workers; the predominant attitude of those attending was anti-religious.[38] At Pré-aux-clercs on November 9, a majority of the audience hissed and booed when Edmond de Pressensé quoted Mirabeau to the effect that God was as necessary to the French people as freedom. At Menilmontant on November 13, a speaker called for the reform of education; "for what has produced despotism for some and slavery for others is that a supernatural being has been introduced, who acts arbitrarily; that the eye has been trained upon the enjoyment of a supposed future life to which humanity has been sacrificed." He was cheered by the audience.[39]

Echoes of the civic morality of the Revolution resounded in these halls. Prolonged applause followed the demand of another speaker at Menilmontant on November 28, that the catechism be replaced by a philosophic history of humanity, and the New Testament by the civil code. A member of the International, speaking against religious training, propounded Proudhonian doctrines of a mutualist education.[40] By this time the ideas of the conscious members of the working class included not only the end of religious education, but a particular view of what education should be. It ought to be close to the realities of life, as in Proudhon's workshop-school; it should produce a culture of solidarity through a moral training independent of religious concepts.

Under the Commune only one member of the Council, Marie Vaillant, worked at secularization of the schools. But there was a popular movement toward this end. On April 2, 1871, the Commune received a delegation from the Société d'éducation nouvelle, demanding that all religious or dogmatic instruction be left to families and immediately eliminated from the schools of both sexes, along with all religious objects.[41] Six days later, in the seventeenth arrondissement, it was ordered that the teaching of *morale* be disengaged from any religious or dogmatic principle. Teachers who could not stand this "principle of freedom" should resign.[42]

The petition brought to the Commune contained language that was significant for the future. It demanded that the schools employ exclusively "the experimental or scientific method, which commences always with the observation of facts, whether natural, physical, moral or intellectual."[43] Clearly the more radical thinkers of the Second Empire had gone beyond spiritualism and were denying altogether the necessity for religious concepts in *morale*. The influence of Proudhon and *morale indépendante* had prepared the way for acceptance of a non-religious morality in the schools, and for the replacement of spiritualist ethics by socially-oriented ethical systems at end of the century.

The most radical spokesmen of the new *morale*—workers, students, and a growing cadre of positivist intellectuals—had gone even further, some to scientific materialism. The claim that *morale* was a science, up to this point made only in the sense that ethics could be philosophically established, was to be extended in new and varying forms during the Third Republic. But first, secular morality had to be institutionalized as part of a national primary school system.

Part III

The
Inauguration of
Morale Laïque

Introduction

The aftermath of the Commune, like that of the June Days of the Second Republic, was a reaffirmation of the old verities—political, social and religious. Through 1873 it seemed almost inevitable that a monarchy of some sort would be restored. Those who had cooperated with the Commune were banished, either from existence, from France, or from the social and political life of the nation. The Church again appeared to the frightened bourgeoisie as the guarantor of moral order in the society; the idea of morality without religious concepts was pushed into the background. Nevertheless, the preoccupation with *morale* continued. Not only were the remaining republicans—moderate, to be sure—concerned with the necessity of universal education, including moral education, as a requirement for universal suffrage; intellectuals in general were meditating on the reason for France's ignoble defeat by the German armies. Moral unity seemed more important than ever.

   New thinking on the subject of ethics resulted in a blend of ideas already present in intellectual circles, modified by the new circumstances in which France found herself. The basic elements of the blend were still Kantian, or neo-Kantian, as represented by Charles Renouvier, and by liberal Protestantism. These Kantian elements were combined with the increasingly popular tenets of positivism which, well after the death of Comte himself, seemed more and more to accord with the needs of republican thinkers. The result, in the *morale laïque* that would prevail in the schools starting in the 1880s, was basically the old spiritualism, combined with republican and anti-clerical fervor, taught by a corps of dedicated *instituteurs* similar to that envisaged in the First Republic.

7

Protestants and Positivists in the Third Republic

Renouvier

CHARLES Renouvier, like so many intellectuals after the disaster of 1870, wasted no time in reviving the discussion about the importance of ethics in society. In 1872 he founded a periodical, *Critique philosophique*, partly to offset the return of Church influence.[1] In the first issue he emphasized the link between the progress of a nation and its *morale*. He pointed out that society must, through education, combat the "weakening sense of duty."[2]

In an article on "l'Education et la morale" he wrote that the Church had pretended to teach morality, but did not teach it, and opposed any one else's teaching it. The schools, on the other hand, were not performing their function in this period of intellectual anarchy, caused by a religion hostile to thought on one hand and a thinking hostile to religion on the other. "Our schools have fallen into moral nothingness." The students were not receiving the slightest teachings on the universal notion of Justice, on its elements of equality and reciprocity, on the correlation of rights and duties. "The absence of a social morality, of a universal morality in education, has contributed more than any thing else to the division of French society into two camps, . . . profoundly separated. . . ." The "morality of the state" must be rational, severe and philosophical, respecting religious faith, even admitting certain universal elements thereof; it must be Kantian critical philosophy. The Church, on the other hand, would have to respect the associations of others if it wished its own

85

rights to be honored. It would have to learn to conciliate its "high pretensions" with the authority of a secular moral state, representing a kind of civic and political religion of reason.[3]

Renouvier and his associate, François Pillon, conceived the purpose of their journal to be the elaboration of such a republican doctrine. It should be free of metaphysical speculations; but it would nevertheless respond to the new political life of the nation as well as to the human need to believe and affirm the primacy of moral law in the universe. Morality would be central to such a doctrine; the task was to seek its basic principles. Noting that the habit of authority in political life remained as a leftover of the defunct Catholic religious teachings, the editors chided the bourgeoisie for desiring peace and order at any price, for being religious hypocrites and denying their faith in justice. Bourgeois reaction against republicanism, they observed, had caused a gulf between the middle and lower classes, resulting in the turn of the latter toward socialism in the worst sense of the word.

Critique philosophique called for a return to the moral doctrine embodied in the republic's essence and teachings, a doctrine transcending all dogma, while subject to none. Its first principle was the dignity of the human person, manifested in freedom and respect.[4] Advocating free, obligatory, secular education, the journal discussed *laïcité* in terms of a program of moral education in primary schools. Eliminating the priest from the school was not enough; as the priest left, the teaching of rights and duties as part of a rational moral system should enter the schoolroom. Ethics should be an essential element in both primary and secondary education.[5] Reviewing Michel Bréal's book[6] claiming that the school should be outside of politics, they wrote, "We think, on the contrary, that the school should be republican, and that the state is obliged to establish a moral and national education," particularly when the republic was fighting for its life. They emphasized that people should be taught their rights as well as their duties, since the teaching of duties was often done in an authoritarian manner. In a free society, duties should be presented as the counterpart of rights, and inseparable from them.[7]

Renouvier's periodical, addressed to republicans laboring to organize the republic, represented the thinking of those who, throughout the century, had felt the necessary link between that form of government and a secular morality independent of the Church. It was no longer enough, as Cousin had done, to insist upon the independence of the moral philosophy taught to the elite. The republic was indeed "fighting for its life" against reactionary forces led by the Church. In January, 1873 the secularists, led by Brisson and Paul Bert, fought to keep clerical representation from the newly-constituted Conseil supérieur de l'instruction publique. But Simon and Vacherot, still viewing religion as the school of popular morality, took the side of the conservatives, who won. The Church also gained freedom in higher education, with even the anticlerical Bert acceding.[8] It was not until the Republic became truly republican, later in the decade, that Renouvier's concept of education began to predominate.

Liberal Protestantism

Renouvier believed that Catholicism was not suited to a republic; political liberty, he noted, had been realized best in Protestant countries, because the reformed religion fostered the concept of individual duty and responsibility. For a while he encouraged free-thinkers and indifferent Catholics to further the cause of secularism by becoming Protestants. To that end he began, in 1879, a periodical called *Critique religieuse*. Although on the face of it, such an attempt seems to have been hopeless, it becomes more understandable by taking into account the disproportionate number of Protestants connected with the republican movement, and particularly with the cause of secular education. They were men who had first worked toward liberalizing their own reformed religion, and who then turned to apply their ideas to *morale laïque*.

By mid-century the French Reformed Church was already split into a party of order and a party of movement on the religious level. The latter group considered itself the natural successor to the Protestant spirit of free inquiry. Under their influence the national Protestant synod had, in 1848, rejected the requirement of a creed for the church, by a vote of 69 to 6.[9] However, by 1863 things had changed enough that the Consistory of Paris had removed Athanase Coquerel from his pastorate for espousing Renan's view of the humanity of Jesus.[10] At this time *Le Protestant libéral*, a weekly periodical, was founded.

One reason for the success of Protestant orthodoxy during the Second Empire may have been that many liberal Protestants were in exile from Paris, where freedom of thought had become difficult. In the provinces or abroad, they awaited a more favorable moment to work for the republic. Macé taught boys and girls in a Protestant school in Alsace and founded popular libraries. Barni took a position at the University of Geneva. Switzerland became the center of a growing group of exiled Protestants that also included Jules Ferry, married to a Protestant in a civil ceremony.[11] Their mentor was Quinet, also in exile, later called by Gambetta the "promoter of secular education in France."[12]

Baptized a Catholic for social reasons by his pious Calvinist mother, Quinet had been raised in an atmosphere of natural religion and toleration for the beliefs of others.[13] He had come to view Catholicism as wholly incompatible with freedom of thought. "Wherever Catholicism encounters freedom, it destroys it; wherever freedom encounters Catholicism, it swears to respect it," he insisted. Nor did he think education would eliminate the problem, since religion was one of the main educators of a people. The Catholic Church had tradition, sentiment, even force on its side. He did not underestimate the difficulty of replacing one religion with another. But he maintained that different sects had different social implications. Other forms of Christianity, more in accord with the principles of the Revolution, could serve the republic. "It is not only Rousseau, Voltaire, Kant who are with us against the eternal religious oppression: there are also Luther, Zwingli, Calvin. . . ."[14]

It was Quinet who obtained for the Methodist Ferdinand Buisson, student of Barni,[15] the chair of philosophy and comparative literature at the University of Neuchatel. Buisson had defended Coquerel in 1864, and had been publishing brochures on liberal Protestantism and contributing to *Le Protestant libéral*. While in exile, he began his thirty-year study of Sebastian Castellio, a defender of religious tolerance during the Reformation. He also gave lectures opposing Bible study for children, which were published in 1869 in book form. He was particularly opposed to telling children that Bible stories were true; this would threaten their intellectual development by making it subservient to authority. He pointed to the many indecent Bible stories that could threaten the moral development of the young. Buisson frequently referred to the current term *morale indépendante,* and believed in a universal innate morality. Some of his greatest indignation was reserved for the story of Abraham and the sacrifice of his son. As Buisson saw it, the story led the child to separate in his mind "those two things that one cannot disunite without impunity: God and the moral law". The idea that there was a will of God, which should be heeded in preference to the voice of conscience, should never be allowed to germinate in a child's mind.[16] Quinet wrote to his friend about this work: "What a bold, decisive blow you have struck in the midst of this seemingly orthodox milieu!"[17]

Other Protestant refugees, oppressed by both political and religious orthodoxy, made their way to Switzerland and joined Buisson in the ranks of the late-Empire republicans, believing that, "for the reborn French republic, education would be the first of all its reforms". In preparing the resurrection of France, they would employ "la foi laïque" as Buisson called it.[18] "How marvelous it would be," wrote Quinet, "to see Neuchâtel arouse Paris!"[19]

They came from all over France. Félix Pécaut, son of an old Huguenot family, was brought up to be a missionary among the Basques in the nearby Pyrenees. By mid-century his orthodoxy had diminished considerably, and he was drawing a large following for his liberal preaching in Saliès. However, his views on the humanity of Christ led to his dismissal by Protestant authorities. Through most of the 1850s he taught his independent brand of ethics in a private Protestant school. Physically frail, he retired to write on his beliefs. *Le Christ et la conscience,* published in 1859, was a manifesto of the extreme left wing of liberal Protestantism, skirting Unitarianism. He did not wish, he wrote, to leave the Reformed Church, even less to leave Jesus, "the first-born of the brothers." His place was with those who, dissatisfied with the world, aspired to peace and perfection, the realm of all the gods—Jewish, Christian, and those of Greek philosophy.[20]

In *l'Avenir du théisme chrétien,* in 1865, Pécaut denied that Jesus was either divinely or humanly perfect. What he said and did was not the unsurpassable limit of moral knowledge; it was good to the extent that conscience approved of it. (In a lecture given later in Geneva, he gave as an example of the primacy of conscience Luther's "I can do no other."[21]) It was this kind of Protestantism that moved Quinet to remark: "Finally, after eighteen centuries, people begin to declare that God has descended into man."[22]

Pécaut was convinced that a liberal Protestantism might solve the problems caused by the inability of the Catholic Church to adjust to the modern world. But he saw orthodox Protestantism as also bound to the past by dogma. In *De l'Avenir du protestantisme en France,* he wrote that only the liberal form of the sect was unconstrained by the authority of a book, a church, a dogma. It had always supported progress.[23] Joining Buisson in Switzerland, Pécaut collaborated on a manifesto of liberal Protestantism in 1869. Ernest Renan said of him that he was the last of the spiritualists, preserving in his secular ethics "the perfume of an evaporated religion."[24] This characterization, at least the last part, seems more apt for Renan himself than for the activist Pécaut.

Another Protestant pastor who made a name for himself with his liberal teachings was Jules Steeg, who served in Libourne, near Bordeaux. He was brought to court for outrage to religion in 1872 because he had tried to explain to the readers of the local newspaper the pagan origins of the local *Fête-Dieu* celebration.[25] He wrote in *Le Protestant libéral* that the time had come to reject the authority of systems, traditions, official hierarchies and orthodoxy. Like Pécaut, he insisted that liberal Protestantism was the religion of the moment; Catholicism had lost ground, not because of any particular doctrine, but because it was "absolutely and fundamentally opposed to freedom," despite pleading its own case in the name of freedom. Addressing his own denomination in *De la Mission du protestantisme dans l'état actuel des esprits* in 1867, he noted that Protestant piety was essentially secular, democratic, profoundly human, and urged that its spirit be spread in France even though the church itself might never have a large membership.[26]

In 1869 Steeg was attracted by the urging of Buisson to Switzerland, where he found his ideal—a Protestantism "without dogma, miracles or priests."[27] He was inspired by the freedom of discussion, the Protestant schools, the numerous periodicals available in this liberal environment. Poor health prevented him from active participation in the liberal movement represented by Buisson and Pécaut. But he resolved to work in his own area of France, as he said, "to consecrate myself to liberal propaganda, to create around myself the air of freedom from old belief and old superstitions." He became editor of the local newspaper in Libourne, *Le Progrés des communes,* and entered the campaign against the plebiscite of 1870. During this time he wrote to Buisson: "More than ever, throughout and within all this political action, I feel myself a

Protestant pastor. In Paris, in Lausanne, I would have remained a theologian. Here and throughout France it is necessary to approach the problem differently.''[28]

After the fall of the Empire all three men—Buisson, Pécaut and Steeg—were to approach the promulgation of their beliefs differently, through political action and public education. As Buisson later explained, they had learned from the Second Republic that it was not enough to try to laicize religion, as Quinet, Lamartine and Victor Hugo had tried to do. Renan had been right: Everything one said or did in the name of religion in France profited Catholicism. Therefore the liberal Protestants, instead of speaking in the name of God, spoke in the name of liberty, solidarity, human dignity, sincerity, uprightness, justice, respect for the rights and duties of the moral life, social progress toward equality and fraternity.[29]

Under the first educational ministry of Jules Simon, Buisson was appointed inspector of primary schools, and was immediately attacked by the Church. When Jules Ferry became Minister of Education in 1879, Buisson was named director of primary education, a post he held for twenty years. He then became professor of pedagogy at the Sorbonne. A member of the Radical party in the Chamber, he served as its president, as well as heading the Ligue de l'enseignement and the Ligue des droits de l'homme during the two groups' most anticlerical period at the turn of the century.

Steeg also entered political life, winning a seat in the Chamber in 1881, where he lent his support to the laic laws of Jules Ferry. He served as rapporteur of the law on primary education in 1886. After Pécaut's death, he took his place as director of the Normal School for Women at Fontenay. But before his career in politics, the frail Steeg fought with his pen, as editor of three newspapers in the Gironde (*Le Progrès, Le Patriote, l'Union républicaine*).

Pécaut also used the first years of the Republic to propagandize on behalf of a liberal republic in France. Profoundly concerned by the implications of the Commune, he questioned in print whether the ruling classes were not in some way responsible for the tragedy. ''These cries of savage hatred against the propertied and against the clergy, do they not trouble your soul?'' he asked the readers of *Le Temps* in one of his first ''Provincial Letters'' in 1871. Thinking of the heroism of the people during the war, he could only feel that the splendid efforts of which they were capable were misdirected by a pernicious milieu and an inadequate education.[30] The special problem of French society was that it had failed to participate in the secularization of the sixteenth century, he wrote. Thus, what divided the French was not forms of government, but two contrary ways of thinking. The upper classes and the clergy, natural leaders of the people, had been unable to forward the movement to democracy because they feared freedom, both social and religious. So the national renewal would come from a small group of liberals working for a basic education for children and adults in every village of France.[31]

In another letter, Pécaut had already warned that the people would learn to read, if not from the wise, then at the instigation of fools. Unfortunately, he observed, the Church had not made use of its control over education since 1850 to prepare the people for democracy. "The day when the liberals see their route clearly, see where they wish to go, the people will follow them; for all the forces of civilization today join on their behalf."[32] The future of the century, he insisted, depended upon "secular popular education distributed under our auspices by our sons and daughters, impregnated with the modern spirit. . . ."[33] Nor was simple instruction the whole answer. Pécaut preached that the components of democracy must include the elements of a new morality that would enable the people to govern themselves wisely.

When the republicans grew stronger, and primary education was established, Pécaut became the director of the first national normal school for women at Fontenay-aux-Roses in 1880. Here he had the opportunity to put his ideas into practice in the training of teachers who would train others for work in primary schools. He himself did not teach the course in morale, but turned it over to the psychologist Henri Marion, who was a spiritualist.

What Pécaut sought to provide was a moral spirit that would pervade the entire educational process. In his daily morning talks to the young women, he urged them to stand back from their tasks and meditate on what they were doing, on how it could be perfected, on the conditions of the moral life. Education, he taught them, could only be worthwhile if it offered some eternal standards for an unstable and precarious existence.[34] Fontenay was the chef d'oeuvre of Pécaut's life. Its admirers called it "the Port-Royal of the école laïque."[35] Sure as he was that the non-confessional school was a necessity to the republic, he was just as certain that it should be imbued with an ethic of its own.

And so it happened, as a critic summed it up, that the old Huguenot spirit made these men republicans before the fact, during the Empire. A free polity and a free conscience seemed to them two sacred causes that they could not separate. In serving one, they served the other.[36] The liberal Protestants belonged to an early stage of the Third Republic's morale laïque because they continued to identify secular morality with religious ideals. As Protestant spiritualists, they were to be sorely tried by the problem of religion versus science that dominated the end of the century. Buisson argued that one could not give predominance to religion as it was because it faulted reason; but science, he insisted, could not answer all human problems. Beside the regularities of nature charted by science there existed "a force which, rightly or wrongly, believed itself free, revolted against necessity, aspired to ends beyond science." It would be wrong for educators to deny these normative, ideal ends. In every situation where knowledge was sought, reason and the scientific method should be used; in situations requiring action, conscience should be the guide. "Science and conscience . . . that is the rock on which all liberal education is founded," he concluded.[37]

Buisson, the longest lived of the Protestant republican contingent, was not an original thinker. His ability to adjust to change enabled him to participate in the various modifications of morale laïque that followed. He praised the doctrine of solidarity in the 'leçon d'ouverture' of his first course in pedagogy at the Sorbonne. He never objected to the sociological morality that followed.[38] But neither did he ever deny his form of religion, which he described, abstracted from its historical manifestations, as "the spontaneous aspiration of humanity toward the true, the good and the beautiful."[39] Thus Buisson, in explaining his position in 1900, returned to the rhetoric of Victor Cousin.

And so it was, as he said, natural that Ferry, seeking to conciliate respect for religion with republican necessity for a non-confessional public school, should choose as his collaborators "those who, in all churches and in all schools of thought, upheld the possibility of deriving an entire education, not from dogma, not from anti-dogma, but from that natural wisdom that lights the way of every person who comes into the world."[40] Indeed, the organization of secular morality in the schools utilized a strange combination of spiritualists, neo-Kantians, followers of *morale indépendante,* liberal Protestants, free-thinkers and positivists.

Positivism

The influence of positivism in France extended from mid-century to the elaboration of the discipline of sociology by Emile Durkheim. However, different aspects of the positivist doctrine were emphasized at different times. In its original formulation, Auguste Comte's philosophy had little to contribute to an ethics for primary education, since he placed the "science of man" at the end of the educational series, after the absorption of all the other sciences.

Comte himself had called for the education of the people in 1848. Under the rubric Order and Progress, he had proposed to develop positive education in free courses open to all, teaching only subjects open to demonstration. These courses would "subordinate intelligence to sociability," because there was basically only one science, "that of humanity, of which all the other genuine studies constitute only the indispensable preambles."[41] In 1850-51, Comte actually conducted a course at the Palais National; it was shut down by the government. Still, Comte's personal influence was minimal, particularly since he reverted to admiration for the Church and even support for the Empire.

Those elements of positivist thought most manifest in the intellectual milieu at the beginning of the Third Republic were the ones connected with his third stage of human development. The idea that humanity had outgrown his theological and metaphysical stages, and was entering a positivist era, based upon facts and demonstration, was reflected in the works of Quinet; but it appealed most to anticlericals who were not spiritualists and who tended toward scientific materialism.

The main spokesman for positivism in the early Third Republic was Emile Littré, a disciple of Comte.[42] In 1852 he had published a book insisting that no radical reform could take place in the social order without a moral and intellectual reform. There must be a common education, the same for all, that inculcated in the student the desire for the common good. Neither the Church nor the state had managed to provide an integral education. Contemporary morality, he wrote, owed its individual cultivation to pagan antiquity and its domestic cultivation to Christianity. Positivism would provide its social cultivation.[43]

Littré had admitted, in an article in *Le National* in August, 1849, that the republic needed education in morality for its youngest children. But in the positivist system of Comte, the students would be exposed to the sciences in a series over five years, culminating in a sixth year of sociology. This final year would include the "methodical exposition of morality" for which all the previous curriculum had been the necessary introduction. This clearly took too long; therefore Littré presented a new scheme. The moral education of the child followed that of humanity—the three stages—and so education should conform to them.

In the first, or theological stage, the child followed his instincts, but was regulated by religious dogma. God was the instinct of the just in humanity; immortality, the instinct of self-preservation. The discipline of instincts should be taught by example, by exhortation, and by influencing the passions.[44] Littré saw Christianity as having regulated the human relations of force within the family, providing "domestic morality."

However, the metaphysical stage would soon modify this initial education. In this stage, the system of guarantees set up within families and small groups was extended to the entire society. Thus the first moral education of the child should be a combination of the theological and metaphysical stages. It should never be in contradiction with incontestable truths, since, if ethics was associated with questionable dogma, the rational disproving of dogma would ruin ethics. However, it should be taught in a poetic, familiar, naive and maternal manner. It would begin in the home and be founded on love of family and other natural sentiments of fraternity and benevolence.[45]

Admitting that the preoccupations of the positivist society, utilitarian and scientific, were not apt to provoke the passion for altruistic sacrifice, Littré advised retaining the cultivation of these first stages while moving into the third. The final step would be, of course, the cultivation of the rational faculties. The student would be led through the sciences to sociology and positivist ethics from his twelfth to eighteenth year. But the three stages would never be clearly separated from one another. There would be some rationality in moral education from the beginning; and at the end instinct and passion would remain to fortify moral reason.[46] The desire to serve humanity would be the emotional replacement for former religious passion.[47]

Littré's actual contribution to *morale laïque* was more in his staunch secularism and his general support for public education than in moral theory. Nevertheless Ferry, the architect of French educational policy in the early Third Republic, was known to be a positivist. (Gabriel Hanotaux called him ''a man of doctrine, the positivist doctrine, not by attraction or by hearsay, but by a meditated adherence.''[48]) If one may view Condorcet and the *idéologues*, who strongly influenced him,[49] as the bridge between the Enlightenment and nineteenth-century positivism,[50] then Ferry's positivism seems a logical development in his personal philosophy. He was also greatly influenced by Quinet's *l'Education du peuple,* which expressed the positivist concept that all the institutions of society must necessarily be freed from theological concepts.[51]

Ferry shared with Littré membership in the Masonic Order. In 1875 the two were initiated into the lodge Le Clément Amitié on the same night. In the seventies freemasonry was gradually turning from deism to positivism, adopting a morality independent of theological concepts. Now violently anticlerical, the Order numbered 203,000 in France, with 15,000 in Paris alone. Almost every politician who was to support secularization laws in the Chamber was a Freemason.[52] Littré chose as his initiation speech the topic of morality.

It was useless, he said, to base morality upon beliefs which, like the belief in God, had become enfeebled. Duties flowed from the fact that humans were creatures partaking of an ensemble. The evolution of ethics was linked to that knowledge of the world, of one's relationship to it and to others. The moral law emanated ''from the very basis of our individual and collective life.'' Conscience embodied ''the sum of moral rules that each civilization, each epoch makes prevail in the social milieu.''[53]

On the anniversary of Littré's initiation he was ill, but sent a speech for the celebration, also dealing with morality. ''One's principal duty to one's self is to educate oneself; our principal duty toward our neighbors is to educate them,'' he wrote. Social morality, still in its infancy, was the doctrine of the duties of society toward its members. The collective improvement of society would come through education. Ferry, in his own speech, insisted that from the positivist viewpoint, morality was ''an essentially human fact, distinct from all belief about the beginning and the end of things . . . . a social fact, which bears in itself its beginning and its end.''[54]

Comte had seen a rational system of education in which moral considerations would predominate as the answer to the social problem.[55] Following him, Ferry and Littré agreed that a universal moral education was absolutely necessary for social progress. Now these men and their cohort were actually faced with the reorganization of society on the basis of republican politics.

Littré himself had become more hesitant about the role of the working class in political life, since the Paris Commune. He now saw the parliamentary republic as a conservative form of government that could restrain the rash tendencies of the working class by indirect rule. Thus, he saw education as a means by which the bourgeois state could consolidate itself, by providing the enlightenment which would weaken both the socialism of the Left and the main bulwark of the Right, the Church.[56] While Comte, the theorist, had seen social organization as relative and progressive, along with knowledge,[57] Littré was willing, at least at this time, to settle for the bourgeois republic.

The entire system of moral education set up by the republic in the 1880's can be seen as a program aimed at guaranteeing, politically, the existence of the republic, and socially, the predominance of the bourgeoisie as the natural leaders of the republic. In other words, although French leadership had moved from teaching secular morality only to the elite under the *monarchie censitaire* to universal moral education under universal suffrage, the goal was similar— the orderly society, administered by those most capable of guaranteeing order. In this light the moral education of the Third Republic seems only the substitution of secular propaganda supporting a bourgeois republic for the old religious propaganda which supported aristocratic monarchy, and thus a political necessity, as it had been in the First Republic. If this is true, Comte's own writings played a role. He had insisted that education be directed to the subordination of the individual (who, he maintained, was only an abstraction) to the society (or Humanity, which was real).[58] Through education the positive spirit would grow and unify the minds of the people, bringing first intellectual, and then social regeneration. Positive education would be organized by a new class of devoted teachers thoroughly trained in the series of the sciences—a class similar to the priesthood of the Church. But the total of positive knowledge could be conveyed to the general population only as demonstrated truths, since all could not attain the education necessary for these truths to be demonstrated to them.[59] Thus, Comte himself provided for an elite group which would lead the rest in positive understanding of the social forces at work. In the Third Republic, and clearly in the minds of Ferry and Littré, this group would consist of republican legislators and government-trained primary school *instituteurs*.

It must be noted, however, that every educational system has as its goal the shaping of its students to conform to the society in which they are expected to live. The new republic was under attack from both the Left and the Right; that it should use education to defend itself was natural. On the other hand, universal education, even with conformity as one of its aims, always produces individuals who, by the very fact of being educated, seek change in their society. And one must remember that Ferry was also an apostle of Condorcet, who believed that education, rather than perpetuating any particular system, would lead to the infinite progress of human society.

8

The Neutral School

Jules Ferry

THROUGHOUT the seventies, the Falloux Law was in force; under it the Church provided religious instruction in the state schools, and had a free hand in establishing its own primary and secondary schools. After 1875 it was able to enter higher education also. But by 1879 the republicans had won majorities in both Chambers; for the first time the state budget for education was larger than that for religion.[1] Anticlerical pressures to laicize the schools grew, particularly in Paris. The Society for Elementary Education, founded in 1875, advocated free, compulsory, secular education for all children, including moral and civic instruction. The Union de France, consisting of one hundred autonomous societies totalling 17,000 members, advocated education for the working class, including women, that would emphasize scientific instruction and an independent morality.[2]

Many of the members of these organizations were Masons and belonged to Macé's Ligue de l'enseignement. Françisque Sarcey wrote in 1879 that the secular primary school was the most important issue of the day.[3] And in that year Jules Ferry became Minister of Education, a post he was to hold in the next five cabinets. The clergy was eliminated from the Conseil supérieur de l'instruction publique. But Ferry did not adopt the language of the most radical secularizers. Instead, he espoused the concept of the "neutral school."

It was at this point that the second important step was taken in the development of *morale laïque*. Cousin had institutionalized spiritualism as a moral philosophy separate from religion in the secondary school system. Ferry was to institutionalize the concept of a secular morality as a part of the new system of universal primary education. The classroom *morale* which resulted was the product of a series of political compromises such as are inevitable when theory is translated into practice in a divided country under a parliamentary regime. In effect, it was the old spiritualism. Ferry's triumph was that he succeeded in establishing in law the principle that a secular morality should be part of the school curriculum.

Ferry's position on the teaching of *morale* in the primary schools can be drawn from the nature of the arguments he used during the debates on the laic laws. His justifications for both the laicization of education and the teaching of secular morality were already common coin among republicans. On the secularization of education, Ferry used the same argument that Quinet had used in 1850. Pointing to the modern development of the secular state, of secular civil society, of secular knowledge, all independent of religion, he maintained that the secularization of education was a natural consequence. He also quoted Guizot's insistence, in the 1844 debates, that the state must be secular in order to preserve the liberties Frenchmen had acquired.

What the republic was doing, Ferry said, was pushing the *laïcité* of that time a little further, by extending secularization from secondary to primary education.[5] He admitted that the republican government preferred secular education because it conformed to a free and democratic society, just as religious education conformed to a monarchy.[6] And in his famous summary of the "oeuvre scolaire" of the Republic, in 1889, he insisted that secularization of the schools was not only the consequence of the secularization of other areas of society; it was "their safeguard and their fundamental guarantee."[7]

The justification of *morale laïque* also followed the familiar republican pattern. But the most difficult task Ferry aimed to accomplish in these debates was to reassure the fainthearted that no one could object to the content of the morality to be taught in the schools. The nature of these arguments illustrates the fact that Ferry was conducting himself, not as a thinker insisting upon his own views, but as a politician seeking to accomplish what he could, at that particular point in the life of the Republic, toward his general goals. The "neutral school" was the most Ferry considered could be attained at that time. Just as he labored for *obligation* first, and then *gratuité,* before even attempting laicization of moral education, so he strove to establish first the principle of a lay morality in the schools, while compromising on the content.[8]

The first discussions of lay morality as a part of the school program came up in the Senate debates on the sensitive subject of secular secondary education for girls, December 21, 1880. The Duc de Broglie insisted that it was unheard of to teach a morality with no religious or philosophic basis. Ferry replied that although the program of *morale* would be detached from confessional dogmas, it would be philosophically grounded. It would only be separated from "those high metaphysical conceptions . . . over which theologians and philosophers have been in discord for six thousand years.'' Nor was such a moral teaching totally new. In the special program of secondary education founded by Victor Duruy under the Empire, students were taught moral obligations to themselves, to the society, and to God. This program had already been adopted for use in the *lycées* for young men.

Ferry insisted that if there was no independent morality, distinct from all the infinitely changing metaphysical theories, then there was no morality that could be taught at all—unless Catholics were claiming, in this day and age, that there was no morality outside the Catholic religion. Although there were controversies over metaphysics, there had been, since the beginning of the world, unity on morality, ''because morality is the very law of society; society could not have existed if it had not contained in itself the force to beget a moral strength and a moral truth superior to all changes of doctrine and all controversies.''

Ferry's use of the term metaphysical, as opposed to philosophical, was clarified in the debates on the primary education law in the Chamber on December 23, 1880. Metaphysical doctrines, Ferry declared, were concerned with ''the origins and ends of things.'' One could teach a moral philosophy at all levels of public education completely independent of metaphysical concepts.[9]

The primary education law provided for ''instruction morale et civique'' in the public schools; in private schools religious instruction would be optional. The lack of any religious education in the primary schools of the state enraged the Right, even though provision was made for the release of the children from school on Thursdays to permit religious instruction in the churches if the parents so desired. Ferry compromised here, allowing for the local priest or minister to give religious instruction on that day in the school if the church was too far away.

The offending paragraph was adopted by the Chamber, only to run into trouble in the more conservative Senate. On June 10, 1881, the Duc de Broglie proposed to change the wording from ''instruction morale et civique'' to ''instruction morale et religieuse.'' A grand debate on the nature of *morale laïque* ensued. Ferry declared that *morale* would be taught in the primary schools, but that it would be ridiculous to attempt to teach young children its bases and postulates. Not theory, but ''the good old morality of our fathers, ours, yours, for we have only one,'' was a proper subject for young children. ''Yes, the secular society can provide a moral training; yes, the teachers can teach *morale* without resorting to metaphysical research . . . . It is not the principle of the thing that they teach, it is the thing itself, it is the good old ancient human morality.''

On July 2, responding to another effort to put the adjective *religieuse* after the term *morale*, Ferry again tried to reassure his listeners. True morality, he insisted, needed no modifying term. "Thanks be to God, morality in our French society, after so many centuries of civilization, has no need to be defined." This morality was not related only to Christianity, but to the philosophers of antiquity, to the human soul itself. When a speaker claimed that there were many moralities—evolutionist, utilitarian, positivist, independent—Ferry insisted that basically they were all the same. What was involved, he maintained, was merely the teaching of "the current morality, domestic morality, social morality." He pointed out that the majority of the teaching corps was spiritualist, a point he had also been careful to make in the Chamber.[10]

Here Ferry was not only playing the politician, soothing the fears of the opposition and trying to convince them of the harmlessness of secular morality. He was undoubtedly perfectly willing that the content of *morale laïque* in the primary schools be, for the present, those spiritualist teachings accepted by most of the society. Littré had spoken of Christian morality as "domestic morality"; it had been modified by metaphysics. He had viewed this combination as the ideal form of moral education for the young, who were themselves still in the theological-metaphysical stage of life. When Ferry described *morale laïque* as the morality "of humanity, of the human conscience,"[11] he might easily have been referring to humanity and the human conscience at its early stage of development, both in terms of the society as a whole and in terms of the tender age of primary school children. The important thing was to keep any limiting phraseology out of the law.

It was Jules Simon who next denied that a course in independent morality could be offered in primary schools.[12] He proposed an amendment to the law: teachers will teach their students their duties toward God and their country. On July 4 Ferry spoke against the amendment. He objected that the notion of a particular religion was being injected into the law. One's duties toward God varied according to what kind of God one conceived of.[13] It was exactly this kind of theoretical discussion of the nature of God which should be avoided in the primary school. Some supporters of the amendment, Ferry declared, were envisioning fifty or sixty thousand teachers as Savoyard vicars. He doubted that the Catholics would relish such a prospect; but beyond that, it was a dream. The *instituteur* could teach concrete morality, but not abstractions. The priest or minister was the authority on duties toward God. Although Ferry tried to avoid bringing the amendment to a vote ("It is not a matter here of voting for or against God: one does not vote on God in assemblies."), a new plea by Simon resulted in a vote by which the amendment was adopted, on July 5.[14]

However, the Chamber refused to accept the Senate's amendment; and the elections of August and September returned even more republicans than before. In March of 1882 the law was returned to the Senate, where Simon spoke again for the amendment. In his reply, Ferry quoted Simon's own words in opposition to press laws aimed at preserving religion—that one could not force doctrine by law or protect belief through the courts. The amendment was finally rejected. Ferry gave the Senate his promise that any teacher who taught anything hostile to religion would be fired.[15] The law on primary education in its final form, including *obligation, gratuité,* and *laïcité* was promulgated on March 28, 1882.

Ferry had insisted that the content of the program of *morale* not be prescribed in the law, that programs were in the province of the Conseil supérieur. In the July 4 session of the Senate, he had pointed out that the program in use did include God as a sanction of morality.[16] Soon after the law was passed, the Section permanente of the Conseil supérieur began to discuss the program in *morale,* which had been assigned to its particular provenance.[17] It was proposed, on the basis of the parliamentary debates and a series of pedagogical conferences held during the year, that *morale* be intermingled with all subjects taught. The value of moral readings was discussed. However, it was agreed that some kind of direction should be given to the teachers.

Buisson favored a kind of morality-in-action program, along the lines of that offered in Belgium, for the lowest grades, with some kind of structured course for the intermediate grades (ages 9-11). He felt that those who left school at this point should take with them some five or six general ideas, linked to one another and forming the embryo of a moral code. Octave Gréard, vice-rector of the Académie de Paris, questioned whether formal courses in *morale* should not be left until the children were older. It was agreed that an "esprit général," fostered by maxims and manuals, should be created for the program. Buisson and Paul Janet (biographer of Cousin and a spiritualist) were delegated to prepare sample programs in *morale* for different levels of primary education.[18]

On June 21, Janet made his report. The law, he noted, imposed the duty of teaching *morale* as a separate subject for its own sake. This would also eliminate the problem of too much latitude for the teacher in a morality generalized throughout the curriculum. Furthermore, moral training should involve, not only the unconscious inculcation of good habits, but a conscious understanding of moral principles. Duties beginning with those to self, family, fellow men and country should be crowned by duties to God. Janet argued that to eliminate all religious ideas from the program of *morale* would be to admit to their adversaries that the state was incompetent in the spiritual domain. "If the state allows itself to be dispossessed of the right to teach religious ideas in their general, human, and natural form, it abandons by that very act a part, and the highest part, of that spiritual domain that they deny it."

Janet also suggested that the *cours moyen* (ages 9-11) should include general principles of social morality. He suggested for it the following program: practical morality: the child in the family—duties to parents and grandparents, to brothers and sisters, to servants; the child in the school—duties to teachers, duties to comrades; duties to old people; duties to the nation; duties to oneself; duties to others; duties to God; brief notions of theoretical morality. In the *cours supérieur* (ages 11-13) social morality would be stressed. The program would include: the family, society, duties of justice, duties of charity, the town and the nation, brief notions of theoretical morality.[19]

Two days later the members of the Section permanente engaged in argument over duties toward God. A committee was appointed to draw up a definition of God which would be a compromise between a personal God and an impersonal force.[20] The following day the discussion resumed; it was suggested that perhaps they should only name God and leave out the details of His nature. Buisson and Gréard opposed this. Janet insisted that it was necessary to make it clear that the idea of God was "laïque, humaine."[21] The next meeting broke up on the issue. Gréard and Edgar Zevort, director of secondary education, feared a program which would produce skepticism. Some philosophy must be agreed upon, they declared, and that of secondary education was clearly spiritualist. Buisson insisted that the Conseil supérieur as a whole would never show a majority for the proposition that there was no morality without God. At 7:45 p.m., after two and one-half hours, Janet said he could not go on; the matter remained unresolved.[22]

A formulation was finally agreed upon two days later: "In this whole course, the teacher supposes and assumes as given the [student's] consciousness of the moral law and of obligation. He appeals to the sentiment and the idea of duty, to the sentiment and the idea of responsibility, and does not undertake to demonstrate by way of theory." As for the subject of God: "The teacher is not charged with giving *ex professo* a course on the nature and attributes of God." He should teach respect to God, should associate God with the First Cause. Duties toward God should be taught mainly as obedience to God's laws as revealed by conscience and reason. The teacher should also foster belief in justice, wisdom and beneficence as divine qualities.[23]

The First Years

It is clear from the discussion which took place in the heart of the educational establishment that the *morale laïque* to be taught in the schools was indeed, as Ferry had put it, "the good old morality of our fathers," that is, spiritualism. Renouvier thought the reformers much too timid; he said they had given in to a melange of eclecticism and positivism.[24] In *Critique philosophique*, Pillon complained that the program would not lead to teaching morality as a science, with principles like justice.[25] Clearly, what Ferry had managed to keep out of the law—precise religious references—had been put back in the programs of the secular school. The need for such a compromise between the radical secularizers and the traditional Catholics and spiritualists of the republic became obvious in the fight over the text books in *morale* which took place in 1883. But even before that, certain difficulties with the program became apparent.

In the debates, Simon had advised eliminating the teaching of *morale* in the primary school because of the lack of teachers trained for such a task.[26] Normal schools for primary teachers had been established to provide for the necessary staffing of the new public schools. The course on "psychologie et morale" was taught by the director of each school, who usually also taught the course in pedagogy. The program, elaborated by Buisson, Marion and Janet, had been presented to the Conseil supérieur in 1881 by Janet. It provided for a first year of psychology and theoretical morality, and a second year of practical and civic morality; in the third year, *morale* was to be related to pedagogy, which was taught separately for the first two years. Two hours a week were devoted to the course in the first and second year.[27] The program, as outlined by Janet, could have been written by Cousin.

In the fall of 1882, meetings of normal school faculties were held in each department to discuss various questions submitted by the Minister of Education on the organization and programs of the normal schools. Question number two, on programs, elicited many responses indicating the inability of the future teachers (aged 16-18) to grasp the theoretical aspects of the course on *morale* and psychology.

One school (Barcelonnette) deplored "the abstractions of psychology placed at the threshold of moral studies." "This course is almost the philosophy course of the *lycée*," complained the school at Ajaccio. In primary education, the school at Lascar pointed out, it was perhaps best not to teach principles before practice, but to reverse the order.[28] This suggestion was seconded by many other schools.[29]

The problem was, according to the reports, the low intellectual level of the students with which the *écoles normales* had to deal. They had no literary education, and had gotten through the primary grades by the use of memory. "In the majority of the normal schools of central France," read the report from Aurillac, "the students of the first year . . . hardly know their native language. . . . How could a teacher put at the level of these minds, hardly opened, the teaching of these difficult matters, which demand such a great stretching of the mind?" In Auxerre they reported pupils "whose faculties of observation and reason have been not at all sufficiently cultivated" for such work. The difficulties of the study of psychology and theoretical morality were almost insurmountable for students "little habituated to reflection and reasoning, absolute strangers to abstractions," at Privas. Some of the schools complained of a lack of simple texts.[30]

The matter of texts had been left open, both at the level of the *école normale* and the primary school; individual teachers chose from a number of texts available to them, with complete freedom.[31] The teachers themselves had expressed a desire to teach morality as an adjunct to all subjects, without making it a special course; they agreed it should be "independent of confessional teachings," and "in harmony with the principles of modern society."[32]

Ferry's first Instructions to them had emphasized practice rather than formal teaching. The *instituteur* was charged with teaching *morale* "as a representative of the society: the secular and democratic society has the most direct interest in initiating in all its members, at an early age and by ineffaceable lessons, the awareness of their own dignity, and a no less profound feeling of their duty and personal responsibility." However, there was no need to teach theoretical morality. Most children had presumably received religious training and the fundamental notions of eternal and universal morality at home. These notions were still fragile, part of memory rather than of conscience, barely exercised. They needed to be matured and developed. This was the task of the *instituteur:*[33]

> His mission then, is well-defined: it consists of fortifying, of rooting in the soul of his students for their whole life these essential notions of human morality, common to all doctrines and necessary to all civilized men, by making them pass into the realm of daily practice. He can fulfill this mission without having personally to either espouse or oppose any of the diverse confessional beliefs with which his students are associated and with which they mingle these general principles of morality. . . .
>
> Secular moral teaching is thus distinct from religious teaching without contradicting it. The teacher does not substitute himself either for the priest or for the paterfamilias; he joins his efforts to theirs to make of each child an honest person.

These instructions mirrored the views of Marion, who taught *morale* to the *institutrices* being trained at the École Normale primaire supérieure at Fontenay-aux-Roses. These students were to become the special corps who would train female teachers in the *écoles normales* of the various departments. In his "leçon de clôture"of 1882, Marion emphasized two points: that the teaching of *morale* in the primary school was first of all a matter of creating "practical habits, that is, ways of acting and thinking"; but that it was also necessary to teach "reflection, which alone makes action enlightened and free." This meant providing students with ways of thinking, with rules for judging, with the idea of personal responsibility. Moral teaching meant supplying general precepts of good and evil which would already be germinating within each student upon arrival at school. What was necessary was to bring them out and to clarify them through reason, developing judgment and conscience together. Discussions of situations in daily life and historical or imaginary anecdotes were preferable to maxims learned by heart.[34]

However, young *instituteurs* with little confidence in their new role were resorting to the printed word, in the form of the numerous text books on *morale* written in the seventies and early eighties. By September, 1882, these texts were being attacked by the Church as irreligious—not so much for the basic morality which they taught, as for such things as emphasis on civil marriage, or failure to introduce the deity. Parents were warned by pastoral letters not to allow the texts to be read by children; in one famous case a father who refused to send his child to school because it was not neutral was upheld by the local school committee.

On December 15, four textbooks were placed on the Index: Steeg's *Instruction morale et civique,* Gabriel Compayré's *Eléments d'instruction morale et civique,* Paul Bert's *l'Instruction civique à l'école,* and Mme. Henri Gréville's *Instruction morale et civique des jeunes filles.* The teachers continued to use the books, however; in some cases they even met to condemn the condemnations.[35] The Conseil d'Etat ruled that school committees could not justify children's being kept home from school because of use of these texts. At this point the Church would have settled for a declaration, which Ferry would have been willing to make, of the neutrality of the public schools. But the republican camp, aroused for battle, would not give in.[36]

The debate reached the Senate on May 31, 1883. Ferry claimed that it was actually a political battle, not a religious one, that the Right was waging. He noted that the forty or fifty textbooks in use in the schools were based on deistic or spiritualist morality, with only a small number reflecting *morale indépendante.* And even those, he claimed, quoting the one by Coignet, were neutral, not antireligious. He announced the intention of his ministry to limit the previous freedom of choice with regard to texts by setting up a list among which they would be chosen.[37]

In July the Section permanente of the Conseil supérieur discussed the subject. It was decided to draw up a list each year from those books presented to it.[38] But Ferry insisted, on the principle of the freedom of the teachers, that the list be recommended, and not required.[39]

In a famous letter to the *instituteurs* of November 17, 1883, Ferry discussed the teaching of *morale* and civics as one of their most essential missions. He emphasized that the moral teaching was to be "simply that good and old morality which we have received from our fathers and mothers, which we all honor ourselves and follow in the relationships of life, without taking the trouble to discuss its philosophic bases." When you propose a precept or maxim to your students, he charged them, "ask yourselves if you know a single honest person who could be offended by what you are going to say. Ask if the father of a family . . . could in good faith refuse his consent to what he would hear you say. If yes, refrain from saying it; if no, speak out." However, he promised them that no text would be forced upon them by school authorities.[40]

Ferry's neutrality was undoubtedly sincere, despite his personal positivism, or perhaps because of it. He claimed from the beginning that his own philosophy was not relevant to questions of state, and that there was in France neither a religion of state nor an irreligion of state.[41] He recognized that moral education at this stage had to be spiritualist, because France was still spiritualist. However, by keeping all religious references out of the law, he left the way open for future developments in moral theory.

And, in truth, the majority of the textbooks used were Kantian, if not spiritualist. Emile Boutroux, respected university philosopher, divided them into three categories: Catholic, deist, and *morale indépendante*. Most fell into the deist category, appealing to God either as the founder or the guarantor of *morale*.[42] *Critique philosophique* ran a series of articles on the texts, approving those, both deist and *morale indépendante*, which emphasized conscience, particularly Renouvier's own *Petit traité de morale*,[43] and the texts of Marion[44] and Coignet.[45] Mme. Gréville's book, which leaned heavily on an interest morality, was not so well accepted.[46] Bert's textbook, although considered a bit strong on the comparison of the barbarous old regime and the just republic, was excused because Bert was a believer who thought that French society would fail without a common republican faith,[47] a position shared by those around Renouvier.

To read the manuals in *morale* of the seventies and eighties is to wonder if any real development in moral theory for education had taken place since Cousin. However, the republican Left was already becoming more radical. Opposition to the prevailing philosophy was expressed in the debate on the 1886 primary education law, dealing with secularization of the teaching staff. The Socialist leader Jean Jaurès questioned why spiritualism should be the philosophy of the schools when the intellectual elite no longer believed in it. Edouard Vaillant, disciple of Proudhon, complained that if the presence of non-Catholics in the schools indicated that religion should not be taught, the presence of atheists indicated that spiritualism should not be.[48] But the influence of Pécaut and Marion at Fontenay-aux-Roses, and the influence of Cousin's pupils and other spiritualists in the secondary schools and on the governing councils of education, extended the sway of spiritualism. The official programs in *morale* continued to include duties to God.

However, the program was foundering. Ferdinand Lichtenberger, member of the Conseil Supérieur, reporting on moral education in primary schools for the 1889 Exposition, used reports of 57 *inspecteurs d'académie*, 337 *inspecteurs primaires*, 62 *directeurs* and 35 *directrices* of *écoles normales*, and 67 *instituteurs* and *institutrices*, besides those of students graduated from primary schools. He found that many teachers doubted the value of formal lessons in *morale*, and claimed to inject moral values into all studies. Most of them were dissatisfied with the lessons they did give in *morale*. The textbooks seemed of little help; the teachers did not know how to use them. The parents did not back up the ethical teachings of the schools.

Lichtenberger admitted that a veritable state of war existed between the clergy and the teachers. More and more they were omitting any mention of

God; in this they were aided by the textbooks, which tended to give literary and historical texts as examples, rather than religious ones. He bemoaned the fact that the word *laïque* seemed to be opposed to the work *religieux*, when the two forces should be collaborators in *morale*.[49]

It was becoming clear that a new formulation of *morale* for education purposes was overdue. The varieties of Kantian morality, from Cousin to Renouvier, were to remain strong in the French education system to the end of the century. But the general spiritualism which resulted from them was being rejected by advanced thinkers, who were turning toward science as the answer to moral and social problems. The assertion that morality was a science, made from the time of the Enlightenment in a philosophical sense, was now to be translated into an attempt to base *morale* on social science, as Comte had insisted.

9

Solidarité

IN the history of science, the seventeenth century is viewed as the century of physics. The political and social theories which corresponded to the seventeenth and eighteenth century emphasis on the physical sciences mirrored the world of individual atoms in motion described by the physicists. Democratic society was viewed as a collection of equal individuals in varying combinations. The nascent social sciences also concentrated on individuals— assumed to be at least potentially equal—as the units of study. Kantian moral theory began with the individual person, who found his morality within himself in the categorical imperative, itself linked to universal reason.

The Organic Society

The nineteenth century, however, was to be the century of biology. Reactionary philosophers of the post-revolutionary period, like de Maistre and de Bonald, posited medieval society as the perfect system in which each man had his function and contributed, according to his position in the hierarchy, to the ensemble known as society. They contrasted this "organic" concept of society with the "atomistic" concepts elaborated during the Enlightenment. But the organic society was not only the product of conservative social theory. The *idéologues* were forced by Cabanis to modify the sensationalism of Locke, with its egalitarian implications, and to recognize that different individuals actually received sensations differently. Their response was to retain the goal of equality by demanding that medical science eliminate individual physical imperfections.

The study of physical and psychological differences led the physiologist Xavier Bichat to divide people into different categories—intellectual, motor and sensory. Society, he said, should develop in each individual his major faculty. This theory led Saint-Simon to his own concept of an organic society based upon differentiated functions of individuals naturally suited to perform different tasks. The analogy was, of course, the human body, whose different organs performed the tasks particularly suited to them, in integral harmony. The utopias of both Saint-Simon and Fourier were based upon this concept, which implied the interdependence of all members of society upon one another and upon the whole.[1]

The implication of the organic theory of society for ethics was the necessity for some sort of devotion by every individual to the society upon which he was dependent and which, in turn, depended in some way upon the role he performed in it—a New Christianity, according to Saint-Simon, a religion of Humanity, according to Comte or Pierre Leroux. (It was Leroux who first described the relations of human beings in such a society by the term *solidarité*, describing it within a religious context.)[2] Both of the latter were in some way disciples of Saint-Simon. But Comte evolved a less visionary religion of Humanity than his mentor's New Christianity; based on positive knowledge, it made ethics the final stage of positivist wisdom. The science of sociology, in which ethics was embodied, was the apex of the series of the sciences, following biology. The positive spirit, Comte declared, was strictly social; it assumed that "man, as such, does not exist, there exists only Humanity, because all our development is owed to society."[3] Each important question would be revealed as dependent upon social cooperation.[4] Personal morality, seen in its true light, would become a matter of general concern and public rule.[5]

However, as we have seen, the predominant moral philosophy of nineteenth century France was Kantian. Although French Kantians, including Cousin and Barni, had criticized Kant for relegating morality to the noumenal world, spiritualist texts in *morale* had always begun with individual morality. It was Renouvier, influenced by Saint-Simon and Fourier, who incorporated into his criticism of Kant the idea of social solidarity. There was, he wrote in 1858, no pure and absolute rational morality. The actions people performed were related to both their personal solidarity, which included everything that had made them what they were, and their social solidarity. The latter he described as "the connection resulting from those motivations of a free act which are attached to anterior acts, repeated and habitual in a given society, and to authorized maxims, and to the institutions and customs of which the same experience and repetition are the sources." However, he insisted that such social influences did not mean that the act was not imputable to a free agent.[6]

Renouvier pointed out that humans were biologically social animals, in that they lived, first in a family, then in a larger interdependent group. Human nature was developed through and within this social life. Mutual services rendered within a group led to notions of reciprocity and equality, and finally, to a notion of justice and obligation to one another—a kind of "contracted duty" to the group from which one had received certain indispensable things. The idea of moral obligations among humans, of reciprocal rights and duties, led to recognition of a tacit social contract, which served as the base for all primitive societies, for all domestic and social order. Only under the rule of law did this contract become formal.

Philosophically, Renouvier declared, the followers of Kant could postulate a morality both rational and historically based. By escaping from the illusion of absolute principles, while continuing to affirm freedom, duty, conscience and justice, they could establish human solidarity while avoiding determinism.[7]

In his second *Essai* of 1859, Renouvier tried to explain the social contract by analogy with the individual, who basically felt a unity of the disparate elements of his self as it had developed in time and space. "To thus reduce plurality to unity is to contract with the self to give thought to the governance of consciousness." Logically, the contract which integrated the moral person would precede the contract which created society. But in fact, since the moral person was not born in isolation, this was not the order of succession. Families, cities, nations were living forms of contract, uniting people throughout their lives. As society became more self-conscious, it recognized the contract that joined its members, and tried to make it conform to the model of justice which developed within it. But conscious participation in group life also brought the realization of what Renouvier called "the first of the social verities: that the imposed authority should not extend beyond duties universally avowed by free consciences, and that all the rest pertains to freedom."[8]

The next development of neo-Kantianism toward a social philosophy was elaborated by Renouvier's disciple Henri Marion, member of the Conseil Supérieur and professor of pedagogy at the Sorbonne after 1883. In his *De la solidarité morale* of 1880, he noted that moral liberty was subject to conditions inherent in the very nature of the individual—heredity and environment; the factors of the individual moral life were interdependent. This was also true in social life. Not only was there an interdependence among members of a group, organized or not, but among generations succeeding one another, and among different societies. "And just as an animal displays phenomena which the cells which compose it do not display separately, so a society conducts itself, as a body, otherwise than its isolated members . . . and thus moral solidarity takes on a new aspect in social life."

Marion also modified Kant's categorical imperative by denying the "morality of good intentions." If the result of acts motivated by a formal sense of duty were bad for the community, the acts themselves could not be good. Since society was the natural sphere of human actions, morality could not be individual. Kantianism was saved by emphasis on the other aspect of the imperative—that one could see one's acts as becoming universal practice. But Marion insisted that both the act itself and the will to action were conditioned by factors which were interdependent. "The ensemble of conditions which concur, along with what freedom we have, to make us morally what we are, that is what I call moral solidarity." He did not believe that changes in public morality could be legislated. The state could favor moral progress only by repression of moral disorder and by the education of youth.[9]

Marion really went no further than Renouvier in his explanation of *solidarité*. His importance lies in the position he held in the educational hierarchy and in the fact that his books were used in the school system. The first to try to break out of the spiritualist mode and arrive at some kind of compromise with positivist views was Alfred Fouillée. Although recognized as a brilliant mind during the Second Empire, the need to support his family at a young age, and later his ill health, kept him from a university career.[10] Nevertheless, his philosophical writings were influential in radical republican circles.[11] Fouillée's contribution to moral philosophy was his new view of the spiritualist concepts of freedom and conscience, which he modified by his own formulation of the *idée-force*.

Like the spiritualists Fouillée began with the irreducible, experiential fact of consciousness, first of ourselves, then of other consciousnesses. This consciousness, he maintained, was not passive but active. In being conscious of ourselves, of others, and of the universe, one conceived an ideal of a universal consciousness, of a universal society of consciousnesses. In this way, the consciousness, projecting itself into others and into the whole, was linked to them by an idea which was at the same time a force, the foundation of justice and fraternity.

Up to this point, Fouillée was purely idealist; but he did not stop there. All the factors cited by the positivist and naturalist schools of thought—mechanical forces, play of interests, laws of life, society and evolution—were part of consciousness. Thus, there was no transcendent categorical imperative; the movement toward the ideal was purely immanent. "One does not think the ideal because it exists, but it exists, rather it tends to be and to realize itself progressively, because I think it."[12] Consciousness then was the basis of conscience. (I think, therefore I have a moral value.) The thinking person created a hierarchy of objective moral values. (I think, therefore I evaluate things.) The *idée-force* of morality began to actualize itself in being conceived. (I think, therefore I realize the ideal.) This was the beginning of the true society. (I think, therefore I begin to create, in and through human society, the universal society of consciousness.) Or, as Fouillée rewrote Descartes; I think, therefore we are.[13]

The idea as force, as motivating ideal, formed a basis for Fouillée's first contribution to the theory of *solidarité* in 1880. Society was "an organism which realizes itself in conceiving itself and willing itself." The role of consciousness was to project an ideal. A group of people became a society when they conceived more or less clearly a type or organism which they could form by uniting, and when they united under the influence of that conception. Because that common idea involved a common will, the society which resulted was a contractual organism.

In this formulation, Fouillée escaped the determinism of biological solidarity, while retaining the concept of society as an organism in nature. The contractual organism, as he called it, united its members in voluntary solidarity rather than in merely mechanical interdependence. It implied democracy, because anything done without the consensus of the participants would break the vital connection.

Fouillée insisted that "the union of consciousnesses in society, which is represented to us as a reality, is only an ideal . . . a directing idea whose very direction should be exactly defined; for as the social idea is, so is the politics." Any absolute unity, such as Comte's great Being, Humanity, would abolish the individuality of persons. The best social ideal was one which would conciliate the greatest individuality of each citizen and the greatest solidarity of all citizens. The directing idea of social evolution was not the subordination of the individual conscience to the group conscience, but the harmony of all consciences in freedom.[14]

As for practical morality, it must accord with reality. The term "ought" implied an ideal in the face of reality, an ideal which was not always possible. There was always a certain amount of injustice in a society. But this injustice was not accepted by Fouillée; rather, it was the basis of his concept of "reparative justice." Heretofore the necessity for reparative justice, he noted, had been neglected, or confused with the idea of charity, or love of humanity. Some socialists had absorbed the idea of justice into the idea of fraternity, which was not a transcendental ideal, but a human one. Actually, it was fraternity which should be absorbed into the idea of justice. The right of reparation was based upon an original violation of rights; justice consisted, not only of abstaining from evil, but of repairing accomplished evil. This was true whether one considered injustice in society as the product of natural fatality or of human freedom. "It is for freedom to make amends, as much as it can, for the evils of fatality, and even more so, for the evils created by freedom itself."[15]

Nor was anyone totally free of the obligations of reparative justice. Fouillée quoted Comte that all of us were born laden with all kinds of obligations toward society. All individuals were linked together in social solidarity and therefore participated in its injustice. Therefore, "each individual should contribute his share in the reparation of the common injustice and in the reestablishment of the true conditions of human society." This duty extended to past injustices which the society inherited from other generations. One of the greatest means of accomplishing reparative justice was the provision of free and obligatory education to all. The foundation of right and of the social contract was the moral will, which required development of the intelligence. Thus, it was the right of all to have sufficient knowledge of the essential conditions of the association.[16]

What Fouillée had accomplished in this work was to eliminate the spiritualists' distinction between justice and charity, by extending the concept of justice to those moral inequities formerly covered by charity. In his next work, *La Propriété sociale et la démocratie*, he pointed out the weakness of Cousin's position that man, through his free will and his labor had brought something new into the world, and therefore had inviolate right to property. Man was always building, Fouillée noted, on something already there; and this natural base, or means of production, could be maintained as property only by the decision of society, because it was social property. Not only that, but the methods of production were passed down to him by previous generations. "He who invented the plough labors still, invisible, at the side of the worker."[17]

Fouillée's social viewpoint here moved closer to that of Proudhon, to a social morality, and away from the individualist moral theory of spiritualism. Thus, he was able to say that his concept of the contractual social organism was both liberalism pushed to the highest degree, because it would demand nothing of the individual without his conscious consent, and a rational socialism, because its object was a social organization where all participants were *solidaires*, united among themselves and to the whole, animated by a common idea.[18] This concept was basic to the formation of the Radical-Socialists' political and social program. It also contributed to the new moral philosophy which was to revitalize *morale laïque* in the schools under the rubric of *solidarité*, as the radical party grew in strength in the 1890's.

Léon Bourgeois

What the newly-developing social philosophy needed, in a democratic age and in an educational system staffed by primary school teachers who were not intellectuals, was popularization. This task was performed by Léon Bourgeois, who replaced Macé as president of the Ligue de l'enseignement, was seated in the Chamber of Deputies from 1888 on, and served as Minister of Public Instruction in the Freycinet and Brisson ministries. Bourgeois' father, like Cousin's, was a watchmaker, but the former was to rise farther—to the presidency of the Senate and of the Radical-Socialist Party.[19] As president of the Ligue, Bourgeois addressed its Bordeaux congress in 1895 on moral education, using the language of Fouillée. Character, he said, was a product of heredity, environment and education. Education should provide a clear idea of the good. "The idea is a force, it is force itself," he declared. But it acted only after being transformed into feeling.[20]

A politician rather than a *universitaire*, Bourgeois wrote his book, *Solidarité*, the following year; it was in a popular style, and ran into seven editions by 1912. In it, he noted a new moral attitude developing, which offered a middle way between classical individualism and collective socialism. This attitude had arisen, just when certain writers had claimed the bankruptcy of science and the divorce between science and morality, out of the convergence of two forces—the scientific method and the moral idea. "There is between each individual and all others a necessary bond of solidarity; only the exact study of the causes, conditions, and limits of that solidarity would produce a standard of the rights and duties of each to all and all to each, and would insure scientific and moral conclusions to the social problem." In the Enlightenment tradition, Bourgeois claimed that what the discovery of physical laws had done for material life, the discovery of moral laws would do for the life of society. Reason would determine "the inevitable laws of [social] action"; will, led by moral sentiments, would undertake that action.[21]

Bourgeois had advanced from an individual to a social morality. Like Fouillée,[22] he refuted social Darwinist arguments for the survival of the fittest with a theory of the "solidarity of beings, or interdependence of nature and all men." But, less careful than Fouillée to preserve individual free will, he tended to refer to the biological and the social as one.

Originally, Bourgeois noted, humans derived their concepts of rights and duties from the supposition that they were unique creatures, ends in themselves, children of God. But it was now known that moral laws cannot be discovered except by the study of the human being, considered, not in metaphysical isolation, but in the reality of his relationship with his milieu, his time, the race from which he derives and the posterity that will derive from him.[23]

Clearly Bourgeois was moving further away from Kantian morality than had Fouillée: He was approaching positivistic views represented by Hippolyte Taine.[24] At the time he was writing, the ideas of Comte himself, interpreted by his disciple Jacques Lafitte to overflow audiences at the Collège de France in the 1880s, were receiving wide recognition in University circles. (By 1898 the man few French intellectuals had read in his lifetime was to have his centenary celebrated at the Sorbonne.[25]) And perhaps of greater importance for Bourgeois's scientism was that expounded by Ernest Renan in *l'Avenir de la science*, written in 1849 but first published in 1892. It named science "the first need of humanity." Through the free and rational operation of the human mind, society must organize itself scientifically to "improve the established order." Renan proclaimed that science was itself a religion. "Science alone will henceforth form the creeds."[26] The influence of this work in the 1890's was enormous.[27]

Bourgeois was perhaps being led by the spirit of the time to express more scientism than may have been natural to him. He did argue against the concept of a state or society superior to its constituents. There was, he said, only a group of people, associated, with reciprocal rights and duties. Laws were deducible, not from a state founded upon formal conventions, but from an "association of fact, pre-existent." Positive law should be a reflection of the society in its most ideal form. Its goal would be freedom for the physical, intellectual and moral development of each person.[28] Thus Bourgeois swung between the determinism of the "natural laws" of society and the traditional concept of individual freedom.

The same problem occurred in the concept of social debt, a derivation of Fouillée's reparative justice. Since one could not live without society, one owed something to it; and this was the basis of duties, which were merely the counterparts of the advantages gained by living in association. But Bourgeois insisted that, although this debt was a limitation on human freedom, it did not negate it. If one paid his debt, he was free. However, the debt was enormous; when first born each individual owed the society the entire heritage passed down to him. Thus, one was already involved in a "quasi-contract of human association." The payment of the social debt would be guaranteed by positive law, based upon the scientific understanding of the natural laws of solidarity. This theory substituted for the Christian morality of charity, and for the even more abstract republican morality of fraternity; it was a quasi-contractual obligation, source and measure of the rigorous duty of social solidarity[29] based on the social debt humans owe one another.

Solidarité in Education

What Bourgeois had done was to outline, in popular form, a social theory which would satisfy the Kantians, by emphasis on the free acquiescence of the individual in a tacit social contract, and at the same time, could claim the "scientific" basis required of a positive social theory. Its various possibilities and emphases were to be worked out in a series of exegeses by intellectuals of the university community. Buisson, in the leçon d'ouverture of his course in pedagogy at the Sorbonne in 1896, referred to it in terms of his predecessor, Marion: "Instead of solidarity submitted to, it is a willed solidarity. . . . The bond of mutual dependence which free beings establish among themselves is an act of wisdom and morality; it supposes the governance of minds by reason, of wills by justice." Therefore, Buisson celebrated solidarisme, as he called it, as a doctrine responding to the needs of educators.[30]

In July of 1899, a Société de l'éducation sociale was formed, with Bourgeois as president and Buisson as one of the vice-presidents. The following March, they held a congress (attended mainly by representatives of workers' and teachers' associations, and including some artists, writers, and Radical senators and deputies) to study the fundamental conditions of existence of human society and the means to inject knowledge of them into general education. Bourgeois addressed the group.

He described the purpose of the organization as research into the proper means to produce, not only the virtuous person, the good citizen, but the veritable social being; this would be an education of the "social sense" in humanity. Children must be taught to recognize the "common consciousness [conscience?]" and to judge their own acts by it. For this education a purely philosophical viewpoint was insufficient; what was necessary was "a precise analysis of the objective conditions of solidarity," to see if the laws of solidarity embodied the makings of a truly social system. He suggested as a basis for discussion three "positive facts" which he said could not be seriously contested: that the individual, as a condition of life, existed in a natural and necessary state of solidarity with all human beings; that human society developed through freedom of the individual (not necessarily, he noted, in a metaphysical sense), which was the condition for progress; and that human beings conceived of and desired justice, which was the condition of order.

He went on to elaborate on the quasi-contract which must be recognized by members of the society, and on the necessity for abolishing man-made inequities through law. But the state could not legislate justice without the consent of society; what was needed therefore was a new development in human consciousness, a recognition of solidarity. "The social problem," he declared, "is, in the last analysis, a problem of education." The object of social education was to create the "social being" in each person, to make him act socially and pay as well as he could his social debt. Social education should teach the laws of natural solidarity and the way in which they constituted an obligation for everyone. It should lead the will of each student to realize his obligations. Bourgeois concluded by emphasizing that no law was sufficient to assure the payment of the social debt unless all were conscious of it and consented. This was the task of education.[31]

The discussion which ensued involved such matters as how much of the social debt each person owed, and how it should be paid. It was agreed that those in misery because of past inequities were hardly liable to any extent; that each should pay his share according to his circumstances; that the debt should be paid to society as a whole, which would in turn guarantee a minimal physical existence and an education to all; that each person, if he paid his just share, would be acquitted of his debt and free.[32] It is interesting to note Buisson's demurral on this occasion. He questioned the concept of debt (dette) and preferred that the word duty (devoir) be used instead, to avoid misunderstanding. He also claimed that "liberty, equality, fraternity" were clearer than "solidarity."[33] This was an early indication of the fact that, although *solidarité* was to encompass the Kantians, it never fully converted them.

The next step on the road to making *solidarité* not just the moral philosophy of the Radical Party, but the official philosophy of French education, was to bring it into the university community. At the turn of the century, Alfred Croiset (renowned Greek scholar and Dean of the Sorbonne) presided over a series of conferences and discussions on moral instruction in secondary education. Gustave Belot, professor of philosophy at Louis-le-Grand, spoke for the necessity of a completely secular morality in an age when religion was suffering under the assault of science. He spoke of the "plasticity" of the human being, and predicted that secular morality would in time be as effective as religious morality once had been. He distinguished moral rules, which related to the ideal, from moral motivation. One must develop in the child the moral motivation which was related as closely as possible to the reasons which determined the rule in the first place, thereby making it an interior motivation. Thus, the child's moral motivation would be objective and rational.

Secular moral pedagogy would also replace the absolute character of religious morality with a relative and progressive one; "The average moral education is achieved in conformity with the exigencies of social life." It should be realistic, linked with real goals—not utopian, but associated with the progressive realization of the good life. Thus, it would have a social character. Gustave Belot criticized contemporary secular morality for attempting to deduce ethics from individual conscience and reason. What was necessary was not a plastering over of old moral theory; for *morale laïque* to fulfill its pedagogical mission, it must be inspired by entirely new premises— "an organic creation in harmony with the critical rationalism and social democracy which solidly dominate contemporary life."[34]

Belot was also present at a series of lectures by Bourgeois at the École des Hautes Études Sociales[35] in 1901-02, and participated in the discussions of *solidarité*. Bourgeois here responded to criticism that labeling solidarity scientific implied that it would operate without the need for human intervention. He admitted that natural solidarity had no moral goal. But just as one used the morally neutral law of gravity to prevent catastrophe by establishing equilibrium, so one could use the law of solidarity to prevent human misery, by establishing justice. Instead of allowing the law of solidarity to work for the ends of nature, one must make it work for the ends of society. In later discussions, however, Bourgeois admitted that the basic principle was justice, not solidarity. But solidarity could add precision to the idea of justice, as in Fouillée's reparative justice. Justice might be the goal, but solidarity was the natural law of society, which must be used to attain justice.

Kant's categorical imperative was extended by solidarity, he claimed. We are responsible not only for our own acts, but for those of others, and they for ours. Neither the freedom nor the responsibility of the individual were absolute. Solidarity, Bourgeois insisted, was a fact anterior to either freedom or justice, and modified both. A social being was one who understood that, by the fact of solidarity, there was a part of his person, his property, his activity, his liberty that derived from the common human effort. Although much of the discussion at this meeting was concerned with social legislation, Bourgeois's closing lecture emphasized education, rather than coercion, as a method of realizing solidarity.[36]

In Buisson's contribution to the lecture series, he strove to retain the Kantian emphasis in solidarity. What was being taught in the schools, he insisted, was the opposite of natural solidarity, which was brutal and born of necessity; the solidarity of law introduced the concepts of personality and responsibility.[37] On the other hand, some positivist participants tried to show the relationship of solidarity and positivism. Alphonse Darlu, Inspector General of Public Instruction, found Bourgeois's thinking too individualistic. Quoting Comte on the concrete reality of society as opposed to the abstract nature of the individual, he complained that Bourgeois shrank from giving too great a role to the state. But did not solidarity constitute the principle of the rights of the state over the individual? He himself would prefer to say that France was a moral person, instead of 39 million inhabitants who had contracted among themselves. The interior life of the individual was quite a different matter from the exterior collective life of solidarity. However, even Darlu agreed that both the interior and the exterior tendencies—conscience and action—should be retained in morality. The progression would be from a personal morality at a very young age to social consciousness in adolescence, he noted,[38] thus conforming to Littré's program.

Emile Boutroux, president of the École, wound up the series of lectures on a critical note. He credited both Comte and Proudhon for the replacement of individual morality by social morality. But as a philosopher, he felt impelled to point out that the idea of an end (justice) weakened the unity and rigorously scientific character of the concept of solidarity: "It is impossible to hold to that somewhat mechanical transposition of the given natural solidarity into an ideal solidarity." There were actual contradictions between the two. Natural solidarity, for instance, led to the survival of the fittest and the elimination of the feeble. Ideal solidarity required the addition of a chosen principle—the idea of justice. "One must then conceive of human solidarity, not as a fatal law of dependence, endured by individuals, but as a mutuality, regulated by justice and freely consented to." Natural solidarity should be studied in order to make ideal society effective; but it was ideal solidarity which pointed man's way to his duties.[39]

It is clear that *solidarité*, while seeming to produce a moral formulation on which all could agree, had logical difficulties. The Kantians reacted against the formula of complete organicism. Others questioned the utility of the concept of social debt. Some critics, who worried about socialism, were disturbed by the tendency to confuse duty, which was moral, with debt, which was juridical.[40] Charles Brunot suggested eliminating from the definition of solidarity the biological analogy, and also individual responsibility for social debt. Noting the dichotomy between natural and social solidarity, he suggested that the transition from one to the other would be made by giving to the individual a social education.[41] Here Boutroux voiced his suspicion that *solidarité* was a system thought up after the fact, to rationalize certain worthy ends, like transforming charity into legal assistance. However, he went on, even if the doctrine rested only upon the sentiments of charity, sympathy, and love of one's neighbors, there was no reason to deny it legal right. What was necessary was to make these sentiments general in the society.[42]

The acceptance of *solidarité* by the University was indicated by the number of lectures and discussions devoted to it in the first decade of the century, and by the favor accorded it by Croiset, Dean of the Sorbonne. In his preface to the collected discussions at the École des Hautes Études in 1907, he wrote that solidarity represented "a fundamental tendency of our time: the consideration of society, of the collectivity, substituted more and more for that of the individual." He saw this as a reaction against the excessive individualism of the old philosophy and political science. The old terms—justice, charity, fraternity—seemed insufficient to a modern generation, "eager for a positive and objective science, feeling the need for a word which would express the scientific character of the moral law." The word solidarity, borrowed from biology, responded to this need. He praised the fact that, although solidarity implied a sentiment for the improvement of the lot of others, this sentiment was not indispensable. However, Croiset would not exclude fraternal feelings as the "necessary cement" of a just society.[43]

An examination of the available *morale* textbooks in use from 1895 to 1914 reveals that the concept of *solidarité* was an important and lasting addition to the predominantly Kantian texts of the earlier Third Republic,[44] although it often appeared as merely an afterthought added to the traditional treatment. The first manual to place duties to society before those to individuals was J. Curé and F. Honzelle, *Sommaire de leçons de morale*. However, while picturing society as necessary to man, it continued to view conscience as innate. E. Abadie, *Manuel d'instruction morale et civique à l'usage des écoles primaires*, written for the upper primary levels, took a solidarist view of society, picturing it as based on mutual interest.[45]

The first clearly *solidariste* text was E. Primaire, *Manuel d'education morale civique et sociale*, which emphasized the necessity of society in order for humans to evolve from bestiality. It spoke of the debt owed to our ancestors, which must be paid to our successors. But it still maintained the Kantian view of the universality of conscience.[46]

There is in the Musée Pédagogique one handwritten student's notebook in *morale* from this period, written by a girl (age 15) attending the sixth section, third year at the Collège Chaptal. It is basically Kantian in theory:

> La morale est la science du devoir, et l'honnête homme est celui qui la respecte, et accomplit le devoir *parce que* c'est le devoir. Le devoir est imposé à l'homme par la loi morale qui devient ainsi la règle unique de ses actions. Le caractère de cette *loi,* qui prend la forme d'un *ordre absolu est d'être obligatoire.*

However, in the section on duties to others, there appears the following:

> L'homme est un être essentiellement *social.* À aucun moment de sa vie, il ne peut se passer de ses semblables. La société au sein de laquelle il est appelé à vivre est composée des personnes liées entre elles par les mêmes droits et par les mêmes devoirs. Le lien, c'est la *solidarité* morale dont le principe est le respect et l'amour des uns envers les autres.

Also, under the heading of duties toward society: "La société n'est donc pas le resultat d'un simple *contrat;* elle est une *nécessité* pour l'homme." However, in these notes, the duties of justice and charity were still described as based on the Kantian principle of the inviolability of the human person.[47]

In 1902 *solidarité* became enshrined in the official secondary school program of *morale.* Pierre-F. Pécaut's *Petit traité de morale sociale,* written to conform to the program, was intended for high school students 15 to 16 years of age. It defined solidarity as "the fact that the individual does not realize the conditions of his organic or spiritual life except by the collaboration, voluntary or involuntary, of his fellow-men." Both economic and scientific solidarity were dealt with. As for *morale,* it was described as an ensemble of feelings which are acquired under the influence of others. The duties resulting from solidarity were outlined, without, however, including reparative justice.[48]

Another work produced to meet the new program, L. Le Chevalier's *l'Idéal moral,* while declaring that "man is a moral person," and that morality did not enter man from without, also maintained that the individual owed everything to society. "All that you are yourself you receive from others," it stated, including ideas and feelings. Therefore, one could only pay one's debt through devotion to society. "Man becomes a moral being only by interaction with his fellow men."[49] This melange of the old spiritualism and the new solidarity was documented by readings from both Kant and Bourgeois. The mixture— *solidarité* superimposed upon the still-influential tenets of individualist Kantian morality—was typical of most of the manuals before 1914. An occasional exception was based totally on spiritualist[50] or totally on *solidariste*[51] doctrine. One can make no distinction along these lines between texts written for primary or secondary schools, except that none of the texts written solely for secondary schools eliminated the old spiritualism. (Few of the primary texts did either.) Clearly, although an important element of *morale laïque* at this time, *solidarité* had not replaced the old spiritualism of Cousin.

Although accepted in this form by the republican establishment, *solidarité's* claim to be "scientific" was not completely successful. And the Radicals who dominated the Third Republic after the turn of the century were devoted to the twin doctrines of democracy and science.[52] Demands for the "single school," merging the primary and secondary systems, were voiced in the parliamentary enquiry on secondary education in 1899.[53] And as for science, the new Minister of Education in 1902, Georges Leygues, stated that it was possible to teach the republic and democracy without attacking religious beliefs, "by making love and respect for scientifically-established truth" the cornerstone of education.[54]

Meanwhile, the search for a scientifically-established *morale* was being conducted at the Sorbonne in the context of a newly-established discipline, called for by Comte—sociology. The results were to be the theoretical culmination of the century-old search for a secular morality.

Part IV

The
Theory and Practice
of *Morale Laïque*

Introduction

The great change that occurred in French thought at the turn of the century was the shift to relativism, a change shocking to many contemporaries, but almost inevitable in the light of previous developments. Since the Enlightenment French thinkers had been interested in *moeurs*, and had noted with fascination the differences in customs encountered as the known world was enlarged. However, in moral theory they had always presumed both the importance of the individual and the identity of human nature. Now practical experience (particularly in the colonies)[1] and academic research were reinforcing the axiom of the positivists and of the theorists of organic society. It was not the individual, but society that had a "nature." And, contrary to the assumption of earlier social philosophies, which presumed an ideal society, of which existing societies were better or worse approximations, observed societies presented a bewildering variety of forms and institutions.

The social preoccupations of the French, viewing their burgeoning neighbor across the Rhine, moved away from the question of the ideal society toward the more pragmatic question: what makes a successful society? Both attracted and repelled by Germany, French intellectuals pinpointed the flaw responsible for France's defeat in 1870 as a weakness of the "scientific spirit." Soon after the war, Ernest Renan wrote, "The victory of Germany was the victory of science and reason." The lack of faith in science was the profound shortcoming of France. This was the intellectual flaw; but Renan detected also a social flaw. "A country is not the simple addition of individuals who compose it; it is a soul, a conscience, a person." He saw in egoism, in "democracy badly understood," another weakness of French society.[2]

French intellectuals did not want France to be like Germany, but they wanted a stable and successful nation. The late nineteenth century saw a series of pilgrimages by French *universitaires* to Germany, where they studied German social sciences and educational practices.[3] By the end of the century, the term "scientific," as applied to the social sciences, indicated the historical method. Out of the merger of the traditional *histoire des moeurs* with scientific empiricism and German historical methodology developed both *science des moeurs* and sociology. They were to have profound implications for *morale laïque*.

Emile Durkheim and Sociological Morality

Social Science

THE leading figure in the development of sociology was Emile Durkheim.[1] Born in Lorraine, the agnostic son of a rabbi, Durkheim retained throughout his life the vocation of a prophet and a missionary. At the Ecole Normale Supérieure he studied philosophy with Boutroux and history with Fustel de Coulanges, both of whom he admired. But he was determined to devote himself to a practical philosophy applicable to the social problems of the Third Republic. He was influenced by Kant, Comte, and Renouvier. In his early years of teaching at provincial *lycées* he also read Herbert Spencer and Alfred Espinas, who described society as analogous to a biological organism.

By 1885, in a review of Albert Schäffle's *Bau und leben des sozialen körpers*, he was posing the problem inherent in *morale laïque* of teaching people to understand rationally their relationship to society, so that they would naturally accept their duties to it.[2] In 1886, Durkheim had a conversation on this subject with Louis Liard, student of Renouvier, professor of philosophy, and Director of Higher Education. Liard emphasized the necessity of a social viewpoint for France more realistic than that provided by speculative philosophy. He and Durkheim agreed that a scientific study of society could provide a secular morality suitable for teaching in secondary and higher education, and in the *écoles normales*. It was he who advised Durkheim to go to Germany and observe what was being accomplished there.[3]

On his return, Durkheim wrote articles linking what he had learned to French needs. Primarily, he seems to have been reinforced in the idea, conveyed to him philosophically by both Boutroux and Renouvier, that the whole was greater than the sum of its parts.[4] By the very fact that individuals were related in a particular manner, something resulted which had special properties, which could have a personality and a self-consciousness. Durkheim was convinced that phrases like "social consciousness" and "collective spirit" expressed concrete facts. Former moral theories deduced ethics from given concepts such as duty, the good, et cetera. But morality was actually a complex function of the social organism; not an immutable abstraction, morality changed as the society changed.

Durkheim had been particularly impressed with Wilhelm Wundt's psychology and ethics. It was from Wundt that Durkheim derived the notion that moral truth was based upon universal consent.[5] He reported that Wundt had broken almost all ties between ethics and metaphysics, and he called for the organization of a "moral science" in France, similar to that which was flowering in Germany. However, he disapproved of the fact that, while moral science was discussed at the universities in Germany, its practical application in the schools was left to the clergy. The French way would be to apply philosophical theory to moral teachings in the schools.[6]

Durkheim also made some general comparisons between French education, which stimulated individualism, and German education, which stimulated life in common. "It is hardly contestable," he commented, "that what we need most at this moment is to reawaken in ourselves the taste for collective life." It was necessary to explain to students that the personality was made up in large part from impressions from the physical and social environment. The individual, he wrote, echoing Comte, was only an abstraction. Thus, students must learn that physical and social phenomena were facts which did not necessarily yield to human will.[7]

It is believed that Durkheim was deliberately chosen by the educational establishment to initiate the science of sociology into the University as an aid to *morale laïque*.[8] Upon his return from Germany in 1887, he was transferred from the *lycée* at Troyes to a post at the University of Bordeaux to teach pedagogy and social science. The initiative for this transfer seems to have come from Liard, and from Espinas, who was at Bordeaux. Durkheim indicated to the dean at Bordeaux that the topic of his first year of teaching would be *la solidarité sociale*. During this period, he was active in organizations like the Fédération des jeunesses laïques, and often spoke at popular meetings on secularization. He clearly associated his concern about *morale* with *laïcisme*.[9]

In the 1880's Durkheim began to write his doctoral dissertation on the relations between the individual and society. His Latin thesis, presented in 1892, was on Montesquieu.[10] He praised Montesquieu for being the first to abandon the concept of an abstract ideal society based upon human nature, and to recognize the different types of social, as opposed to political, organizations. His French thesis, *De la division du travail social,* was presented in 1893. In the preface, he wrote that it was no longer possible to believe that moral evolution consisted in the development of a single idea in time. Rather, changes in social structure had given rise to changes in customs, and these could by observed by the social scientist.[11]

To Durkheim, sociology was primarily a science dealing with "moral facts," a science which could provide a new ethic for modern man, based on reason rather than on revelation, a science which could replace the worn-out moral criteria of the nineteenth century. He posited the division of labor as the new source of moral values. The individual must no longer try to realize in himself the qualities of some abstract "man" in general, but the special qualities of his *métier*. The greatest moral value in the modern world, he declared, was in usefully fulfilling a determined function in society.

Originally, societies were bound together by "social solidarity through similarity," a solidarity embodied in the common consciousness and represented by the whole body of criminal law. "The ensemble of beliefs and sentiments common to the average members of a single society forms a distinct system which has its own life. . . . It is independent of the particular conditions in which individuals find themselves. . . . It is the psychic symbol of the society." An act is criminal when it offends the collective consciousness. "We do not disapprove of it because it is a crime; it is a crime because we disapprove of it." Durkheim refused to say that this disapproval necessarily related either to the vital interests of the society, as in utilitarianism, or to an abstract idea of justice. The function of punishment in a society was simply "to maintain intact the social cohesion by maintaining the common consciousness [and therefore social solidarity] in all its vitality."[12]

In the modern world, solidarity through similarity was giving way to an organic solidarity based on the division of labor and represented by civil law. The more social functions were divided, the more dependent upon society each person was, while at the same time he gained a kind of autonomy in his special task. Thus, organic solidarity promoted the growth of individualism and the decline of religion, which had been the expression of the collective consciousness of the past.[13] In a modern organic society, morality would tend to pertain more and more to professional groups. Durkheim refused to view solidarity as mechanical and analogous to that of a biological organism. In society, the functions of individuals were changeable. Nor did he accept the analogy with animal societies. Human societies progressed because of the greater sociability of people. Special enlargement and diversification gave rise to new kinds of psychic life. Thus, Durkheim rejected both the classical notion of the ideal society and the reduction of psychological life to purely physical origins. This did not mean, he pointed out, that our psychic life stood outside nature; it derived from social life, which was itself natural, and observable by science.[14]

As for morality, it was dependent upon life in society. There was no such thing as individual morality. The current moral crisis, Durkheim stated, was the result of the change in social structure away from solidarity by similarity. The common consciousness had been destroyed and no new basis for ethics had been clearly formulated. The remedy was not to revive old traditions which were not in accord with the new social structure, but to build anew on the basis of a scientific understanding of the facts of social life. "To regulate our human relationships, it is necessary only to revert to the means which aid us in regulating our relationships with things: reflection, methodically employed." A social science which understood the developmental laws of society could predict the direction of moral tendencies.[15]

It is clear that Durkheim's thesis made a strong contribution to the growing ideology of *solidarité*. The final section of the work discussed abnormal forms of the division of labor, where division led to disintegration of the society, and the individual sought only his own ends. He advocated action by society as a whole to regulate social relationships in the direction of justice and the greater use of natural talents.[16]

Associated with both the Radicals and the socialists, he participated in discussions of solidarity.[17] Bourgeois' own work was published after Durkheim's. However, there were already divergences between them. *Solidarité*, as described by its various adherents, oscillated between the analogy with biological organisms and the still-powerful belief in the Kantian individual conscience. The first supported the assertion that *solidarité* was a scientific moral theory; the second preserved the individualism so prized by the French. Durkheim, in effect, denied both. His sociology was to transcend *solidarité*. What he wanted was "to extend scientific rationalism to [the study of] human conduct," by demonstrating that, "considered in the past, it is reducible to cause and effect relationships which another rational operation can transform into rules of action for the future."[18] This social science was to be both descriptive, as *science des moeurs*, and normative, as moral philosophy.

Durkheim warned that social facts must be regarded as pure data—as things, not as ideas. In morals, for instance, it was not the conception of the morally ideal which must be studied, but the actual rules regulating conduct. However distasteful it might be, one must eliminate all preconceived notions and treat phenomena objectively according to their visible exterior characteristics. These could be established, not by concepts, but "by means of sensation . . . the primary and necessary material of all concepts." Only then could sociology be truly scientific.[19]

It was this part of Durkheim's work which was incorporated into the new *science des moeurs*. Represented by Lucien Lévy-Bruhl, this cultural science seemed closer to the old *histoire des moeurs*, in that it involved observation of the customs of a society, and the ordering of these customs into a system. As Lévy-Bruhl put it, "practice [of morality] is not here then deduced from theory; but on the contrary, theory is compelled to rationalize the existing practice.'' Thus, he claimed that what should be studied was not the evolution of theory, but the evolution of moral practice which caused new elements to appear in moral theory. He, too, criticized the postulate that human nature was identical in all times and places, and that therefore there was an absolute morality. ''It is not because we know it to be absolute that duty appears to us as imperative; it is because it appears to us as imperative that we believe it to be absolute,'' he wrote,[20] thereby reversing Kant. It followed that science could not found *morale,* it could only find it, as a given. But there was no such thing as ''morale naturelle.'' One could only say that humans were naturally moral if one meant by it that all humans lived in society and all societies had moral codes. Systems of morality did not express the eternal essence of justice; their content emerged from the given social reality. Although Lévy-Bruhl listed economic, political, intellectual, geographic and historical factors as making up the context in which a moral code developed, he attributed changes in morality predominantly to changes in economic organization.[21]

As so described, *science des moeurs* was merely descriptive; in order to apply it, but only after the science had progressed, one would have to add *l'art moral rationnel.* This practical application, in Lévy-Bruhl's terms, implied bringing moral practice, which tended to lag behind, in line with the other social variables.[22]

However, Albert Bayet, who was to become Director of Primary Education after Buisson, and who was active in the Radical Party, saw *l'art moral rationnel* as a branch of politics, just as *science des moeurs* was a branch of sociology.[23] Theoretical morality should bend its efforts, not toward elaborating a code of duties, but toward improving ceaselessly the moral reality. This would involve action on the levels both of ideas and of social mechanisms, adapting each to fit the needs of the group involved, enlarging them to meet new social problems, rectifying them to adjust to new sociological discoveries. Sociologists could not create moral ideas, which created themselves in accordance with facts. They could only study their origin and direction. It was then up to the enlightened social practitioner, presumably the politician, to make use of this knowledge. Bayet spoke of the necessary connection between the educational system, which taught *morale,* and the state, which practiced it.[24]

Lévy-Bruhl himself was not willing to go so far. *Science des moeurs* could not be theoretical and normative at the same time. It was completely objective and indifferent to politics, although politicians might find its results interesting. He disavowed Bayet's applications of morality as valid interpretations of his doctrine.[25]

Science des moeurs was a natural outgrowth of a tendency toward social relativism which, as Durkheim had noted, began with Montesquieu. The difference was that it now clearly espoused moral relativism. But its prescriptive value for ethics was limited; it remained merely descriptive. As Bayet pointed out, it was a part of sociology, and an important part. It remained for Durkheim to develop the observation of customs into a theory of morality.

Social Morality

At this point, Durkheim had also outlined a descriptive science. How could it prescribe for the future? As he himself admitted, science explains but does not judge. It would be necessary to find a criterion by which to judge impartial facts in order to indicate normative solutions to social problems. But to preserve objectivity, this criterion must be one "inherent in the facts themselves," as he put it, one which would permit the observer to distinguish scientifically between health and sickness in the different orders of social phenomena.

Durkheim's choice was the norm. A social fact must by judged by the standard of what was normal for the social type to which it belonged, at its particular phase of development, in the average society of its kind. Instead of "desperately pursuing an end which recedes as one advances," men should work to "maintain the normal state, to reestablish it when it is disturbed, to search out the conditions thereof if they have just changed." Obviously, the norm was always evolving along with the society itself, and therefore, morality was constantly in a process of change.[26]

Durkheim's version of social solidarity was not immediately accepted by the university. He confounded his dissertation committee, which included the spiritualists Janet and Marion.[27] Lucien Herr, librarian at the École Normale Supérieure, who profoundly influenced a whole generation of normaliens, wrote of *Les Règles,* "not only do I not adhere, I do not comprehend and refuse to recognize as scientific anything that could be constructed on such a foundation, with these materials." He particularly objected to Durkheim's positing of society as exterior and anterior to individuals, his attempt to assign an imperative coercive power to rules of interpersonal relationships, his view of social feelings as originating in the mass rather than in the individuals composing it—in general, to his slighting of the individual in favor of society.[28] This criticism corresponds to neo-Kantian reservations about *solidarité.*

Durkheim's whole sociology, and consequently his moral theory, did in fact rest upon his view of society. He saw social forces as originating in the common life and not in the individual. The whole was more than the sum of its parts; society was a reality *sui generis,* with an existence distinct from that of the individuals who composed it, with a particular nature of its own.[29] A social force, he maintained, was not general in the society because it existed in the individual; rather, it existed in the individual because it was general in the society.[30] The collectively shared ideas of a society could not be explained by factors less complex than those regulating the social life. In an article of 1898, Durkheim claimed that, just as the chemical properties of atoms were insufficient to account for physiological phenomena, so the nature of individuals was insufficient to explain social phenomena. In the combination of individuals, something entirely new was produced, irreducible to its components.[31]

This has sometimes been seen as the beginning of Durkheim's idealization of society.[32] In 1906, speaking to the Société française de philosophie, he noted that morality required disinterestedness and devotion. To inspire these qualities, the object of morality must be higher in value than the individual. If society were merely the sum of its individuals, no moral value could be embodied in it. Therefore, if a system of morality existed, it meant that the society was a moral being qualitatively distinct from individual beings. The only alternative to society, he postulated, was God; and "I myself am indifferent to this choice, since I see in the Divinity only society transfigured and symbolically expressed." Emphasizing the debt the individual owed to society, he declared: "The believer bows before God, because it is from God that he believes he has his being, and particularly his mental being, his soul. We have the same reason for feeling that sentiment for the collectivity."[33]

In 1912 Durkheim gave definitive form to the theory of "totemism" which he had been developing over the years. In Les formes élémentaires de la vie religieuse, he concluded, on the basis of a study of primitive societies, that the totem was simultaneously a symbol of God and a symbol of the clan, or society. Thus, God was society symbolically conceived. To Durkheim, society occupied the same honored position as had nature to his eighteenth century predecessors. Society, he declared,

> . . . is of nature, yet dominates it. Not only do all the forces of the universe converge in society, but they also form a new synthesis which surpasses in richness, complexity and power of action all that went to form it. In a word, society is nature arrived at a higher point in its development, concentrating all its energies to surpass itself.[34]

The idealization of society, as opposed to the individual, was being promoted at the turn of the century by conservatives,[35] particularly anti-Dreyfusards, who believed that even if Dreyfus was innocent, his exoneration would cause great harm to the nation. Yet Durkheim was one of the intellectuals who defended Dreyfus.[36] Durkheim's defense of individualism was written in 1898, in the midst of the Affair. He agreed with the conservatives that a religion was needed to unite France. But the only religion on which all could agree was the religion of humanity, of which the rational expression was individualism.[37] (It is notable that Durkheim did not, like his mentors Comte and Saint-Simon, whom he credited with first conceiving of sociology,[38] capitalize Humanity, although he often did so with Society. Neither Comte nor Saint-Simon would have made individualism the content of his religion of Humanity.)

However, by individualism, Durkheim did not mean the "deification of private interests," but rather the Kantian sacredness of the human person. One could have this kind of individualism, he wrote, as an ideal, while recognizing that the individual was more a social product than a social cause. The moral beliefs which made the individual sacred were derived by the individual from society.[39] This formulation—that society dictates to the individual the sacredness of persons—would seem to solve the problem of the conflict between the two better that Rousseau had.

In lectures given the same year, Durkheim defined the role of the state as one of moralizing and organizing the society, to the end that each of its members was treated as an individual and that each maintained his obligation to others.[40] In a course given at the Sorbonne in 1913-14 on "Pragmatism and Sociology," he commented again on the individual role in morality. Moral truth was a social fact, superior to individual conscience. "But even that which is collective in it exists only through the individual conscience: the truth only realizes itself through individuals."[41]

However, later in 1914, Durkheim handled the problem of the individual versus society in a more characteristic way, in a essay on the dualism of human nature. Collective ideals, he wrote, were the effects of "that singularly creative and fertile psychic operation—which is scientifically analyzable—by which a plurality of individual consciousnesses enter into communion and are fused into a common consciousness." These ideals penetrated the individual consciousness, where they were themselves individualized. (Psychologists today would say internalized.) Thus, each person had two natures: one was rooted in his individual organism; the other was social, an extension of society that had become part of his self. There was often a conflict between the interests of society and those of the individual; thus, it was clear that the maintenance of society required individual sacrifice.[42] Put in this way, Durkheim's "common consciousness" sounds more like Rousseau's "general will" than it did in the 1898 article.

Durkheim had a unique opportunity to set his ideas in motion through his position at the university. By means of sociology, the "moral facts" would become known; they would be disseminated through education. Durkheim introduced sociology into the curriculum at Bordeaux in 1887; in 1896 he founded l'Année sociologique, which published sociological monographs until 1916; in 1902 he replaced Buisson as professor of pedagogy in Paris, teaching a course required of all students for the agrégation; in 1906 he was made full professor in the chair of Ethics and the Science of Education. Only in 1913 was this chair given its more accurate title—Sociology and the Science of Education.

Although it might seem from Durkheim's theory that the individual was helpless in changing the society which had produced him, one loophole had been left for progress. While it would be denying society, and consequently oneself, to desire a morality other than that which grew out of the social conditions of a given time, an individual or group could effect change under certain conditions. If there were a scientific (sociological) recognition of the disparity between the rules of morality and the actual state of society, an attempt to change the situation would be, not the individual fighting society, but "the collective itself, more and better aware of itself."[43] Durkheim saw this as the current situation in French society. The education crisis in France[44] seemed to be, not only a prime manifestation of the general moral crisis, but an opportunity for sociology to work toward a solution.

Moral Education

Durkheim saw each school generation as material for the re-creation of morality. Already at Bordeaux, he had begun a work tentatively entitled "Les raisons de l'être moral de la société en général," which exists only as a fragment. "The child must first be made to feel the moral forces which draw men together and which thus give birth to human societies," he wrote, comparing these forces to the law of gravitation. One must explain to the child the moral causes of this action: first, that we are attracted to those who think and feel as we do ("the man who lives in a group has more moral energy than the isolated man, since he draws perpetually on that common reservoir of life. . . . "); and second, because people depend upon one another ("there is the origin of the division of labor. . . . "). One must show the child the "absolute universality of human society," and demonstrate the significance of that universality.[45]

Durkheim believed that sociology could provide a theory of social institutions and of the role of the individual in society which would replace the mythologies on which former moral education was based.[46] The required course in pedagogy was Durkheim's means for introducing sociology into the citadel of letters. "It is above all as a sociologist that I will speak to you of education," he told his first class. The individual, he taught, was not predestined to a determined function in society by his intellectual or moral temperament; the average person was eminently plastic. It was society which divided labor among its members in a way which best suited its needs.

Thus, the education that society provided was one which constantly renewed the conditions of its own existence. The ends of education were above all social; therefore, it must respond to social necessity, must express collective feelings. Durkheim stressed the necessity for a body of directing ideas in education to replace those which were no longer valid, and assured his students that sociology could provide them.[47] He keyed his discussion of *morale laïque* in this course to the present. They were not seeking a *morale* for mankind in general, but for "the people of our time and of our country." He lauded the decision of the nation to provide a purely rational education, eliminating all the dogmas of revealed religion. Science, he said, denied that any category of reality was beyond the reach of human reason. Moral phenomena were no exception.

Durkheim pointed out how theological conceptions had been diminished, first in Protestantism, then in spiritualism, until even religious believers were willing to admit that morality could be constructed independent of theology. However, it was not simply a matter of teaching the old morality, minus religious notions. To eliminate religion *in toto* would be to eliminate morality also. What was necessary was to discover the rational substitutes for the religious ideas which in the past served as vehicles for essential moral ideas. Morality was based on a higher reality, which had previously been symbolized by God, but which might turn out to be a purely empirical reality. This reality must be disengaged from its symbols and presented to students in a rational form.[48]

The immediate object of moral education would be the guidance of conduct, not in a general sense, but in the sense of conduct for a particular time and society. One characteristic of moral rules was that they were obligatory; therefore, discipline itself was a basic factor of education. Another characteristic of moral rules was that they were collective in nature, pertaining to the society rather than the individual. "If society is the end of morality, it is also the medium. The individual does not bear in himself the precepts of morality . . . they can only be derived from the relationships established among associated individuals." The latter was borne out by the fact that morality varied in different societies. The ethics of each people varied directly with variations in the social structure. Each type of society had the morality which was necessary to it, just as each biological species had the nervous system essential to its maintenance. Actually, then, the two characteristics of moral regulations were one: society was the source and the disciplinary authority of morality, providing both of the traditional moral elements—the rule, and a sense of duty.

Durkheim saw European society as having lost the sense of authority and discipline. Therefore, moral renewal must be sought in the other element of morality—the good. This element must be emphasized by setting up great collective goals to which individuals could devote themselves; "Above all, we must seek to evoke faith in a common ideal." New concepts of justice and solidarity were in the process of elaboration, which would sooner or later produce appropriate institutions. The educator must work to clarify these ideas, to make the children love them, without turning them against the traditional ideas and practices which nurtured the new ones. "Above all," he insisted, "we must create for ourselves a soul, and we must prepare that soul in the heart of the child.''[49]

Durkheim pointed out that the new morality, which would substitute society for divinity and other-worldly sanctions, differed from the old in that it was liable to indefinite development along with the society. This made possible a third characteristic, possible only in a rational morality: free will. The seeming passivity of the individual in the face of socially dictated moral regulations was contradicted by the growing tendency to view the human person as sacrosanct and free in conscience. Kant had found man's moral autonomy in the area of reason, but he had made of reason a metaphysical conception, beyond the real world. Real autonomy, according to Durkheim, derived from a scientific ability to free the self from physical submission to nature, by controlling one's relationships to natural forces. The result was an acceptance of the laws of nature, not by constraint, but because it was reasonable—not a ''passive resignation,'' but an ''enlightened adhesion,'' since to wish freely was ''to wish to act in accordance with the nature of things.''

Durkheim pointed out that the believer saw the world as the creation of a good God; science permitted us to establish *a posteriori* what faith established *a priori*. In this way, science was the source of human autonomy. When science was complete, a true science of morals could be erected, based on the nature of social facts. That individuals would adhere to this morality voluntarily would not change the imperative nature of ethical rules. It would only mean that one would participate in morality actively, rather than passively. ''Such is the only autonomy to which we can pretend. . . . It is not an autonomy that we receive ready-made from nature. . . . But we ourselves make it, to the extent that we attain a more complete understanding of things.'' In this reasoned autonomy, Durkheim claimed, lay the distinctive characteristic of *morale laïque*.[50]

To teach *morale*, then, was not to preach it, not to inculcate it, but to explain it. As a positivist, Durkheim found the physical and natural sciences the best preparation for this task, because they oriented the mind to representations of reality. Frenchmen would have to be weaned away from the simplistic Cartesian rationality, which saw things in terms of clear and distinct ideas, before they could view society as a whole rather than in terms of individuals. It was lucky for France, Durkheim noted, that the Revolution had modified this Cartesian tendency by imparting to the French a sense of the supremacy of collective over individual interests. Life sciences, like biology, should be used to show the complexity of the methods needed to understand them. However, while teaching students that neither life nor science was a simple aggregation of elements, one should never indicate in any way that there was in them any ''irreducible basis of unintelligibility'' forever refractory to reason.[51]

History could also be used to teach students about society and its relationship to the individual. Society should never be depicted as the creation of a great man; collective forces were the most important factors in historical development. The objective of teaching history was to make students see how at each stage the individual existed under the collective influence of his contemporaries, how each generation depended upon preceding ones, how each century continued the work of those who went before. Durkheim admonished:

> But to attach the child to the social group he belongs to, it is not sufficient to make him feel the reality of it, he must actually adhere to it with all the fibers of his being. . . . Society is, above all, a consciousness: it is the consciousness of the collectivity. It is, then this collective consciousness which must be made to pass into the soul of the child.[52]

In Durkheim's course on the evolution of education in France, first given in 1904–05, and repeated each year until 1914 to all candidates for the *agrégation,* he also spoke of moral education. It was no solution, he said in his *leçon d'ouverture,* to say that education should make men out of boys; the question was, what kind of man for the existing society? In the current educational disarray, Durkheim saw "a certain tendency toward skepticism, a sort of disenchantment, a veritable moral malaise. . . . A teaching body without a pedagogic faith is a body without a soul." What was necessary was to provide the soul. Only a study of the society that education was called upon to serve could point the way. And this study should be scientific; Durkheim promised that he would speak to them as a social scientist.[53]

In the course, he traced the development of French humanistic education and then subjected humanism to criticism. Its basic postulate, that human nature was always the same, and that ancient literature was the true educator of humanity, did not, he maintained, accord with the findings of modern social science. Not only did humanity remake itself ceaselessly in infinitely diverse ways, but morality was also in a perpetual process of transformation. "The idea that there exists a single morality, valuable for all men, is no longer sustainable today."[54] Man might rather be conceived as an infinitely flexible Protean force, capable of taking on the most diverse characteristics under the pressure of constantly renewed circumstances. If this view of humanity was taught, it would broaden students' views of their own potentialities. When psychology and sociology had passed their rudimentary stages, these disciplines would convey the new view of humanity to students; meanwhile, the task must be accomplished through the historical study of the diversity of human beings.

Again, Durkheim spoke of the natural sciences. One could not know himself without knowing his universe. In order for lay education to replace the former religious education, which taught us our place in the universe, educators must perform the same function through science. Some day, he predicted, the separation between the sciences of nature and the human sciences would disappear, and the idea that one could form an historian or a linguist without a previous initiation into scientific disciplines would seem an aberration.[55]

Durkheim had provided the first really new moral philosophy in France since Cousin, a philosophy which incorporated the main developments of nineteenth century thinking on *morale,* and transcended them. He had replaced the spiritualists' psychological empiricism with a sociological empiricism; the intuition of good and evil which Cousin had considered an empirical fact yielded to the satisfaction and security the individual felt while thinking and feeling as part of a group which provided its members with mutual physical and psychic aid. The existence of a collective consciousness and its influence upon members of a society were considered "social facts." The "moral reason" of the spiritualists was transformed into an ensemble of psychic reflexes elaborated gradually over generations of social life. The new moral theory also incorporated Darwinism; only those moral regulations survived which facilitated social life.

The great change was that any individualism in ethics was rejected, even that surviving in the social ethics of *morale indépendante,* where morality arose out of the relationship among individuals. Durkheim specifically relegated all acts of charity and sacrifice on behalf of individuals to a secondary level of morality.[56] He recognized the necessity for an external authority to replace God; but all of those moral elements which the spiritualists had found in the individual he found in the society. The individual was determined in his psychic life by society, and this determinism could only be modified by knowledge of social science. It was then society, not the individual, that had a psychic life not totally determined by physical or economic factors. It was society, not the individual, that had an ideal, which it then inculcated into the individual. Thus morality, according to Durkheim, was both socially derived and socially directed. The individual's moral values were socially induced; his actions were moral only insofar as they were in conformity with social ends.

However, as Durkheim pointed out in his introduction to what was to be his *magnum opus* on morality, *science des moeurs* revealed only what moral rules were actually observed by human beings at a particular moment in society. These observed rules comprised ethics in a degraded form, "confined to the scope of human mediocrity," with all the compromises that occurred when translating ideals into action. *Science de la morale* should seek to uncover the moral ideals behind the action, in all their purity and impersonality.[57] Here the *morale idéale* of nineteenth century ethics reappeared in Durkheim's thought as the product of society, not of the individual or of some transcendent moral realm.

The Fortunes of Durkheim's Morale

THE opposition to Durkheim's morality came from a broad range of society at large, within and without the University. For one thing, Durkheim became identified with the concept of secular morality, which was widely resisted. In 1905 *La Revue* sponsored an *enquête* on whether it was possible to have a morality without God, based completely on reason. In his answer, Durkheim claimed that even in the current rudimentary state of social science, it could furnish the necessary information for an elementary education that would teach children, in broad perspective, why they should be attached to their family, their country, humanity. "In fact," he wrote, "this method is applied today in primary schools and the lycées by a certain number of my former students, and it does not seem that the experiment has yielded poor results."[1]

These results will be discussed below. It was true that Durkheim's students were on the whole excited by the task presented to them—the scientific study of society that would lead to a new morality. "His ascendancy over us was unique," a student later recalled, "and not to be confused with that of any of our other teachers. . . .This teacher, imperious, yet so scrupulous, appeared to provide and be provided against error."[2]

Opposition Outside the University

However, one result of the teaching of *morale laïque* was the furor of the Catholic Church, the principal opponent of any form of secular morality. The clergy continued their fight against the secular school, particularly after 1905, when the Law on Associations closed a large portion of their own schools.

They saw the public schools now attended by the majority of their children as the seedbed of anti-religion. *La Croix* called the secular school "the mortal wound that eats at the heart of our France." *L'Ami du clergé* labeled *morale laïque* "a morality of forms in the air." Pastoral letters went further, reproaching the schools for presenting children with "a peril close to moral subversion."

One parish bulletin claimed that the public school was "a school of vice and murder . . . destructive of all morality . . . destined to become licentious from head to foot." The basic complaint was stated in a pastoral letter by the Bishop of Avignon in 1912: "What could be the efficacy of a morality in the school that is separated from the idea of God? Morality independent of religion," he concluded, "has the inevitable consequence of making humanity independent of morality."[3]

The issue that stirred the Church to action on a national level was, once again, the texts used in the public schools. In September, 1909, a group of bishops published a pastoral letter directed specifically against some forty primary school textbooks, including some in *morale laïque*, prohibiting the faithful to use, read or even possess them, or to allow them in the hands of their children. At the same time a letter was directed to all Catholic parents, informing them that children belonged to their parents, who had a right to insure that they received an education according to religious principles. As parents began to resist use of the prohibited books, the local educational officials sent circulars to the teachers, warning them not to yield to pressure from outside the school system.[4]

Thousands of children were sent home from school for refusing to use the texts. Some of the authors, including Bayet and Payot (see below), claimed damages, and members of the higher clergy were actually assessed damages in civil suits. Local priests throughout France took up the struggle, occasionally making inflammatory statements that came close to urging violence against teachers. Student strikes and book burnings took place.[5]

By the end of the year enough indignation had been aroused on both sides to occasion eight days of debate in the Chamber of Deputies. The Catholic faction accused the University of being the instrument of anti-Catholic government propaganda aimed at destroying the faith of Catholic children too young to have intellectual defenses, and of actively seeking to destroy the Church and religion through a monopoly in education. Defenders of the educational system alleged that the bishops' letter was a political maneuver designed to make the administration pay for the separation of Church and State.

Republican deputies who favored a neutral, reasonable position complained of the imposition of a "doctrinal authority" in the choice of texts. They pointed out that, since state schools were in many areas virtually the only schools, all citizens, even bishops, had a right to be concerned with them. One deputy also pointed out that the question of free will versus determinism had no place in a primary school text, particularly when summarily resolved in favor of the latter.[6]

One of the high spots of the debate was the speech of Maurice Barrès, well-known author and non-religious opponent of secularism.[7] The schools were not neutral, he insisted, they were anti-Catholic. He painted the sad picture of the *instituteur,* isolated in his "demi-culture," torn from traditional morality by his secular education, turning toward the light of reason that filtered down to him from the University in ever-changing systems—the neutrality of Ferry, the neo-Kantianism of Renouvier, the solidarity of Bourgeois, and the sociological morality of the current period. He quoted derisively an invocation by one of the authors, Jules Payot, used in the primary schools:

> Ignorant, we were slaves of prejudice and the customs of our environment.
> Now we can enter into relations with the thinkers of all times and places. . . .
> Let us, freed from ignorance, love him who has liberated us, as a prisoner
> loves him who helps in his escape. It is ever he who, by making us understand
> how men are freed from their base instinct, from their violent passions, from
> their pride, helps us in turn to free ourselves from our backwardness and leave
> the cave of an animal. . . .

This new doctrine of original sin, Barrès pointed out, differed from the biblical doctrine only in that the sin was to be exorcized by the teacher rather than the priest.[8]

The University's defense was summed up by Théodore Steeg, who became Minister of Education in 1911: "What the Church wants is that the school abdicate from secularism and underwrite its own suicide." The foundation of the secular school, he noted, had been an act of faith on the part of the Republic—"faith that justice and reason are harmonious, and that in the end reason will triumph."[9]

Many Catholic and right-wing intellectuals targeted their attacks on Durkheim. The series of articles written by Pierre Lasserre in *Action française* from June, 1910 to March, 1912, constituted a systematic attack on the Sorbonne as the fountainhead of a new University doctrine. Lasserre began, significantly, with the subject of the new sociology. Unfortunately, he wrote, the term had been loosely applied since Comte invented it. In its ill-defined form it was now placing the doctoral degree "at the disposal of fools, busybodies, visionaries, and charlatans of the social and political Utopia". Aiming specifically at Durkheim, he labeled the discipline a "Jewish invention."[10]

In an article examining Durkheim's *La Division du travail social,* Lasserre objected to the sociological view of ethics. The individual's fundamental duties to the community were unchanging; it had always been a duty to subordinate oneself to the community. But this was not accomplished by suppressing the common (Catholic) education that preserved the traditional beliefs of the community. Nor was morality relative. It was the consciousness of a universal idea, applied to different situations according to the times and social conditions.[11]

Simon Deploige, president of the Institut supérieur de philosophie at the Catholic University of Louvain, wrote an attack on Durkheim's *morale* in 1911, which had a second edition in 1912 and ran into four editions by 1927. Among other criticisms, he accused Durkheim of adopting Germanic methods in social science.[12] (Durkheim saw fit to answer this charge in a review of the book. The main influences on him, he declared, were Comte and Renouvier.[13]) Deploige pointed to other criticisms of Durkheim's work in the 1890s, by Gabriel Tarde, Charles Andler and Fouillée. And he noted approvingly that Durkheim's *morale* had not been accepted by the Académie des sciences morales et politiques as a subject for an essay contest. Still spiritualist, they had objected to Durkheim's denial of the universality of moral principles.[14]

Two opponents from the opposite camp outside the University were Georges Sorel and Charles Péguy, both followers of the philosopher Henri Bergson. Sorel blamed Durkheim for the "petite science" (scientism?) that he saw rampant in the intellectual culture of the Sorbonne. "Sociology," he wrote, "is in the hands of people who are incapable of any philosophical reasoning." It had engendered sophistries that consisted of "putting very different things on the same plane, from a love of logical simplicity: thus sexual morality is reduced to equitable relations between contracting parties."[15]

Disliked and distrusted by the establishment, Sorel had a considerable student following, including Péguy, who had dropped out of the Sorbonne a few months before his *agrégation* and founded *Cahiers de la quinzaine*.[16] The first number bore the triumphant inscription: "The social revolution will be moral or it will not be." But Péguy did not approve of the moral theory of the new sociology. "The metaphysics of our masters. . .is above all the metaphysics of science. . .it is a positivist metaphysics, it is the celebrated metaphysics of progress."[17] In late 1901 he wrote: "Reason does not proceed from authority. . . . It is not decided by majority rule. . . . Reason does not proceed from pedagogy. We touch here upon the gravest danger of our present time."[18]

Nor was Péguy the last student rebel. In 1910 Henri Massis, with the aid of Alfred Tarde, son of Gabriel Tarde, launched an attack on the Sorbonne under the pen name Agathon. They charged that there was no course at the Sorbonne anymore that could properly be called philosophy. Durkheim was preaching a social catechism. Sociology ruled the University and was in the process of creating a "science of morality."[19] In these articles they charged, even before Deploige, that the new scientific method of the University was Germanic. The French spirit, they said, was based on classical culture, and tended to emphasize philosophy and literature. The Germanic spirit stressed facts and history. The malaise at the Sorbonne was due to the imposition of "German erudition" upon French students not temperamentally disposed to it. Agathon also charged that Durkheim had fostered the concept of specialization, as opposed to the education of the whole man, thereby sacrificing the elite individual to the mass man.[20]

The whole argument was part of a larger conflict over classical versus modern education; but Durkheim and his sociology were singled out as the evil influence.

Opposition in the University

That the Church should be so sensitive to secular ethics, in a period that saw the closing down of so many of their own schools, is understandable. That sociology should be viewed as a threat to traditional and idealistic forms of knowledge is also logical. But Durkheim had by no means convinced the reigning intellectuals of the University, as his opposition was assuming he had, of the virtues of his sociological morality. Emile Faguet, reviewing Deploige's book, commented:

> That there is something more, really something more in the thinking of 100 men besides the sum of the thoughts of those 100 men means an effect without a cause. . . . It is supposing that a Holy Spirit has descended upon us because we are united; it is a kind of theological metaphysics which I truly do not understand at all.

The truth was, Faguet declared, wrongly assuming that Durkheim had equated society with the state, that Durkheim's *âme sociale* was merely the soul of the majority of the nation; his theory was "democratic mysticism." All new ideas, all great movements came from individual consciences.

Faguet pointed out Durkheim's own admission that the norm was not always moral. Therefore he reverted to the ideal, which he considered ultra-collective, but which was actually an individual creation. As for social change, Faguet insisted that society itself could not foster change, only individuals could. To limit oneself to the ethics derived from sociology was to be totally conservative; it would be the death of morality.[21]

Faguet's criticism incorporated one of the basic objections to sociological morality—the subordination of the individual to society—that was shared by those in the humanist camp. The secondary schools were, for the most part, bastions of the old humanism,[22] and their personnel did not take kindly to Durkheim's attacks on it. Even those *lycée* professors who accepted sociology did not agree with Durkheim's view of *morale*. Belot, who had participated in the debates on *solidarité* in the 1890s (see Ch. 9), published his own work on ethics in 1907. His aim was to conciliate the roles of fact and ideal in a "positive morality."[23]

Like another admirer of Comte, Alphonse Darlu,[24] Belot did not think that those who had proposed a moral practice based on *science des moeurs* had achieved it. Certainly morality was essentially social in its origins; but the fact that it could be observed sociologically did not mean that it could be assimilated to a technique founded on sociology. Denying, in effect, any relativity in the moral sphere, he claimed that "no given, as such, can be a sufficient principle of moral judgment." The rationality he insisted upon in morality could not be derived from the source of moral rules, but only from their ends.[25]

Belot's critique, while insisting upon the individual, emphasized even more strongly the rationality of moral rules. Durkheim's concept of a society reacting almost unconsciously in matters of right and wrong distressed him. He rejected the relativity of morality in the name of the "essential will" of humanity, which he considered, in the humanist context, to be the same everywhere and aimed toward a rational goal.[26]

In 1908, an exchange between Belot and Durkheim took place at the Société française de philosophie. Durkheim charged Belot with using the term rationality in two senses. The first, with which Durkheim agreed, was as a systematization of given realities. The other, which Durkheim felt to be extraneous to nature, was the construct created by mind. Belot argued that conduct was more moral as it was more reflective, more reasonable, and that this was not a given, but an ideal rationality. If one could not determine moral ends rationally, and if moral goals were not given in reality, how was ethical progress possible? In fact, if societies could be the object of a complete and definite science, moral ends could never be deduced at all. We would merely continue that fixed and analyzed reality, and there would be no moral progress.[27]

Durkheim replied that if morality could never be completely analyzed, it could never be completely rational. But why should rationality be essential to ethics? Belot answered that, in social reality, individual consciences almost always surged against collective imperatives, conceiving new imperatives, discovering new hypotheses. Sociology he said, tended to neglect the individual conscience.[28] Belot continued to stand for an objective morality at the same time as he defended individual conscience. When asked, at a meeting of the Union des Libres-Penseurs et des Libres-Croyants in 1926, in what name morality could be imposed upon students, he answered, "In the name of excellence."[29]

The secondary school system, bound by classicist and humanist principles, was not a place where sociological morality could be expected to replace traditional moral philosophy. Nevertheless, Durkheim found followers there. Dominique Parodi, professor of philosophy at the Lycée Michelet, was insisting in 1910 that Durkheim's morality was not revolutionary, except in eschewing two inadmissible postulates of the old morality—that human nature was always the same, and that the moral consciousness formed a harmonious organic ensemble. But he quoted Durkheim as saying that the essential characteristic of a moral rule was obligation, in the Kantian sense of the word. The problem was, how could one be sure that sociological enlightenment on the direction society was taking would induce people to help it on in that direction?[30]

Parodi also admitted to a problem with the norm, particularly since Durkheim seemed to make choices between good and bad norms. If one could judge the norm by its rationality (in an immediate sense, discoverable in the nature of things), then the effort to criticize, founded in reason, legitimized by present or future utility the collective consciousness. But this was inevitably, Parodi pointed out, "the old theoretical morality." And he noted that the debate over sociological morality seemed to turn on the eternal question of free will versus determinism.[31]

Besides justifying and explaining his ideas, some of Durkheim's followers had a wider agenda—reforming society through education and politics. At an international congress of Philosophy in 1905, Célestin Bouglé, professor of philosophy at Toulouse, related sociology to social action. Describing Durkheim's collective consciousness as an ensemble of psychological forces projected into institutional forms, he insisted that new moral ideas could only be translated into action if they were in line with the social forces of the time. The task of sociology was to analyze those forces. Thus, institutional reform, not appeal to ideas, was the way to act upon the collective consciousness. There was an interaction between the individual and society that affected both.[32]

This was Bouglé's first modification of sociological theory in an effort to attain desired social reforms. By 1914 he was trying to delimit the role of sociology in morality. "Sociology does not appear to us ready, if it should ever be ready, to substitute itself for morality," he wrote. Previously there had been great hopes in this direction—hopes that sociology could study society as an organism, dispensing with psychology and history, and come up with laws that would not only explain the past, but the future, hopes that sociology could produce a wholly new morality. But sociology never had such pretensions, Bouglé declared. It could, however, render some service in the moral area. What was perhaps possible was the classification of societies into different types, so that for each type one could postulate a normal, healthy state, and therefore an ideal morality. One might debate whether the science of sociology was developed enough to do this; but it was at least in a state to clarify situations and permit methodical action, if not in a state to oblige people morally.[33]

Turning to textbooks on *morale,* one finds very little of what could be called Durkheimian theory. Jules Payot, whose texts were among those most widely used before 1914, was more *solidariste* than sociological. His *Cours de morale,* written for teachers to go with a manual of the same name, was dedicated to Bourgeois. Under the heading, "La morale est une science," he discussed social debt and pointed out the misery of savages and primitive peoples. Under the heading "La cooperation a tiré l'homme de l'animalité," he proved that, without the development of cooperative labor, humanity would still be living in a state of bestiality. This constituted the so-called scientific basis of morality.

In the second section, the text proceeded with traditional duties to the self, then duties to others, divided into the negative duties of justice and the positive duties of solidarity. In the section on religion, agnosticism prevailed; only science and morality could save humanity from evil. In the chapter on sanctions for behavior, penal law and public opinion were preferred over those of a life hereafter.[34] Payot's 1907 set of texts, *La Morale à l'école,* generally repeated these concepts. He was sociological only in his emphasis on development away from the savage state and on the division of labor.

The only clearly sociological text to be published before 1914 was, strangely enough, by Arthur Bauer, a professor of philosophy and member of the Société sociologique de Paris, an organization hostile to Durkheim. His project for a common course on ethics, to be taught in all schools, went beyond solidarity to include Durkheim's concepts of professional groups within the society, each with its particular morality, and of society as a "great moral personality." Bauer urged that, beside a common course on *morale* for all, specific courses should be prepared for categories of students who would play different roles in society, teaching the virtues appropriate to each profession.[35] But it does not, nor does any available textbook before the war, reflect faithfully Durkheim's whole moral philosophy.

With this exception, it seems that the secular republic, in a dominant position from the first years of the twentieth century, remained relatively conservative in its use of textbooks for *morale,* failing even to incorporate the latest methods of sociology, and relying to a surprising extent on "the good old morality of our fathers," or spiritualism, right up to 1914. One might, of course, look for evidence of Durkheim's influence in the post-war years. Despite the fact that he himself died in 1917, he left a number of disciples who might be expected to carry on his ideas in the area of morality. And indeed, the new program of 1920 for the primary schools prescribed for the second year a course in social morality. Nevertheless, only one textbook that could be called Durkheimian has survived, written for the primary normal schools by J. Boucher.

After a section on scientific method, this book grounded the principles of morality in the primacy of society. In almost all circumstances, "the individual conscience prescribes or condemns what the collective conscience prescribes or condemns." Social customs *(moeurs)* summed up the conduct of members of the society; morality consisted of the rules of conduct considered moral by the collective consciousness. Pure reason in morality might be too abstract to relate to the conditions of life at a particular time. The function of reason in *morale* was rather to systematize the givens of the collective consciousness. However, sometimes the superficial clarity of an insufficiently formed reason was less valid in morality than the obscure depths of instinct.

Sociological morality was inductive and relative. The norm of collective consciousness might be changed by virtue of an ideal. Therefore morality could not, strictly speaking, be called a science. Scientific law was a relationship between facts; moral law, a relationship between fact and idea. But morality could be studied scientifically.

Boucher followed Durkheim in emphasizing the obligatory nature of morality and also the enforcement of moral rules by society. Of all those written for the schools, his text is the closest to Durkheim's moral philosophy, even in his retention of much traditional Kantianism. His section on the "idées directrices" of morality listed human dignity, social interest, justice, solidarity, and happiness. The final section dealt with freedom and responsibility.[36]

Adaptations

It was in the primary schools that the need for morale *laïque* was felt most keenly. Albert Bayet, Director of Primary Education from 1895 and prominent in the Radical party, seemed at first to welcome sociological morality with open arms. Lévy-Bruhl and Durkheim, he announced in 1905, had made the most solid advances in morale since Comte.[37] In his own textbook of 1902, he had connected changes of morality with modification of social groups, had pointed to the progress brought about by the division of labor, and had named solidarity as the highest duty prescribed by modern morality.[38]

Bayet was eager to believe that morality could be empirical if it rested on a methodical study of facts and laws. He saw no difficulty in dispensing with individual morality; morality should attempt to ameliorate the social situation without preliminary definitions of the Good. Its particular field of action should be, not the eternal universe, but particular groups at particular times. In any group, Bayet stated, the moral reality would include mechanisms responding to generally admitted ideas, mechanisms corresponding to ideas that had outlived their time, and new currents of ideas from which new mechanisms would arise. Improvement of the social reality should take place at the level of both ideas and mechanisms, adapting them more closely to the needs of the particular group, enlarging them to fit new social problems, rectifying them according to new sociological discoveries. Bayet's attempt here was clearly to use "scientific" language appropriate to his sociological approach.

His enthusiasm went further, however. The moralist must "sell" his ideas, through publications and education. He saw moral education as a good instrument for this purpose. It should consist, not in teaching a moral code to children, but in making them understand why particular moral values fit their country and their time. The teacher would act upon the intelligence of the students as a "social engineer." The aim was not to make the children 'better,' in some metaphysical and absolute sense of the word, but to make them better conform to the needs of the society.[39] In the name of what, then, would morality be taught? Belot's "In the name of excellence," was traditional, idealistic, but impractical for mass education. Bayet chose the good of the society at that time as the only possible end of morality.

Bayet was more sanguine about the effects of moral education than Durkheim, who had expressed some doubts about the ability of *morale laïque* to do more than reflect the current society.[40] Bayet insisted that the new, reforming ideas might already exist in the society in a confused state, and need only to be clarified. Undisturbed by the problem of individual conscience, he noted only that, where a social interest was not involved, the individual should be allowed free development.[41] For objective moral values, he obviously had no regrets. In his next book Bayet was even more specific about the relativity of *morale*.

However, this book, written in 1908, also included Bayet's first criticism of Durkheim. Arguing that morality did not involve the idea of obligation, he stated that it was impossible to transform positive social laws discovered by sociology into morally binding laws. He also denied the usefulness of Durkheim's norm. Why should the normal be considered preferable to the abnormal if the abnormal might be better? As a man who wished to transform social theory into political and pedagogical action, Bayet was also impatient with Durkheim's assumption that societies evolved slowly. Why not quickly?[42] The social activist was winning out over the social scientist in Bayet.

In complete opposition to Belot, Bayet insisted that morality was rational if the means employed were deduced from scientific research, provided that such research had nothing to do with ends. He also stated that the real moral ideas of a society were often unconscious. But he did not necessarily agree with Durkheim that a common consciousness could be gleaned from the often uncoordinated ideas of the good that existed in a society. Perhaps in each society, he said, speaking now as a politician, there was one morality for the majority and one for the minority. Insisting that there was no superior principle to regulate moral practice, he left it to the individual practitioners to choose from the real ideas present in the society those that should be preferred. The social scientist, he noted, again disagreeing with Belot, could tell the practitioner of the moral art whether his ideas would work or not.[43]

Who, then, would write the educational programs in *morale?* Bayet was quite clear about this. "In fact, it is the party that holds the power which directs the education." It would teach the morality proper to the groups and classes in power.[44] Writing when the Radicals were in control, Bayet came as close as anyone ever did to stating the basic goals of moral education in the Third Republic.

Bayet, the practitioner of morals in the early years of *morale laïque,* raised questions that would have to be answered by any society that engaged itself in teaching a secular morality in its schools. French secularists at the turn of the century saw clearly that to teach a morality based on ends would be to involve the schools in matters that were clearly the province of religion. In the name of what, therefore, should morality be taught? In the name of the good of that particular society, according to followers of Durkheim. But even in a society as homogeneous as France, Bayet recognized the existence of a majority and a minority morality. The logic of the situation was, then, that the morality of the majority would be the one taught in the schools. The difficulties involved therein are more manifest in our own society, with its failure in the twentieth century to amalgamate its minorities as the national myth prescribes, than they were then in France.

In 1924, Bayet was moving even further from Durkheim. He complained that, unlike Lévy-Bruhl, Durkheim had never really distinguished *science des moeurs* from *art moral.* Under the influence of philosophy, he had made value judgments in distinguishing the normal from the pathological in society.[45] It was, he wrote, necessary to renounce the concept that beyond the diversities of moral practice there was a true morality.[46] He again criticized the term 'common consciousness,' which, he said, perhaps exaggerated the difference between an individual and a group. He also denied that obligation was attached to moral rules.[47]

Bayet's problem was that he found Durkheim too philosophical and not "scientific" enough. There was no proof, he wrote, that only disinterested acts were moral; therefore there was no proof that only acts pertaining to society were moral.[48] However, if a science of morality was not possible, what about a morality of science? As others had before him, Bayet suggested that the ideals of science itself might be used as a basis for morality. In the light of science, human dignity was located in thought, a continued, progressive, unlimited thought. Therefore all should be educated. Unity or the accord of intelligences, was also a scientific goal. A third was freedom of the mind. And, if one included the science of sociology, another ideal became evident— toleration of others who were socially programmed to act in different ways.[49] In 1926 Bayet wrote that, although Durkheim had tried to make sociology more positive than that of Comte, he still remained, in certain cases, a logician, a philosopher. This orientation should be rectified by social science.[50]

If Bayet's moral theory was inadequate, his texts, written and used over three decades, were worse. They included no discussion of the bases of morality, since he clearly did not believe there were any. Thus he was reduced to providing chapters headed, e.g., "Thou shalt not kill," in which the moral lesson provided appealed to sentiment.[51] But his position in the University, first as director of primary, and later of higher education, render his views on the subject highly relevant.

The inclusion of sociological *morale* in the program of the normal schools in 1920 brought charges that ethics was being suffocated with a new dogma. Bouglé came to the defense in *Leçons de sociologie sur l'évolution de valeurs.* The "pensée maîtresse" of Durkheim's sociological work, he wrote, had been that society was essentially the creator of the ideal, through forces stemming from the union of persons in society. Social values were objective, because they were imperative; they were imperative because they were collective. Defending Durkheim's emphasis on society against the charge of materialism, Bouglé said that society was involved not only with the material, but also with the spiritual life of its members. Thus, sociology had deepened the concept of solidarity. Society meant not only an exchange of services or a collaboration of forces, but a communication of feelings. "Intellectual *rapprochement* is one of the conditions of the social *entente.*"[52]

Bouglé emphasized the ideal, spiritual aspect of Durkheim's *morale.* Still doubting that all the moral needs of society could be deduced from scientific investigation (to make someone know something is not yet to make him love it, was his un-Platonic observation), he insisted that no moral education could succeed without a communication of feelings. Dividing values into end-values and means-values, he pointed out that some values might begin as ends and then become recognized as means to yet higher ends. Others that started out as means became ends in themselves. Bouglé also tried to claim for morality a scientific nature; he noted that the scientific virtues (sincerity, impartiality, and disinterestedness, for him) were also moral truths. But he was still wary as to whether science could actually produce moral values.

One of Bouglé's overriding concerns was French national unity, and he sought to use sociological *morale* to buttress it. A nation, he wrote, had a certain mental and spiritual unity, a certain way of collectively ordering its values. The French might be divided in their metaphysics, but they were united in their value system. This was proof that the source of moral goals was in the consciousness of the society. It was the lay educator who must teach those values that the society held in common.[53] Here Bouglé, remaining close to Durkheim, was emphasizing the idealistic aspects of sociological morality. In his 1924 article on the "spiritualism" of Durkheim, he defended him against the charge of materialism. One could not reduce the collective consciousness to biology. Bouglé noted that Durkheim had always opposed the purely utilitarian and the purely organic in morality. The collective representations of a society served to preserve not only the physical, but also the psychic life of the society.[54]

Paul Lapie, another disciple of Durkheim, also defended *sociologie*, as the objective study of social facts, unlike *sociologisme*, which he called the attempt to explain everything in the human realm through social causation. Sociology, he said, respected the autonomy of morality, and confined itself to offering the solid support of scientific induction.[55]

Lapie was not only an associate of Durkheim on *L'Année sociologique*, as was Bouglé; he was a prime mover at the *Revue pédagogique* (changed to *L'Enseignement public* in 1924). He had started out with an ethics based on justice—not as a metaphysical ideal, but as a law of relations between persons, made manifest by reason. He spoke of human rights as resting upon the dignity of the individual, whose dignity rested, in turn, upon possession of reason.[56] By the time he had become Director of Primary Education in the early twenties, his views had become more sociological. Individualism was now against nature: "Humans are only relative, dependent beings, fragments of beings who live only in completing one another, in giving themselves to one another".[57]

The problem left by Durkheim to his followers was to work out the application of sociological morality to education, while at the same time adjusting it to meet the most cogent objections of the opposition. How he himself would have fashioned *morale laïque* for primary schools was indicated by an unedited manuscript, "l'Education morale à l'école primaire," which was revealed in 1922 by Paul Fauconnet on taking over the Sorbonne chair that had been Durkheim's.

It began with an introduction, mainly for the teacher. Lessons were divided into two parts. The first treated the general characteristics of morality, the definition of moral facts, the obligatory nature of moral rules, and the collective character of ethical systems. The second emphasized a psychological method used to teach the child he was part of a larger community.[58] In this opening lecture, Fauconnet defended Durkheim from objections, current at the time, to his conception of education as the socialization of the child.

Lapie presided over a series of conferences for directors of *écoles normales primaires* in the twenties. At one of these, Parodi, now an inspector-general of public instruction, emphasized that the obligations linking members of society made sense only if there were individual consciences in which the obligation was felt, and individuals capable of obeying or disobeying its dictates. He saw the duality of the individual and society reflected in the duality of the self, where reason judged and will willed. The social commandment was the received order, morality the conceived order. The one involved constraint; the other, consent.[59] His position was very close to that of Belot before the war.

Throughout these lectures, speakers continued to express themselves in the name of Durkheim in one breath, while modifying his moral theories in the next. Pierre-Félix Pécaut, after describing the social origins of morality, went on to say that Durkheim's philosophy was an insufficient guide to action in situations where it was not simply a matter of adjusting to a given society, but of making the society different. One could be trapped in a wholly relative morality. "There is, in our nature, an aspiration superior to the given," he declared. Justice was a social ideal; but it was not merely a product of the society, it was higher. "We feel that a *morale,* which is in fact logically anterior to the Society, works on us, wishes a certain kind of society, instead of wishing what exists," Pécaut insisted.[60]

Reading the lectures of these annual series, one is struck by the attempt to make sociological morality fit into the mold of nineteenth century philosophy. Bouglé claimed that Durkheim never said changes in the collective consciousness depended only on social change. There was a proper logic to the development of moral beliefs, whose key was not provided either by social morphology or by individual psychology.[61]

Lapie maintained that the moral ideal itself was a fact that could be observed by the sociologist; however, he saw the moral law as only "the resonance in individual spirits of the necessities of the social life." In attempting to deal with the resulting problem of changes in morality, Lapie fell back again on individual psychology. "I think it possible to demonstrate that all humans who obey the moral conscience obey what one might call the will to justice." So much for Durkheim! In order to retain science somehow, Lapie defined the idea of justice as the translation, in the domain of voluntary actions, of principles that were those of science—identity and causality.[62]

Lapie co-authored a textbook in *morale* that went into three editions and presumably expressed what he thought should be taught to students of the fourth and third classes (roughly, age thirteen and fourteen). It began with a series of conversations: on various moral virtues for the fourth class, on social life and civic institutions for the third. The book declared that in one sense all duties were social duties; in another, they were also duties to the self. *Solidarité* was "the duty of justice applied to the collectivity." And justice was defined as the golden rule in the negative.[63]

The final portion of the book was a collection of readings, first on the various classical virtues, then on social life. All the readings on *solidarité* were from the classics and the eighteenth and nineteenth centuries, the most recent from Marion. The readings on justice followed the same pattern, including Cousin and Proudhon. Readings on *humanité* included Simon, Kant and Littré. No Durkheim. French moral philosophy, for education at least, seemed to have returned to eclecticism.

In 1930 a group of Durkheim's associates wrote about him in *L'Europe.* Here Bouglé, after describing Durkheimian morality as "still Kantian, revised and completed by Comtism," admitted that the group around Durkheim were never all convinced that an advanced sociology would render a "meta-morale" useless.[64] Georges Davy recalled the opposition to Durkheim's collective consciousness, which seemed to deny individualism, attributing to the society what had formerly been seen as inherent in the individual.[65]

René Maublanc felt that Durkheim was basically a philosopher who chose to confine himself within the scientific discipline of sociology; both his enemies and his friends agreed that he was really a man of metaphysics. Recalling that Durkheim had never thought empiricism sufficient, or that experience could explain all that was found within the individual, Maublanc pronounced him an idealist. And, according to Maublanc, Durkheim's moral theory underwent an eclipse after his death, despite the efforts of his disciples, because people did not accept his elimination of both God and freedom.[66]

Although this may not have been true of all Durkheim's disciples in sociology, it certainly was the case with those in the school system involved with *morale laïque,* whether on a personal or a pragmatic basis. But the more immediate problem, to all of them, was whether one could teach morality at all.

12

Teaching Morale Laïque

THE difficulties of teaching *morale laïque* on the primary school level did not, of course, end with the theoretical conclusions arrived at in the Sorbonne. As in the neutral school of Jules Ferry, what was decided at the highest levels of the University was not necessarily reflected at the lower ones. In order to envision the actual teaching of the subject in the primary schools, one must examine the programs laid out for the teaching of *morale*, and the methods that were prescribed for teaching it. Then one must try to evaluate what actually went on in the classrooms of France.

The programs began in the *écoles normales supérieures* that were to produce teachers for the ordinary normal schools in each department of France. Henri Marion himself taught the course at Fontenay-aux-Roses, the new *École Normale Supérieure* for women, beginning in 1881. Basically Kantian, it stressed conscience, freedom and moral responsibility, and used solidarity for social morality. Marion closed his course by admitting that the aim of the primary school teacher should be less to propound knowledge and ideas on the subject than to "create practical habits, that is, ways of acting and thinking." Morality could not be taught in the ordinary sense, it must be inculcated. Good habits, which should already have been learned in the family, should be encouraged.

However, more was required. The teacher must show the children how to think about what they did, provide them with ways of thinking, general rules to judge by, and a strong sense of responsibility. This involved learning moral precepts, but not, he emphasized, rote learning of maxims. The teacher should rather develop the judgment and appeal to the natural sentiments of good and

155

evil that every child has. The moral sense, he declared, was "in part a judgment of reason, in part an instinct of the heart."[1] In the discussions of everyday occurrences, of history, even of imaginary incidents that move the imagination of children, moral precepts could be uncovered.[2]

The course, as elaborated for the *écoles normales primaires* in the Program of January 22, 1881, took two years, and began with a half year of elementary psychology. The second half of the year was devoted to the principles of theoretical morality: moral conscience, liberty and responsibility, obligation and duty, the good and pure duty, rights and duties, sanctions of *morale*. Only then did the students arrive, in their second year, at "practical morality—applications". This included the individual and social duties to be taught. (See Appendix for complete program.)

In the elementary schools themselves, the Program of 24 November, 1883 starting with the class aged 5 to 7 years, made use of simple conversations, little stories with moral meanings, poems and songs learned by heart, and general moral supervision. This extended in the next two years to readings with commentary by the teacher, application of moral precepts in class, elimination of irrational superstition. Teachers were instructed to make a constant appeal to the judgment of the students themselves in moral matters, to make them draw conclusions from things that they themselves observed, and to produce in them the proper moral sentiments.

In the next two years, the same methods, with more difficult readings and exercises, were now coordinated to produce the specific moral teachings, about duties of the child in the family and in the school, with particular duties to siblings, parents, friends, servants; duties to one's country and one's society; duties to oneself, including care of the body, economic prudence, personal dignity, honesty; and duties toward others, both of justice and charity. The course ended, according to the law, with duties toward God. The teacher was urged to associate God with the first cause and with perfection, and to teach the respect owed to such a concept, without enlarging on different views of God. The important lesson was "that the first homage one owes to the divinity is obedience to the divine laws revealed by one's conscience and reason." Critics complained that some teachers never mentioned God at all; that section, left to the end, was often not reached before the end of term.[3]

Since most children left school at this point, this was the basic moral education they were meant to receive. However, those who stayed for the higher level, from 11 to 13, were to go more deeply into the topics of the family, the society, the nation. At each level, the teacher was ordered to make clear, without entering into metaphysical discussions, the difference between duty and interest, "that is, the imperative and disinterested character of duty"; and the distinction between written law and the moral law, that "the one fixes a minimum of prescriptions that society imposes on all its members under various sanctions, the other imposes on each of us in the secrecy of our conscience a duty that no one will constrain us to fulfill, but which cannot be overlooked without feeling guilty towards oneself and toward God."[4] This program was preserved, almost unchanged, until the new program of 1923. (For an example of how it was put into practice in one department in 1891, see Appendix.)

The pedagogy of *morale laïque* was first laid down by Jules Ferry in that famous circular to the teachers of November 17, 1883. "One condition is indispensable, that this teaching reach the living soul of the child" he wrote, and that it not be confused in any way—form, character, tone—with a regular lesson. "You must succeed in bringing to flower in [the child] feelings true enough and strong enough to help some day, in the struggle of life, to triumph over passions and vices. We ask the teacher, not to adorn the memory, but to touch the heart of the child." The necessity to communicate this subject with real conviction and emotion led to the observance on the part of many that female teachers were more effective at it than were males.[5]

Marion emphasized the necessity to instill good habits into the child, but at the same time to provoke thought about the principles of one's actions. He assumed, as did all of the educational establishment, that the child had an instinct for what was good or bad, that could be cultivated. One could use everyday events, or history, to arouse positive emotions on behalf of the good and indignation concerning evil. Poetry also offered examples of moral grandeur. The worst thing to do would be, Marion observed, to provide children with a new catechism that they would mindlessly learn by heart.[6]

Traditionally, of course, French education had relied primarily on committing material to memory. However, since the mid-nineteenth century, the theories of Pestalozzi had become popular. (The article on Pestalozzi in the 1887 edition of the *Dictionnaire pédagogique*, edited by Buisson, ran to almost 60 pages, longer by far than that devoted to any other single figure.) Teachers were now urged to explain, to demonstrate. The system of *leçons de choses*, also called *enseignement intuitif*, in which children learned through their senses, became the origin of *musées scolaires* and outings whereby students could learn things at first hand.[7]

The article on Pedagogy in the 1911 edition of the *Dictionnaire* was written by Durkheim. Outlining the course he gave as Professor of Pedagogy at the Sorbonne, an application of psychology to education, he talked of training the senses, of using the child's curiosity, interest in stories and imitation. The teacher must develop in the student good habits and obedience, but also the feelings of generosity and sympathy for others. He indicated that it was difficult to reconcile the necessity for obedience and discipline with the imperative of developing the child's own personality.[8]

There were other theorists at the University who recognized problems. Ernest Lavisse, historian, inaugurating a primary school in Nouvion-en-Thiérache (Aisne) in 1895, admitted that a child would not be moral just because he knew how to reason. Therefore there must be a moral instruction, distinct from other learning. In the old days, teachers relied on punishment; but the French had given up corporal punishment in the schools. Therefore the teacher, "both priest and father," must lead the child firmly, showing him his duties, cultivating the good instincts and correcting the bad, giving a good example. It was, he said, a matter of "délicatesse morale."[9,10]

The first attempts to teach the new course in *morale* on the primary level had mixed results. As we have seen (See Chapter 8) the teachers were often inadequate to the task. However, an English observer pointed out in 1908 that the Lichtenberger report (q.v. same chapter) in 1889 had been much too early to look for success. The complete laicization of the schools was effected only in 1886, and substitution of lay teachers for clerics in many of them only in 1891. Having interviewed a number of teachers in his journeys about France, he found no one "who did not more or less believe in the efficacy, within limits, of moral instruction."[11]

By this time, of course, a whole support system for the teachers had been established, including yearly pedagogical conferences and courses in the summer, both national and departmental, as well as tutoring and exhortation by a corps of school inspectors, whose relationship with the teachers was at times paternal.[12]

Problems in Practice

This leads us to the problems faced by young teachers, sent out to the villages of France to spread morality. Our British observer noted that alcoholism was rife in the provinces, with some children bringing their wine to school in little bottles. In Normandy, he reported, they drank hard cider for breakfast. Also, he found the local inhabitants of a market town undisturbed by the open sale of immoral postcards.[13] Another Briton found an *instituteur* in the Nord who calculated that only one tenth of his pupils had never drunk strong liquor. Lessons on being kind to animals might still fall flat, as Laurence Wylie noted in 1957, where "Let us be friends and protectors of the little birds," was learned by heart in an area where a grown man boasted of eating fifty or sixty from a spit in one sitting. Not only were the parents, as school inspectors noted, not always supportive of the lesson in *morale*;[14] the entire culture of the region might make the task difficult for the teacher.

France, in the last decades of the nineteenth century, was still a predominantly rural country, particularly in the border areas, and consisted of small villages having little contact with the outside world. Food shortages were still a factor in the violence that persisted in the family even after it receded on the inter-village level. In an economy of scarcity, both the old and the young might be denied their needs; and certainly there was no thought of generosity outside the family circle. Kinship was important, and there was a certain amount of inbreeding in order to keep land in the family. But in its extended form, a family might make up almost the total population of the village. Therefore, there was a hierarchy of rich and poor members of the same family, who did not necessarily help one another. Assault and battery were the rural crimes, within families on a continual basis, but applied particularly to strangers.[15]

This picture, drawn by Eugene Weber, does not apply, of course, to the towns and their neighboring areas. But it describes the sector that was the foremost target of the educational establishment, as well as the most difficult one to transform. The task of the primary school was to create patriotic French citizens, speaking the French language, and adhering to a common moral standard. Leaving aside the first two difficulties, which were considerable, there were problems in creating a *morale* in such an environment.

The picture drawn by Weber bears a certain resemblance to that described by the sociologist Edward C. Banfield in the town of Montegrano, in an isolated area of southern Italy, in the early 1950s. Although the death rate had fallen, along with the birth rate, there was still great poverty. Inheritance had reduced the size of the family plots, as had the end of primogeniture in France. The belief in witchcraft lingered on, although one might try the local doctor first in matters of health.[16] And, as we now know for France, in the most backward areas, more people could read than write, particularly women.[17]

The morality of Montegrano was described by Banfield as one where "good" was equated with "personally advantageous". This might possibly be extended to include some idea of service to the immediate family. But he found that, basically, nothing was sacred, and therefore there were no accepted obligations of one person to another. Force comprised the only restraints on individual actions in such a community; and indeed, those interviewed preferred a strong government as the only possible arbiter. Children were brought up to be selfish, as a means of survival in a harsh moral environment. Banfield concluded that the sense of community responsibility totally lacking in Montegrano could only be developed through education. But it would also be necessary to use the absolute power of the regional prefect to develop local institutions that would aid in planning for the public interest. This was the task that the French had given to the schoolteacher.

No matter how well or how poorly the teachers had learned their moral theory at the *écoles normales*, expounding it was a problem. Sent out alone to the rural villages of France, idealistic young teachers found themselves swamped by the ignorance and lack of initial moral training of their students. The director of a normal school in the Corrèze in 1889 wrote that his students came mostly from the countryside, and that their families, "who gain their living painfully . . . seek above and beyond all, their own interest."[18] Organized into *amicales,* the teachers corresponded with one another about their difficulties and some of the ways they found to solve them, in a collection that can be found in the pages of *Correspondance générale de l'instruction primaire*, founded in 1892.

The letters, describing the conditions that faced them, are moving and sometimes heart-rending. One letter from an *institutrice* to her friends: "I have never felt the responsibility of my task as I do today [after one month]; my expectations were not as heavy as the reality. I have 63 children from 4 to 6 years; I find them a band of urchins, badly raised, without discipline, wild and full of mischief. I must truly civilize them, but will I ever manage it?" Another wrote: "I try to instill some order, but the task is difficult, because the parents uphold the children against me."[19]

But many remained full of hope. One *institutrice* described how she began each day with the lesson in *morale*, because the children were fresh then, their young, innocent faces inspired her.[20] A contest was held for a collection of maxims that teachers could use for teaching *morale*; later, a book of inspirational songs was the subject of another competition.[21] Both competitions turned out to be connected to the founding of l'Union pour l'action morale by Paul Desjardins the following year. The teachers had also the support of Macé's Ligue de l'enseignement and the Freemasons allied with it, who were now fighting the remnants of spiritualism in *morale laïque*.

One of the first problems was the survival of irrationality and superstition. Ernest Lavisse's text (see below) adjured his young readers: "Do not believe in witches. . . . Do not imagine you can avoid harm or accident through the use of amulets, talismans, fetishes." Weber reports that in some towns in Loir-et-Cher priests themselves believed in witches, and were believed to be sorcerers themselves, since they had books.[22]

Another problem was, of course, the Church. The teacher of the Third Republic was supposed to represent the secular Republic in the village.[23] Nevertheless, there was great pressure in many areas, such as Morbihan in Brittany, to go on teaching the catechism, as late as 1895.[24] In girls' schools in strongly Catholic areas, there might still be prayers and crucifixes, and a teacher who took them to mass.[25] One reason for this was that most female teachers at the end of the nineteenth century had been educated, as Ida Berger pointed out, by nuns, and were often hostile to *morale laïque*.[26] But even male teachers who were freethinkers married in the church and baptized their children in strongly Catholic areas.[27]

Another Breton school inspector at Vannes remembered the inauguration of *morale laïque* in Brittany, when the male religious, as well as a few lay teachers, had to be constrained to obey the law. However the women religious in public schools, notably at Saint-Brieuc, made no difficulty. In fact, when some schools were later returned to congregational control, the lessons in *morale laïque* were preserved. However, the area was gradually brought around. A cantonal conference of *instituteurs* at Ploërmel in early March of 1896 featured a lecture on the teaching of *morale*, emphasizing the necessity to handle the subject with a feeling that would convince the students of one's personal love of virtue.[28] These teachers' conventions discussed texts in *morale*, and considered the value of songs introduced into the lesson to intensify feeling for virtue. Societies for the protection of animals and the Ligue antialcoolique were also deemed useful.

The conference followed the pattern of many by outlining the proceeding of a moral lesson. By 1900, the standard class went like this: First the teacher would write the maxim on the board, and explain it briefly, and the children would copy it into their notebooks. Then the teacher would provide, in simple language, and exposition of the topic, ideally with participation of the class. A summary of this exposition would be written on the blackboard, and in the children's notebooks, and often learned by heart. However, it was also considered important to inject ethical discussion into other lessons where possible. "One does it *[morale]* the way M. Jourdain did prose, without knowing it," wrote inspector Rolland of Lorient.[29]

In order to raise the students' awareness, the educational bulletin at the department began to publish accounts of "'acts of probity and devotion,'" which teachers were to read out each week in a solemn atmosphere. The name of the student would go on the blackboard, with his school, the moral precept that he had represented, often his teacher's name. Then the children would sing a song and copy the whole into their notebooks. (Examples given were almost exclusively of children saving others from drowning, or returning to authorities money they found, which, in a poor district, and in large amounts, was truly noteworthy.)

At the secondary level, the Lycée of Pontivy founded a Committee for Charity to the Poor and made visits to bring things bought with their own donations. The inspector reported that they had begun to develop sentiments of generosity. Hearing a child marvel that he could eat meat, the school principal wrote "Our students are thus coming to recognize that they are favored by fortune, without ever having done anything to deserve that favor, no more than these others have deserved their misfortune."[30]

At the Paris Exposition of 1900 there was an exhibit on the schools, including the teaching of *morale*. In covering it for the *Revue pédagogique*, A. Pierre reported that it was customary to write some precept on the blackboard each day, in words understandable to the children of that grade, and to begin the day with a commentary on it. It remained there to be copied into notebooks. While the smallest children only carried on a familiar conversation about it, perhaps drawing pictures to illustrate it, older children got a regular lesson, outlined in advance on the board, to be developed and explicated, used for dictation and summary. Some schools started with the moral maxim and then enlarged on it; others led up to it by reading and discussions.[31]

Of course this was an ideal picture. There is also in the Archives an entire lesson plan by some unnamed teacher in about 1910 for the first part of the third year of primary school, involving reading aloud each day a story from a text, drawing the moral meaning from the story, using the pictures in the book, and a weekly composition whose purpose was to group the ideas logically. One example goes thus: summary of story about Paul, who gets up early because he has to replace his father, a gardener, who has hurt his leg. He waters the borders. Father and son are happy. Discussion on why Paul gets up early, why the father is happy, and why Paul is. Pictures show Paul getting up, watering of the flowers, the tools of a gardener. In the weekly composition, students are asked to think about the five stories, all about the family, and draw from them moral principles. Those expected were fraternal love, obedience, and gratitude for family support.

Unfortunately, all the stories in the book seem not to be of the same moral value. One is entitled ''Say thank-you.'' Some of the best compositions are included in the presentation. In the eighth week students were required to use the last five stories to tell what qualities they would like to have, and which they would seek to avoid. One student wrote that he wanted to serve and learn willingly, like the cultivated vine, and not be like the wild vine, ''la vigne sauvage.'' At the end they were to group the virtues taught in the book under various headings.[32]

This lesson plan, pasted on heavy blue paper, was clearly intended for display. Other lessons were more problematic. In the Musée pédagogique was deposited a document intended to aid lower-level primary school teachers to set up lessons in *morale*. First, take the lesson as you learned it in the higher elementary school and eliminate everything not understandable to your pupils. However, the teacher must know much more than is ever in the lesson for the children. Using as an example the lesson on duties to animals, the teacher was urged to seek for the theoretical basis (the difference between animals and humans, duties toward whom will have already been studied, and between domestic and other animals); then to put the ideas in order of development for the lesson, in the language of the student. Luckily, the teacher would have by this time the aid of the national organization for kindness to animals, with numerous chapters in schools.[33] This was also true in the matter of anti-alcohol teachings, pushed nation-wide through organizations of school children.

There is some evidence that simple conduct could be a problem. A student notebook from an *école communale* in Chartres records the first lesson on the necessity of instruction—benefits, obligation, comparison with older schools. The maxim was ''Ignorance is the worst of slaveries.'' Next followed duties to the self: attendance at school, cleanliness, making good use of time, developing good friends and good habits. Maxim: ''Lost time is never regained.'' There follow a series of lessons on duties to the teacher, who is compared to the father of the family; reciprocal affection between teacher and students; gratitude of student to parents, who provide bodily life, and to the teacher, who provides the life of the intellect. The main maxim on all this is: "Who knows not how to obey will never be worthy to command." Even after the duties of justice and charity, the lessons return to duties of the student at school. One suspects that this teacher was having difficulty controlling his class.[34]

Reports of school inspectors reveal that teachers were often confused about their moral teaching, and preferred to use textbooks that laid it out clearly, rather than rely on their own resources.[35] Lavisse's *La première année d'instruction morale et civique*, written under the name Pierre Laloi, was a favorite. One difficulty noted by the inspectors was the tendency to use self-interest to teach moral lessons. With students in the Creuse the threat of prison was used. Inspectors agreed that only the highest, disinterested standards could be taught as true morality, and opposed utilitarian justifications.[36] Inspectors also deplored any tendency to teach lay morality in a "congregational spirit," as rules laid down by authority. They urged both questioning and commenting by the students, so as to exercise their reason: they also insisted upon the fervent exposition of morality by the teacher. Students had a tendency to laugh at morality, reported one normal school professor; it was up to the teacher to depict for the students the sufferings caused by human injustice in a real and living way. Inspectors particularly objected to disciplinary methods that had "no moral value." Inspectors were generally impressed with the women teachers' handling of *morale*.[37]

The use of school histories and personal notebooks recording morality in action was a widespread method. Notebooks of good resolutions seemed to be particularly favored by girls' schools. Often they would be titled "Exercises of the Will," and would record the resolutions made, and the success in keeping them, attested by mother and teacher. If the student fell short the first month, the resolution would be repeated. Not lying, respecting parents, helping parents were typical resolutions. Sometimes the whole class would make a resolution at the end of an important lesson in *morale*. Put on the blackboard, it could be pointed to by teachers or other students when it was broken. Teachers had societies of model students and good conduct lists; some even conducted examinations of conscience, in the style of Benjamin Franklin.[38]

It may have been these little exercises that helped to bring parents to support moral teachings in the school. In the early days of *morale laïque*, inspectors reported, the parents were "generally indifferent" in some areas (Savoy), in "blind and angry opposition" in others (Clermont). Not only that, the families themselves provided bad moral examples for the children (Allier). In one town on the Seine it was reported that parents didn't object to the teaching, but did nothing to raise their children themselves, and "the street destroys what the teacher builds." There were reports, however, that the children enjoyed the lessons. In the Ardèche they had begun to arrive on time so as not to miss the opening class in *morale*. Gradually the parents too began to rally to the cause. In the last year of the century inspectors reported that the teachers had gained confidence, at least in some places, and were taking advantage of everyday life for examples of virtue and vice (Haute-Loire).[39]

Another reason for the growing acceptance of *morale laïque* in the community was the establishment of mutual aid societies in elementary schools, with all students contributing their *sou* for the family that might need it someday. By 1905, 662,000 children were insured at 2 sous each.[40] Clothes were also supplied for children who did not have them.

Although it took time for the teachers to learn to teach *morale laïque*, and even longer for parents in many areas to accept it, many teachers were proud of their role as the true "instituters of the republic" and even, sometimes, jealous of the status it conferred upon them. As early as 1887, when the Conseil Supérieur de l'Instruction Publique considered taking the course away from school directors to put it in the hands of experts, they queried the directors. Among the overwhelmingly negative responses was one from the director of a girls' school:

> Morality cannot be considered an ordinary course; it does not involve methodological exposition, or pursuit of theoretical results, or preparing students for an exam. It matters little that they "know" morality if they do not practice it; that their intelligence is exercised if their conscience is not aroused; what is necessary is to force them to look inward, to lead them to control their actions, to judge themselves and to take in hand their own direction. But we cannot succeed without fitting the course to our students, not to just any students; it isn't to human nature that we are addressing ourselves, but to particular natures, having certain tendencies, certain faults, certain dispositions. . . . Only the principal can maintain the lesson in *morale* on such a high level and yet so close to reality . . . only she does not specialize, only she puts a general cultivation ["culture générale"] and education before all the rest. And finally, her situation gives her counsels more weight and more authority . . .
> In removing from her this course, by that very act you will diminish her authority and seriously weaken her influence over the students. It is actually necessary that they feel. . . . that we raise them above the preoccupations of everyday life, above their studies, to a higher region, and that the truths we teach them are of another order and importance than what they learn in their ordinary lessons. . . . In effect, it is like a revelation, an initiation into a higher life, an apostolate; therefore are we truly shepherds of souls.

In comparing her role to that of a superior in a convent, she concluded that the lay teacher of morality also preaches the ideal, the important human questions, and that they also spoke in the name of a sacred law, before which consciences bowed. She pleaded, therefore: "Do not close to us that area."[41]

Roger Thabaut, writing about education in his village, described his teacher as believing implicitly in progress, trying but not always succeeding to be neutral toward religion. (He never taught duties to God.) Morality was emphasized, not only in the time set aside for it, but in other lessons also. In arithmetic, the class figured how much one could save by not smoking, or not going to the café for a year, with the conclusion that enough years of prudence would produce savings to buy a home in which to retire. "Thus he prepared us to dominate our instincts and our desires in the name of enlightened self interest."[42]

Many inspectors after the turn of the century reported that the lessons in *morale* seemed to make some difference in the students' behavior. One reported that it had improved the treatment of the old in his area. In fact, one sick elderly woman had come twice to thank the teacher because the children did not torment her any more.[43] And in many areas the children shared the appreciation of the above-quoted *directrice* about the solemn and serious discussion of high moral truths.

One would suspect that this would be true more of girls than of boys, since the evidence is that the female teachers were more effective in providing the appropriate moral tone. However, a poll taken in Lyon in 1891 of 400 primary school students, evenly divided by sex, aged 9 and 10, showed the following results: Asked what courses they preferred, over half listed *morale* (followed at some distance by French, history, geography and arithmetic). There was little difference between the sexes, except that the older girls rated history higher. The reasons given were, of course, those their teachers had told them. *Morale* was necessary, they wrote, in order to know how to conduct oneself as an adult. Alcoholism was mentioned often, also patriotism.

But the most interesting answers came from the girls. They would learn how "to act from their hearts," to "perform their duties with tact." One girl wrote "I like *morale*, which teaches me to be a model and virtuous young lady who will be the joy of her family and a good mother, who will teach her children uprightness, economy, work and many other qualities. Without the good moral lessons our teachers give us, France, so prosperous, would fall into anarchy."[44] Another one told how the lessons helped them to "have recourse to our hearts" for means of helping those in misery "without offending the dignity" of the recipient.[45]

There is, therefore, some evidence to support the increasing optimism of school inspectors on the efficacy of *morale laïque*, aside from the fact that they knew what their superiors wished to hear. The evidence is overwhelming that the teachers, male and female, were "adored by their students," who corresponded with them as adults, even when they had grown to disagree with them.[46] Of course, the males of this generation, who had fervently taught patriotism in the classroom, died on the battlefield in World War I.

Perhaps that teaching corps may be viewed as a nineteenth-century phenomenon. Lacking a modern understanding of what was possible in the moral training of young children, they relied heavily on discipline, on the memorizing of maxims, on competition, all traditional aspects of French education. Where the teaching of *morale* was successful, it was undoubtedly because of a talented teacher, admired by the students, who had an instinct for the possible. Where it did not, no teachers' conferences, no manuals sent out from Paris, no exhortations from school inspectors could make much difference. The areas which succeeded best may have been those that dealt with the most pragmatic issues—alcoholism, thrift—where negative results could be seen. But it is impossible to know. And it is even more impossible to know whether the exhortations to hard work and frugal living that have been found in so many of the manuals bore much fruit.[47]

The most modern method seems to have been that of presenting the student with a moral situation, and asking for a personal reaction, which could then be discussed. (This has been recently used in the United States in Holocaust Studies.) One notebook from the Collège Chaptal commercial course for women contains an essay on such a problem, having to do with moral responsibility. (The cruel mother of the story, who was discovered to be mentally deranged, was judged by the student not to be responsible for her acts.)[48]

In any case, many teachers of the early Third Republic devoted themselves fervently to the task of training the new generation of French citizens in moral values. For them the role of *instituteur* or *institutrice* was indeed what leaders of the Revolution, one hundred years before, had envisioned it to be. It also represented, for the large number drawn from the primary school system, upward mobility. However, this acquired position was to prove a disappointment to many. Not only were the conditions of their work difficult, their pay was inadequate.[49] In areas where Catholicism remained strong, teachers trained by the state, particularly women teachers, often sought positions in vain. Moreover, those very teachers who had succeeded as bearers of republican values became, by the end of the century, progressively more radicalized. The original *amicales* gave way to *syndicats*, through which the teaching corps began to make demands of their own on the republic.[50] By the time the war was over, the working class movement, including the teachers' unions, was questioning the value of state schools that taught its children to conform to bourgeois order and coopted potential leaders to its own ranks.[51]

Twentieth Century Changes

Morale laïque continues to be taught in French public schools, but there are important differences. In general, while nineteenth-century texts continued to be used until the end of the Third Republic, the nineteenth-century spirit, (one might say spiritualism) was usually lacking. It was, of course, still possible for an inspired teacher to infuse the old lessons with the old fervor. But it was less likely, given the world of the twentieth century, more concerned with pragmatic social issues.

The main change, as seen in the textbooks, was a shift to the more pragmatic, utilitarian approach that had been so deplored by pre-war inspectors.[52] Hygiene and anti-alcoholism played increasingly larger roles. The old values were enshrined in maxims to be committed to memory, often as banal as the "Soyons assidus" or "Aimons nos grands-parents" of one 1935 text.[53] *Solidarité* was still strong, although often difficult to distinguish from charity; in some texts it was reserved for the end of the semester, as duties to God had been at the turn of the century.

Aside from the loss of fervor, there was also a gradual recognition that nineteenth-century pedagogical methods usually assumed too much maturity on the part of the child, and that, particularly in the field of ethics, new methods would be needed. The work of John Dewey in the United States indicated that children learned a new thing best when they had developed to a certain stage of readiness for learning it. Therefore he counseled following the child's cues. Since 1945 this line has been pursued in both France and the United States with regard to the teaching of ethics.

In France, Jean Piaget and his associates have tried to plot the moral development of the child. They have established that children go through different stages of understanding moral concepts, of which the Kantian heights essayed by the Third Republic form only the last stage.[54] Therefore one expects less of young children; and those who commit actions considered immoral in their elders but normal at their stage are not considered intractable, as was the case in the Third Republic.[55] Piaget's work has revolutionized our knowledge of how children learn to become responsible persons.

In the United States, Lawrence Kohlberg has worked out similar stages of moral development, based on the pedagogy of Piaget and John Dewey. He has developed some programs graded for school children, and has even supervised an experiment based on this program in one school system.[56] The difficulty is still one of evaluating the results. One expert estimated that a semester course provides up to one-quarter of a Kohlberg stage for about one-half of the participating children, except perhaps with younger children or at the transition ages. But even, so, there is no hard data on how this change affects moral action.[57]

French experience may nevertheless have some relevance for the late twentieth century. Any contemporary society that decides to inculcate a non-religious morality in its youth would need to proceed down some of the paths, both philosophical and pedagogical, already traveled by the French thinkers herein described. Indeed, it is natural that those considering a modern ethical theory, like John Rawls in *A Theory of Justice*, find themselves using many of the same arguments used in the French debate.

Like virtually all French thinkers, Rawls rejects utilitarianism in favor of a neo-Kantian interpretation of justice. Like the *solidaristes* and Durkheim, he sees it as intimately bound up with the life of human beings in society. And he seems to have arrived at solutions to some of the problems hotly argued in the turn-of-the-century debates on *solidarité*. He also conceives of justice as necessitating no support from theological or metaphysical doctrines, particularly not those referring to any life but that led in community with others.

In the matter of moral training, Rawls favors the theory of stages in moral development, referring to both Piaget and Kohlberg. Like Kohlberg, Rawls posits a stage where the person may outgrow, not only the authoritarian morality of those on whom he depends and whom he loves, but also the group morality he derives from association with others. At this point it becomes possible for the person to be inspired by the principles of justice themselves, through the rational understanding of their value in a well-ordered society.[58]

Although there is a common base for morality shared by Rawls and the majority of French thinkers of the nineteenth century, there is a world of psychological research between their time and his. It is possible that this new knowledge might make the teaching of a secular morality in the schools less problematic than it was for the French; however, the years between have also brought greater complexity to our society, next to which *fin-de-siècle* France seems almost pastoral in its simplicity.

Conclusion

The development of *morale laïque* presents us with a picture of continual interpenetration between theory and practice, from the end of the eighteenth century to the beginning of the twentieth. As a theory, it is one aspect of the development of secular moralities during that period; as practice, it is a part of the constant tug-of-war between the Church and the liberalizing forces of the society over the *pouvoir éducateur*.

To preserve the social contract, Rousseau had posited a civic religion with a minimum of dogma, to which all citizens must subscribe. The "republican morality" of the French revolution had the same aim—the preservation of the new social and political order. Thus, it was a direct ancestor of the *morale laïque* of the Third Republic. In both cases, the moral theorists were anticlerical. But this was not the only link between the two. The theorists of the Third Republic returned to the concept of the social contract as a basis for ethics. There is also a clear relationship between Rousseau's "general will" and Durkheim's "collective consciousness", particularly when the latter is raised to the ideal level. As for political connections, Ferry and others often quoted Condorcet in their efforts to establish *morale laïque* in the educational system.

The second step in the development took place in a non-republican atmosphere. The secular, philosophic morality of Cousin, known as spiritualism, was elaborated in a conscious effort to make the Church unnecessary in the education of that limited portion of the society participating in the *monarchie censitaire*. Therefore it was tailored for the secondary school system that educated the elite of the nation. It was this limited political outlook which resulted in the unpopularity of Cousin, although not of his basic moral theory, after the 1848 revolution.

The failure of the Second Republic led to a slow recognition, throughout the Second Empire, that the success of any future republic depended upon weaning the entire population away from the Church. This would necessitate universal education and the extension of secular morality to the curriculum of the primary school system. This program was in fact accomplished in the early Third Republic. But, despite more radical theories of *morale* propounded during the Second Empire, *morale laïque* at first consisted essentially of spiritualism. It was only toward the end of the century that the movement away from spiritualism resulted in an acceptable moral theory based on social interaction, rather than on abstract philosophical concepts.

Although social bases for morality had been enunciated during the Enlightenment and by the partisans of *morale indépendante*, the first to be accepted by the educational establishment was *solidarité*, based on an organic theory of society. Like the radicalization of *morale* during the First Republic, that of the Third was connected with politics. Through individuals such as Bourgeois and Buisson, *morale laïque* became closely identified with the Radical party in the Chamber. The difference between the two republics was that the republicans of the Third, unlike those of the First, had a viable school system over which they had some control.

In the attempt to found a morality on non-religious concepts, French thinkers of the nineteenth century made great use of the revolutionary slogans of liberty, equality and fraternity. Each of these concepts developed through the century in the light of moral theory. The moral freedom of the rational human being in Kantian theory became in Proudhon a thoroughgoing liberty, in which persons freely associated with each other without the strictures of Church or state. Then, in the social theories of the turn of the century, it was modified, first by the necessary interdependence of society, and then by the internalization of the common consciousness.

Equality also, existing on a theoretical level in spiritualism, became absolute in Proudhonian thought on every level. Later theories of solidarity recognized that social and economic disabilities must be mitigated in the direction of greater equality. However, that there was little real acceptance of this fact was evidenced by the lack of actual social legislation in that direction. Fraternity, appearing in spiritualist thought as charity, became to Proudhon one-to-one relationships of justice. The *solidaristes* recognized that, in a good society, acts formerly viewed as individual charity would fall into the category of social justice. But again they failed to translate this theory into action.

One reason for this failure can be found in the nature of *morale laïque* itself. Moral theory with a purpose, its aim was not to change the nature or organization of French society; it was to preserve the bourgeois republic, for reasons as diverse as the groups that supported it. Another of the avowed purposes of *morale laïque* was to unify France under a single moral system, in which case it could only be the predominant, bourgeois variety, "the good old morality of our fathers," as Ferry put it. Therefore, any theory radically different from the traditional, whether Proudhon's or Durkheim's, was not likely to serve the purpose.

By the end of the century, the Radicals were insisting upon a close association between democracy and science, that is, between the republic and formal learning. They claimed that solidarity was scientific. But it was only Durkheim who attempted the true union of scientific method and ethics, in the form of the new sociology. Sociological morality was in accord, not only with anthropological studies, but with the growing specialization taking place as France slowly modernized. Nevertheless, it failed to make a real mark on *morale laïque*. Not only was its scientific nature questioned; there was also in the society a strong residual influence of traditional Kantian ethical concepts.

In the development of *morale laïque* were revealed both the consistencies and the tensions of French thought in the nineteenth century. The most consistent element was the psychological emphasis on consciousness. This might be depicted as consciousness of good and evil, as in Cousin and the other Kantians; or of one's own rights and dignity, as in Proudhon and the *morale indépendante* group; or simply of one's own needs, leading to a recognition of the interdependence of individuals in society, as with Destutt de Tracy and the *solidaristes*. Consciousness enlightened by reason became conscience. From the feelings of one's own rights and dignity one logically derived the rights and dignity of others. The admission of one's need for others in a structured society made reasonable the performance of one's duties to others.

Another consistency was the pervasive insistence upon the empirical nature of *morale*, its basis in facts. There were the psychological facts of individual consciousness, referred to by Cousin, Proudhon and Renouvier. There were also the facts of social life, as expounded by the *solidaristes* and Durkheim. From facts, theory could be induced; therefore morality was a science. Thus, although influenced by Kant, the French consistently denied that morality was beyond the grasp of the rational mind, working inductively. It was this insistence on empirical method that eventually made it possible for some theorists to give up Kant's necessary postulates for morality, God and the immortal soul.

The idea of *morale* as a kind of social exchange was manifested in Rousseau, Proudhon, Renouvier, the *solidaristes* and Durkheim. However, in each theory, the role of the individual differed slightly. In Rousseau's social contract, the individual was totally identified with the society. For Proudhon, the social contract was a series of conscious, freely-made individual contracts. *Solidarité*, with its "quasi-contract," considered the individual as bound to the society at birth; however, adherents of the doctrine never totally accepted the subordination of the individual to society. In Durkheim's sociological morality, the contract was not so much willed as felt, a given in the individual psyche. It was experienced as the *conscience collective*, an unconscious *a priori* element of human life, although susceptible to scientific analysis *a posteriori*.

The controversial concept of common or collective consciousness was, in fact, described by Proudhon in his early writings. Conscience, he said, was the social essence, the collective being which penetrated the individual; morality was the revelation that society made to the individual. However, in *Justice*, while describing the person as Durkheim later did, with both an individual and a social nature, Proudhon denied that morality derived from the society and placed it in the individual. Marion, a forerunner of *solidarité*, came closer to Durkheim's picture of society than did Proudhon, describing it as more than the sum of the individuals composing it. Fouillée, author of the quasi-contract, demurred. Agreeing with Proudhon that in the individual the elements were determined but the person was free, he denied Durkheim's assertion that in social life the individual was determined but the society was free. Any abridgement of individual autonomy was unacceptable to the majority of French theorists; this was one of the elements of Durkheim's moral theory that was never really accepted.

A related area of tension was the general question of freedom versus determinism. Throughout the nineteenth century, it was declared that *morale* was a science; yet only Durkheim drew the inevitable conclusion from this—that individuals were not free, but determined by the society, which could be scientifically studied. Society not the individual, was the independent moral agent who felt the strictures of the common consciousness with the same rigor as the Kantian subject felt those of the categorical imperative. But Durkheim's conclusion was unacceptable to the French in general.

Closely related to this problem was the sociologist's insistence on the relativity of morality to the society. Once it was admitted that morality was social, it seemed inevitable that its objective, absolute nature should be questioned. Yet even Proudhon, while admitting that the just act might differ in time and place, maintained that it was always derived from the idea of justice, which was innate, not in the society, but in the individual. In the discussions on *solidarité*, many participants emphasized that, although science might be a means, a tool for moral understanding, justice was the end, the moral goal. Durkheim went so far as to postulate the ideal as a goal; but he claimed that this ideal would differ from society to society. It is questionable, however, that he himself ever solved the problem of postulating the ideal for a society without the use of some transcendent values. This failure was noted, even by his disciples, as a weakness in his *morale*.

As regards theory, Durkheim seems to have completed all the tendencies of *morale laïque* in the nineteenth century: the total disengagement of ethics from religious dogma, the connection of morality with society, the development of a "moral science." He had accomplished this while refusing to be reductionist in moral matters; in some sense, morality remained for him transcendent and ideal. Yet even these remnants of Kant could not save his theory from the obloquy of his opponents and the reservations of his followers. The latter approved his secularism, his emphasis on social values, his empirical approach. But they could not entirely dispense with objective morality and the free will of the rational individual. Or, if they could personally do so, they knew they could not "sell" sociological morality to the French public. And figures like Bouglé, along with other leading Radicals, were most concerned with French unity.

Thus, although Durkheim completed the theoretical development of *morale laïque*, we must conclude that the last moral philosophy actually accepted by the French for use in education was that of Renouvier. Republican, secular, even anti-clerical, Renouvier altered the Kantian view of morality to fit the French tradition. That is, he located it in the phenomenal world, in actual relations between persons. Justice was innate in human beings, but not transcendent. Although God and the immortal soul were implied in morality, he did not consider them the bases for it. He admitted that the freedom of the individual could not be proved, but asserted it nevertheless. Renouvier thus preserved in some sense all of the traditional components of French ethical theory, while insisting, like Proudhon, on the immanence, rather than the transcendence, of morality. By doing so, he was able to extend individual morality to the social level, since justice was manifested in actual human relations.

There was, in fact, a social contract in every society; but, according to Renouvier and Fouillée, it was based on the individual. Society was the sum of the moral individuals composing it. Therefore social solidarity did not imply social determinism, but rather a contract to which individuals freely subscribed. The collective consciousness, as Fouillée would say, was not a consciousness in itself, but only the result of the multiplication of individual consciousnesses. This was as far as the French mainstream was willing to go toward a social morality.

Contemplating France at the turn of the century, one can easily see why this was so. One of the most individualistic societies in the world, it was dominated by men of the Radical persuasion in the Chamber, who represented the small property holder. However they might approve of morality, these men were not likely to acquiesce in any moral teaching implying that society should have control over their individual lives or over the use of their property. Even Fouillée's "reparative justice," in the form of a graduated income tax for purposes of social welfare, was not accepted by the property-owning classes that controlled the nation. Of the three republican revolutionary slogans, the only one to which they truly subscribed was liberty.

One might say, then, that Durkheim was the last French thinker to produce a moral theory intended for propagation in the school system, and that this theory was never really adopted by the University for use in the schools. Aside from the philosophical objections to the theory itself, there was a weakening of the sense of urgency that had spurred the development of *morale laïque* in the first place, as patriotism increased with the German threat. One of the reasons for the development of a secular morality had always been the unifying role it was to play in the nation. Therefore a great number of the best French minds had devoted themselves to moral theory for over one hundred years. But already by the turn of the century, the majority of writing on the subject was being left to the educationists.[1] And as the German threat increased, French unity grew apace. During the prewar and wartime periods, French thinkers confined themselves more and more to pure patriotism. After World War I they never returned to the emphasis on *morale*. The body of writings and discussions on the subject after 1918 is as nothing next to the material between 1848 and 1914.

Another likely reason for the decline in writing on the subject is that the enemy *morale laïque* was designed to combat was now a helpless giant. The Church, disestablished in 1905, continued its adversary relationship with the secular school. But, stripped of its power, it was no longer a threat against which fervent generations of lay teachers were graduated from normal schools to do combat. Thus the lack of challenge by a powerful Church seems to have ended the constant thinking and rethinking of *morale* that had persisted throughout the nineteenth century. And the decline in philosophical discussion about *morale* implied a concomitant decline in *morale laïque*.

In January of 1910 Buisson addressed the Chamber of Deputies on *morale laïque*, claiming that it proved the originality of France, the only country that had tried to found a morality outside of religion and of metaphysics.[2] In this he was right, although the problems that secular morality was intended to solve were not unique to France. Efforts to use the tool of education for the benefit of liberal government in Italy and Spain were not successful before World War II, perhaps because other aspects of modernization were not as advanced as those in France. Protestantism, as Renouvier had remarked, was not as hostile to liberal government as was Catholicism. But the struggle between the Anglican Church in England and the dissenters had delayed the inauguration of universal education in England until late in the nineteenth century, leaving primary education still under local control, and therefore subject to some kind of religious influence.

In Germany and Scandinavia also, Protestant churches continued to play a major role in the moral education of public school children. In the United States, because of its historical experience, the wall between Church and State was maintained in theory. But school prayer and Bible reading continued in many areas throughout the nineteenth century; the issue is still hard fought between proponents and opponents of school prayer. There has also been some discussion of the necessity for teaching a secular morality at all levels of the school system.

In the thirties, moral training in the schools had become part of totalitarian propaganda in both Catholic Italy and Protestant Germany. The French continued to teach secular morality in the schools, although it was no longer so clearly in support of the republic; *morale laïque* seemed to have lost direction. In 1936, at an international conference, it was described as follows: *"Morale laïque* has become progressively frozen into rites and habits. They continue to practice it, but only at school, only during the period of the lesson in *morale*, the way others go mechanically to mass on Sundays; it is more by tradition than by conviction."[3] The Vichy government, during World War II, restored state subsidies to Catholic education; and even the socialist government of François Mitterand in the 1980s was unable to reduce the independence of these subsidized schools.

Yet *morale laïque* persists. In 1974 historian François Goguel, maintained that the French secondary school had "at the same time a mission of instruction and of education." (As in the Enlightenment, the latter term still implies character-building.) Goguel spoke of the necessity to form persons "whose knowledge, whose capacities to develop this knowledge, whose aptitude to put it into practice in their vocation and social life, as well as their character, their comportment and their qualities of judgment, make them at the same time persons responsible for their own existence, free persons." The context in which this person is to be developed is the school itself, through student self-government, among other things.

Goguel also urged that the *"nouvelle laicïté"* of the fifth Republic abandon the false neutrality of the Third, where the instruction "was conceived in such a way as to make the political system then in force the definitive crowning of an evolution that needed only to be pursued to its end." Nor, he remarked, should education be at the service of certain future social and political forms desired by some, but not by all. "There exists in France," he wrote then, "no consensus comparable to that of the first years of the century."[4] There is, of course, some question about the extent to which such a consensus ever existed.

It may be more useful, then, to look at the development of *morale laïque* as an aspect of the modernization that was in progress in all of Western Europe during the nineteenth century. As viewed by contemporary sociologists, the secularization involved depends to a great extent upon the religious makeup of the population. Martin[5] has noted that the absolute governments of Catholic countries in the early modern period imitated the autocracy of the Church, while putting it under their control. In those countries, where Catholicism has a religious monopoly, modernization usually takes the form of civil war, rather than of revolt against an outside power. This split is irreconcilable, and the Church lines up with the powers of legitimacy, thus acknowledging in some sense the secularization of political life. The religious minorities side with the modernizing forces, even when these begin to include overt secularization.

One then finds the same extremism on an intellectual level that previously existed on the political, and also the same imitation. The anticlericals elaborate broad social and philosophical systems—in effect subverting religion by replacing it. The development of *morale laïque* is a good example. France, and to some extent, Belgium, were the only Catholic countries in the nineteenth century where Church control of the moral education of children was contested. These were also the Catholic countries where other aspects of modernization were well advanced.

Secularization theory also helps to account for the diminishing role of *morale laïque* after the war. According to Martin's theory, the final stage of secularization takes place within the once-dominant Church itself, with the same extremism of radicalism and reaction that marked the political revolution and the secularization of the modernizing society. If one considers, as many French thinkers did, that the Reformation was the first step in the modernization of the Catholic Church, then one can point to a new polarization in French Catholicism before 1914, between those who backed the Sillon and those who backed the Action Française. And the secularizing trend within the church has grown apace in the last half-century.

As far as the control of the minds of children is concerned, the French Church still insists, in the 1980s, that its rights be respected; but many who have backed its demands have done so as much in the name of secular as of religious rights.

Perhaps, then, rather than regarding the development of *morale laïque* as merely a political effort to preserve the rights of the newly-dominant bourgeoisie, one may see it as a normal development—unique to France, but not wholly without connection to general European developments. Nor is it without relevance to a society which, torn between conservative, "born-again religion" and liberal "secular humanism," is experiencing a precipitate decline in public and private morality.

Appendix I
Morals Curriculum 1881

Early Childhood Section
Age 5-7

Very simple talks interspersed throughout all class exercises and recess.

Short poems explained and learnt by heart. Short moral stories to be told and followed by questions apt to bring out their meanings and verify that the children understood them. Little songs.

Special care to be given by the (woman) teacher to those children in whom the beginnings of a fault or vice were observed.

Elementary School
Age 7-9

Informal conversations. Readings with explanations (stories, examples, precepts, parables and fables). Learning through the feelings.

Practical exercises aimed at putting morality in action in the class itself:

    1. Through the observation of individual characters. (Take into account the children's predispositions so as to correct their faults gently, or develop their qualities);
    2. Through the intelligent use of the school's discipline as a tool of education (i.e. moral education). (Be careful to distinguish failings towards duty from

Source: Georges Compayré *Organisation pédagogique et législative des écoles primaires.* Paris, 1900, pp. 68–71.

simple infractions to regulations; make clear the relationship between misdeed and punishment; provide a living example of scrupulous fairness in the governance of the class; inspire the horror of tattle-telling, dissimulation and hypocrisy; put frankness and rectitude above all, and toward that goal never discourage children in their outspokenness, complaints, questioning, etc. . .);

3. Through an incessant appeal to the child's own feeling and moral judgment (Make the children the judges of their own conduct; especially lead them to appreciate, in themselves and in others, moral and intellectual effort; know how to let them act and speak, provided they are led to discover by themselves their mistakes or their wrongdoings);

4. Through the correction of gross errors (prejudices and popular superstitions, beliefs in witches, ghosts, the influence of numbers, mad terrors);

5. Through the teachings to be derived from the facts that the children themselves observe; if the occasion arises, make them aware of the sad consequences of vices which they themselves witness, of drunkenness, laziness, disorder, cruelty, brutal appetites, etc. Inspire compassion for the victims as much as horror for the evil itself; similarly, proceed through the use of concrete examples and appeals to the children's immediate experience so as to inspire them to moral feeling: for instance, elevate them to the sentiment of admiration for universal order and to religious feeling through the contemplation of majestic scenes of nature; to the feeling of charity, by bringing to their attention a misery to be alleviated, by giving them occasions for effective acts of charity performed with discretion; to the feelings of thankfulness and sympathy by recounting an act of bravery, visiting a charitable institution, etc.

Middle School
Age 9-11

Conversations, readings with comment, practical exercises—same mode and methods as previously, some what more precise. Coordinate lessons and readings so that no important point of the program below is omitted:

I.

The child in the family. Duties towards parents and grandparents. Obedience, respect, love, thankfulness. Helpfulness towards parents in their labors; care in their illnesses; help in their old age.

Duties of brothers and sisters. Mutual love; protection of the younger by the older; influence of good examples.

Duties towards servants. Treat them with politeness and kindness.

The child at school. Assiduity, docility, hard work, good manners. Duties toward the teacher. Duties towards school mates.

The Nation. France, its glory and its sorrows. Duties towards the nation and society.

II.

Duties to the self. The body, cleanliness, sobriety and temperance, (dangers of drunkenness), gymnastics.

External Possessions. Economy; avoid debts, fatal effects of the passion for games; avoid excessive love of money and profit; prodigality, avarice. Work (do not waste time, obligation of all men to work, nobility of manual labor).

The soul. Truthfulness and sincerity; never lie. Personal dignity, self-respect. Modesty: avoid blindness to one's own faults. Avoid pride, vanity, frivolity. Shame of ignorance and laziness. Courage in danger and adversity; patience, initiative. Dangers of anger. Treat animals kindly; avoid useless suffering. Loi Grammont, SPCA.

Duties towards other men. Justice and charity (do not do to others what you would not want others to do to you, do to others what you would want others to do for you). Do not attack others' life, person, properties, or reputation. Kindness, fraternity. Tolerance, respect of others' beliefs.

Nota Bene. Throughout this course, the teacher takes as his starting point the existence of conscience, of moral law and of obligation. He appeals to the feeling and idea of duty, to the feeling and idea of responsibility; he doesn't attempt to demonstrate them through a theoretical presentation.

Duties toward God. The teacher is not expected to give a course ex professo on the nature and attributes of God; the teaching to be given to all without distinction is limited to two points:

First, he teaches them not to pronounce lightly the name of God; he associates closely in their minds the ideas of a First Cause and a Perfect Being with a sentiment of respect and veneration; and he habituates each of them to surround that notion of God with the same respect, although it may present itself to him under forms different from those of his own religion.

Further, and without concerning himself with the special prescriptions of various confessions, the teacher strives to make the child understand that the first homage due to God is obedience to God's laws as they are revealed to him by his own conscience and reason.

Upper School
Age 11-13

Talks, readings, practical exercises, as in the previous sections. Furthermore, this course includes a regular series of lessons, the number and order of which may vary, about the elementary teaching of morality, and in particular *social morality*, according to the program below:

> *1. The family*. Duties of parents and children; reciprocal duties of masters and servants; family spirit.
> *2. Society*. Need for and benefits of society. Justice, a condition of all society. Solidarity, human brotherhood. Applications and development of the idea of *justice*: respect for life and human liberty, respect for property, respect of given word, respect of other people's honor or reputation. Honesty, fairness, loyalty, delicacy. Respect of others' opinions and beliefs. Applications and developments of the idea of *charity, or fraternity*. Its degrees; duty of benevolence, tolerance, clemency etc. Devotion to others the supreme form of charity; show that it has its place in everyday life.
> *3. The Nation*. What one owes to the nation (obedience to law, discipline, devotion, faithfulness to the flag). Taxes (condemnation of all fraud toward the State). Voting is a moral obligation, it must be free, conscientious, disinterested, enlightened. Rights corresponding to these duties: individual freedom, freedom of conscience, freedom of work, freedom of association. Guarantee of the security of all citizens' life and possessions. National sovereignty. Explanation of the Republican motto: Liberty, Equality, Fraternity.

In each of these chapters on social morality, the student's attention will be brought to the following points, without going into metaphysical discussions:

1. The difference between duty and interest, even when they seem to coincide, i.e. the imperative and disinterested character of duty.

2. The distinction between written law and moral law: the one sets a maximum of prescriptions which society imposes on all its members under pain of various punishments; the other imposes on each in the secrecy of his own conscience a duty that no one forces him to fulfill, but that he cannot fail in without feeling guilty towards himself and towards God.

Appendix II

Morals Curriculum 1891 Department of the Somme, August 1st, 1891

Preparatory and Elementary School

Note. There is no need here to set a distribution by trimester; the official instructions reproduced below indicate perfectly the limits of moral education for the very young children:

Informal conversations. Readings with explanations (stories, examples, precepts, parables and fables). Teaching through sentiment.

Practical exercises tending to put morality in action in the class itself:

1. Through the observation of individual characters (take into account the children's predispositions, so as to correct gently their faults or develop their qualities);

2. Through the intelligent application of school discipline as a tool of moral education (be careful to distinguish between failure to perform one's duty and simple infractions of regulations, make clear the relation between the misdeed and the punishment, be an example of scrupulous fairness in the governance of the class, inspire the horror of denunciation, dissimulation and hypocrisy, above all frankness and rectitude, and to this goal never discourage the children's outspokenness, their complaints, their questions, requests, etc.);

3. Through incessant appeal to the children's own feelings and moral judgment (make the children the judges of their own conduct, teach them to appreciate moral and intellectual effort in others, know how to let them do and say, provided they are led to discover by themselves their errors and

wrongdoings);

4. Through the correction of crude notions (prejudices and popular superstitions, beliefs in witches and ghosts, the influence of numbers, mad terrors, etc.);

5. Through the teachings to be derived from the children's own experience; when the occasion arises, make them aware of the sad consequences of the vice, whose examples may be in front of their very eyes: drunkenness, laziness, disorder, cruelty, brutal appetites, etc., while inspiring in them compassion for the victims as well as horror for the evil itself; similarly, proceed through concrete examples and appeals to the children's immediate experience to initiate them to moral feelings: for instance, elevate them to a feeling of admiration for universal order, and to religious feeling by having them contemplate some majestic scenes of nature; to the feeling of charity, by bringing to their attention a misery to alleviate, by giving them occasions for effective acts of charity to be accomplished discreetly; to feelings of gratitude and sympathy by the account of an act of bravery, a visit to a charitable institution, etc.)

END

Middle and High School

Note. The methods of teaching are the same for these two levels in the primary schools (where there is no 'High' School in the proper meaning of the word); for the rest, since classes will be held in common, one curriculum will suffice: however, the teacher may spend time with the more advanced students on questions of social morality, give them some examples of theoretical morals, pointing out in particular:

1. The difference between duty and interest, even when they seem to coincide, i.e. the imperative and disinterested nature of duty;

2. The distinction between written law and moral law: while the one sets minimum prescriptions which society imposes on all its members under pain of predetermined punishments, the other imposes on each individual in the secrecy of his conscience a duty that no one can force him to accomplish, but the neglect of which must make him guilty towards himself and towards God.

1st Trimester

The child in the family. Definition of the family, in Antiquity, before the Revolution, today. Primogeniture. Modern family based on justice and equality. Duties of parents to their children. Duties of children to their parents: filial love, gratitude, respect (feelings), obedience, devotion, help and protection in old age (actions). Duties to grandparents and collateral relatives. Duties of brothers and sisters: brothers and sisters are natural friends; mutual affection, obligingness, politeness; protection and good example on the part of the older; trust and obedience on the part of the younger; role of the oldest child if parents are absent. Family spirit. Respect for the family name. Duties towards servants: treat them politely, kindly; old servants are truly members of the family.

The child in the school. The school of olden times and the school of today; advantages of instruction; difference between instruction and education. The need for work, and its results. Primary Studies Certificate. Duties of assiduity, exactitude and hard work in return for the benefits of the State. Duties to the teacher. Duties towards comrades: analogy to duties to brothers. Friendship must stem from mutual esteem. Benevolence, obligingness, frankness. Good company (vs. 'bad'-translator's note).

2nd Trimester

The Nation. The family, first image of the nation. Definition: agreement between feelings and will; community of territory, language, interests, laws; same historical past. Patriotism. Need for young Frenchmen to study the language, history and geography of their county, as well as its administration. Chauvinism. Cosmopolitanism. The State. The Citizens. The Constitution. The Laws. Duties toward the nation. 1. Schooling duty; 2. Obedience to the laws; 3. Military duty (discipline, courage, devotion, loyalty to the flag); 4. Taxes (their legitimacy, condemnation of any fraud toward the State); 5. The Vote (it is morally obligatory; it must be free, conscientious, disinterested, enlightened). Rights of the citizen: political freedoms; individual freedom; freedom of conscience; freedom of work; freedom of security for each person's life and possessions. National sovereignty. Explanation of the Republican motto: Liberty, Equality, Fraternity. France: its justice; its generosity; its multiple glories: sciences, letters, arts, industry, etc. Its sorrows; the war of 1870.

The duties of children. Love the fatherland and work toward its greatness.

Duties to the self. Awaken the idea of self-respect, honor, personal dignity. Conscience. Good and evil. Human nature: physical and moral. Close solidarity between body and soul.

The body. Preserve and develop physical strengths. Hygiene, cleanliness; Temperance, the dangers of drunkenness. Good habits. Combating sensuality, gluttony, laziness. Usefulness of gymnastics.

External possessions. Property. Economy: the advice of Franklin (bonhomme Richard); avoiding debt, fatal effects of passion for gambling games; prodigality; avarice. Work: it is born from need and becomes man's honor and society's salvation. All work is noble and legitimate, whether manual or

intellectual, paid or unpaid. Laziness and its consequences: boredom, disorder, ruin. Work is a duty, it insures the person's dignity.
The Soul. Duty to cultivate its faculties. Truthfulness and sincerity; never lie, even as a joke. Hold one's promises; respect the given word; be discreet. Personal dignity and self-respect produce legitimate pride, which does not exclude modesty and simplicity. Strive to be courageous, constant, firm, prudent, patient, resignated in unhappiness, severe to oneself and indulgent to others; combat egoism, vanity, envy, jealousy, anger, hatred.
Be good to animals. Do not make animals suffer unnecessarily (Grammont Law, SPCA) School associations for the protection of nests.

3rd Trimester

Society. School, the first image of society. Natural origins (need and sympathy); need for and benefits of social living. Equality and natural inequalities. Justice, a condition of all society. Social solidarity; human brotherhood.
Duties to others. Distinguishing between duties of justice and duties of charity (do not do unto others … do unto others…).

1. *Application and development of the idea of justice.* Justice is absolute, without exception, it obliges us:

   a) To respect human life. Homicide, legitimate defense (death penalty), duelling.
   b) To respect human freedom. Inviolability of the person; freedom, a condition of morality; slavery (slave trade), serfdom.
   c) To respect property. Property is sacred; it is a right founded on individual freedom and work. Theft (various kinds: fraud, poaching, etc.) Donation and transmission of property, inheritance.
   d) To respect the honor and reputation of others. Calumny, defamation, ill-gossip, insult, indiscretion, envy, ingratitude are counter to the idea of justice. Benevolence towards others. What is meant by public opinion.
   e) To respect the given word (see above, under Soul). Sincerity, honesty, loyalty are absolutely indispensable in social life.
   f) To respect the opinion and beliefs of others, more commonly called tolerance.

2. *Application and development of the idea of charity and fraternity.* Charity is no less obligatory than justice. Benevolence and beneficence. Different forms of philanthropy. Alms (private and public assistance), advice to the ignorant, consolation to those in pain, care of the sick, etc. Kindness, service, philanthropy, devotion, heroism.
Nota Bene. In all this course, the teacher takes as his starting point the existence of conscience, of moral law and obligation. He calls upon the sense and idea of duty, the feeling and idea of responsibility, he does not attempt

theoretical demonstrations.

Duties toward God. The teacher is not expected to give a course ex professo on the nature and attributes of God; the teaching which he must give to all bears on two points only:

> "First, he teaches them not to pronounce lightly the name of God; he creates a close association between the ideas of a First Cause and a Perfect Being and a feeling of respect and veneration, and he habituates all students to surround this notion of God with the same respect, even though it might come in forms different from those of one's own religion.
>
> Second, and without bothering with the special prescriptions of various confessions, the teacher strives to help the child understand and feel that the first homage he owes to the divinity is obedience to the laws of God, as they are revealed to him by his own conscience and reason."

Notes

PART I INTRODUCTION

1. See Stanley Mellon, *The Political Uses of History: A Study of Historians in the French Restoration* (Stanford: 1958).

CHAPTER 1

1. For such a survey, see Lester G. Crocker, *Nature and Culture* (Baltimore: 1913).

2. Bayle drew his examples from the Stoics. Toward the end of the seventeenth century, there was considerable discussion of the problem of the damnation of virtuous pagans. See Pierre Hermand, *Les Idées morales de Diderot* (Paris: 1923).

3. Despite such pleas, born of prudence rather than conviction, Bayles's books were condemned as irreligious and obscene in France, where all references to him were censored until the 1760's. Two editions of the *Dictionnaire* were published in Rotterdam, in 1697 and 1702.

4. This subject is well covered in the monograph of Robert R. Palmer, *Catholics and Unbelievers in Eighteenth Century France* (Princeton: 1939).

5. Jean-Jacques Rousseau, *Emile, Oeuvres complètes* (Paris: 1873), 2:257.

6. Ibid., pp. 258-61. In *L'Etat de guerre*, Rousseau wrote that if natural law were written only in human reason, it would hardly be capable of directing our actions. "Mais elle est encore graveé dans le coeur de l'homme en caractères inéffacables," and thus more effective than "tous les préceptes des philosophes." *Jean-Jacques Rousseau, the Political Writings*, ed. C. E. Vaughan, 2 vols., 1:294.

7. Jean-Jacques Rousseau, *Emile*, op. cit., 2:352-53.

8. Ibid., p. 6.

9. Ibid., pp. 35-36.

10. Vaughan, op. cit., 1:159-175.

11. Rousseau, *Emile*, op. cit., p. 65.

12. Denis Diderot, *Réfutation de l'homme d'Helvétius, Oeuvres* (Paris: 1821), vol. 3. See also Diderot's *Encyclopǒdie* article, "Droit natural," which enunciates the concept of reciprocity in moral relations.

13. Jean-Jacques Rousseau, *De l'économie politique,* ed. Vaughan, op. cit., p. 105.

14. Ibid., *Histoire des moeurs,* fragment, p. 335.

15. Crocker, op. cit., p. 105.

16. Claude-Adrien Helvétius, *De l'esprit* (Paris: 1909), p. 33.

17. Claude-Adrien Helvétius, *De l'homme* (Paris: 1909), pp. 230, 257-58.

18. See Voltaire's articles on Conscience, Law, Virtue and Vice, and Diderot's *Apologie de l'abbé des Prades, Oeuvres,* op. cit., vol. 1.

19. It has been suggested that the morality expressed by the Savoyard Vicar was for Rousseau only a personal morality in a time when there was no social morality, and not a universally applicable solution to the ethical problem.

20. This comparison is made by Crocker, op. cit., pp. 247-48.

21. *De l'économie politique,* Vaughan, op, cit., 1:241-42.

22. Vaughan, op. cit., 2:48.

23. Vaughan, op. cit., 1:494.

24. Ibid., p. 450.

25. Vaughan, op. cit., 2:40-42.

26. See Immanuel Kant, *The Metaphysical Elements of Justice,* trans. John Ladd (New York: 1965), pp. 13-23. See also Ernst Cassirer, *Rousseau, Kant and Goethe* (New York: 1965), pp. 30, 32, 48.

27. Vaughan, op. cit., 2:50-52.

28. Ibid., p. 132.

29. Helvétius, *De l'homme,* op, cit., p. 230.

30. "Instruire une nation, c'est la civiliser," wrote Diderot, adding that among the goals of education should be the inculcation of social values. *Plan d'une université pour le gouvernement de Russie, Oeuvres,* op. cit., 12:174.

31. Vaughan, op. cit., 2:142, 382.

32. Ibid., pp. 437-41.

33. F. de la Fontainerie, ed. and trans., *French Liberalism and Education in the Eighteenth Century* (New York: 1932), p. 149.

34. Anne-Robert Jacques Turgot, *Les Oeuvres de Turgot* (Paris: 1844), 2:605ff.

Chapter 2

1. Robert J. Vignery, *The French Revolution and the Schools* (Madison: 1965), p. 7.

2. Maurice Gontard, *L'Enseignement en France de la révolution à la loi Guizot* (Lyon: 1959), pp. 72ff.

3. Vignery, op. cit., p. 19.

4. Victor Boisdé, *L'Enseignement primaire sous la révolution* (Paris: 1908), pp. 27-34.

5. J. Guillaume, ed. *Procès-verbaux du Comité d'instruction publique de l'Assemblée législative* (Paris: 1889), p. x.

6. J.-B. Duvergier, *Collection complète des dècrets, ordonnances, règlements et avis du conseil d'état publiés en France depuis 1789* (Paris: 1824), 1:91.

7. Boisdé, op. cit., pp. 47-48.

8. Talleyrand-Périgord, "Rapport sur l'Instruction publique," *Procès-verbaux de l'assemblée constituante* DXX, p. 763.

9. Guillaume, op. cit., p. xvii.

10. Marie-Jean Antoine Nicolas Caritat de Condorcet, *Oeuvres choisies* (Paris: 1893), 2:1ff.

11. Guillaume, op. cit., pp. 188-89.

12. Ibid., p. 191. Condorcet pointed out that in a society where some receive their ideas through reason and others through revelation, there would always be two classes—those who reason and those who believe, or in other words, masters and slaves.

13. Ibid., pp. 193, 201.

14. Ibid., pp. 202, 204-206.

15. J. Guillaume, ed., *Procès-verbaux du Comité d'instruction publique de la convention nationale* (Paris: 1889), 1:613.

16. In referring to the section of higher education called moral and political sciences, he noted: "Il est superflu, sans doute, de prouver qu'elles ne doivent pas etre séparées." J. Guillame, *Procès-verbaux . . . de l'assemblée législative,* op. cit., p. 214.

17. Ibid., p. 223.

18. Ibid., pp. 227, 229, 239. In the secondary schools, one professor would teach the analysis of sensations and ideas, *morale,* logic, and general principles of political constitutions, which gives an insight into the relationship which Condorcet presumed to exist among these topics. In the section on mathematical and physical sciences, there would be a professor of "application du calcul aux sciences morales et politiques," which Condorcet explained in a note to the 1793 edition, in terms of the relationship of politics and political economy to morality. Ibid., pp. 230, 232-35.

19. Ibid., pp. 228, 192.

20. Guillaume, *Procès-verbaux . . . de la convention nationale*, op. cit., 1:121, 151-52. This was the period when republican rituals, with their own iconography, were being celebrated. See Alphonse Aulard, *Christianity and the French Revolution* (New York: 1966) and John McManners, *The French Revolution and the Church* (New York: 1969).

21. Ibid., pp. 123-25, 127-28. Supporting speeches appeared later, pp. 181-82.

22. Gontard, op. cit., p. 159.

23. Guillaume, *Procès-verbaux . . . de la convention nationale*, 1:191.

24. Ibid., 1:419, 206. This is a persistent verbal distinction made by the French, although it was always considered necessary that the schools provide both.

25. Ernest Allain, *l'Oeuvre scolaire de la révolution* (Paris: 1891), p. 36.

26. Boisdé, op. cit., pp. 116-18.

27. Guillaume, *Procès-verbaux . . . de la convention nationale*, 1:272-75, 630.

28. Ibid., pp. 68, 525ff., 569ff., 557.

29. Ibid., 2:34, 45-46. The project was actually the work of one Michel Lepéletier, by then deceased.

30. Ibid., 4:239-40.

31. Vignery, op. cit., p. 110.

32. The most complete study of this group is François Picavet, *Les Idéologues* (Paris: 1891).

33. Emile Caillet, *La Tradition litteraire des idéologues* (Philadelphia: 1943), p. 250.

34. Picavet, op. cit., pp. 75-79, 307-309, 322-23.

35. Destutt de Tracy, *A Treatise on Political Economy* vol. 2 of *Elemens d'idéologie* (Georgetown: 1817), Introduction.

36. Destutt de Tracy, *Quels sont les moyens de fonder la morale d'un peuple?* (Paris: 1798), pp. 455, 462-63.

37. Destutt de Tracy, *Rapports du physique et de la morale de l'homme, extrait raisonné servant de table analytique de l'oeuvre de P. J. Cabanis* (Paris: 1815), pp. lxxi, c-ci.

38. Destutt de Tracy, *A Commentary and Review of Montesquieu's Spirit of the Laws* (Philadelphia: 1811), p. 23.

39. Gontard, op. cit., pp. 281, 311-15, 318.

40. Georges Weill, *Histoire de l'idée laïque au dix-neuvième siècle* (Paris: 1925),

pp. 34-38.

41. Jules Simon, *Victor Cousin* (Paris: 1887), p. 21.

42. Victor Cousin, *Du bien,* with Introduction by Paul Janet (Paris: 1895), p. 18.

43. Victor Cousin, *Cours d'histoire de la philosophie moderne* (Paris: 1841), p. 1. About 2,000 people attended this course, with almost no diminution over thirty weeks.

44. Victor Cousin, *Fragments de philosophie cartésienne* (Paris: 1845), p. iv.

45. Paul Janet, *Victor Cousin et son oeuvre* (Paris: 1885), pp. 217, 475, 281-282.

46. Cousin, in fact professionalized the teaching of philosophy, giving it great prestige and raising it to a position where philosophers could not only declare their independence from theology, but could promote the desired unifying values. See Doris Goldstein, ''Official Philosophies in Modern France: The Example of Victor Cousin,'' *Journal of Social History,* Spring 1968, p. 73.

47. Simon, op. cit., pp. 124-128.

48. J. Barthélemy Saint Hilaire, *Victor Cousin, sa vie et sa correspondance,* 3 vols. (Paris: 1895), pp. 132, 42, 66, 70-72.

Chapter 3

1. Victor Cousin, *Cours de philosophie professé à la faculté des lettres pendant l'anneé 1818 sur le fondement des idées absolues du vrai, du beau, et du bien* (Paris: 1836).

2. Victor Cousin, *Du Bien,* op. cit., pp. 42-48.

3. Ibid., pp. 57, 130, 55-56, 131, 134.

4. Ibid., pp. 137, 155ff., 161-63.

5. Victor Cousin, *Cours d'histoire de la philosophie morale au dix-huitième siècle* (Paris: 1848), pp. 7, 11.

6. Victor Cousin, *Justice et charité* (Paris: 1848), pp. 7, 17, 30, 31, 21-22.

7. Ibid., pp. 40, 41, 42.

8. Victor Cousin, *Philosophie populaire* (Paris: 1848), pp. 16ff.

9. See the complete course, *Du Vrai, du Beau et du Bien* (Paris: 1853.)

10. Cousin, *Justice et charité* op. cit., pp. 44-46.

11. See Doris Goldstein, op. cit.

12. Victor Cousin, *Oeuvres de Platon* (Paris:1846), 1:3-5.

13. He claimed to have enforced respect in his university students for all faiths, and especially for Catholicism, by his vigilance over philosophy professors, his inspection

of their writings, his emphasis on the respect owed to religion by teachers of philosophy. Victor Cousin, *Défense de l'université* (Paris: 1845), pp. 62–63.

14. Hester Eisenstein, ''Victor Cousin and the War on the University of France'' (Ph.D. dissertation, Yale University: 1967), chapter 7.

15. Victor Cousin, *Les Pensées de Pascal: Rapport à l'Académie sur la nécessité d'une nouvelle édition de cet ouvrage* (Paris: 1843), pp. 156-58.

16. Victor Cousin, ''Sur le scepticisme de Pascal'' (RDM, 15 December 1844), 1:10-14, 2:354-56.

17. This work was printed in Henri Maret et. al., *Le Catholicisme et le rationalisme en France* (Louvain: 1845).

18. Paul Thureau-Dangin, *Histoire de la monarchie de juillet,* 7 vols. (Paris: 1880-1900), 5:468.

19. Cousin, *Défense, op. cit.,* p. 399.

20. Ibid., pp. 67, 81, 83.

21. *Journal générale de l'instruction publique* (November 1880).

22. Saint-Hilaire, op. cit., 3:472.

23. Janet, op. cit., pp. 251-52.

24. *Journal des écoles* (June 1847; July 1847).

25. Jules Michelet, *Cours professé au Collège de France* (Paris: 1848), pp. xii, xv, 243, 263ff.

26. *L'Avant-garde,* 1:1-2, 102.

27. Hippolyte Carnot, *Le Ministère de l'instruction publique et des cultes depuis le 24 février jusqu'au 5 juillet, 1848* (Paris: 1848), p. 7.

28. Paul Carnot, *Hippolyte Carnot et le ministère de l'instruction publique de la deuxième république* (Paris: 1948), p. 43.

29. Hippolyte Carnot, op. cit., pp. 10, 11.

30. Ibid., p. 26.

31. *Journal général de l'instruction publique,* 17:244.

32. Hippolyte Carnot, op. cit., pp. 49, 52. The most popular classics of the working man were reported to be the works of Corneille.

33. Ibid., pp. 12-14.

34. Ferdinand-Dreyfus, *L'Ecole en 1848 et le ministère de Hippolyte Carnot* (Paris: 1908), p. 14.

35. *L'Education républicaine* (May 1848; June 1848).

36. *Journal général de l'instruction publique,* 17:322.

37. Inaugurated in December, 1847, the journal included as participants Jules Simon and the young Ernest Renan, who had just left the seminary. A subscription drive in the University community was unsuccessful. Cousin did not subscribe, although the purpose of the review was to defend the spiritualist philosophy and the independence of the University. Paul Gerbod, *La Condition universitaire en France au xixe siècle* (Paris: 1965), pp. 184-85.

38. *Liberté de Penser,* 1:494-95. These arguments were first used by Condorcet.

39. Ibid., 2:174-75.

40. Edgar Quinet, *Oeuvres complètes* (Paris: 1870), 11:3ff., 11, 512, 24, 67, 81, 93, 117, 89, 107. It was Quinet who first used the term *morale laïque.*

41. Edgar Quinet, *Lettres d'exil,* 4 vols. (Paris: 1855-56). Volume 3 contains letters to those who corresponded with him in Switzerland.

42. J. Tchernoff, *Le Parti républicain au coup d'état et sous le second empire* (Paris: 1906), p. 167; Georges Cogniot, *La Question scolaire en 1848 et la loi Falloux* (Paris: 1948), pp. 109, 114–15.

CHAPTER 4

1. Joseph Ferrari, *Les Philosophes salariés* (Paris: 1849), pp. 100, 101-04.

2. *La Liberté de Penser* (March 15, 1849), 8:313-20, 439.

3. Ibid., 6:164. Jules Simon left the journal in 1850 because he believed in property rights. Georges Weill, op. cit., pp. 110-11.

4. *La Liberté de Penser* 7:1-71, 377, 625; 8:340, 601.

5. Gerbod, op. cit., pp. 264-65. Vacherot, in the Avertissement of Cousin's published course on *morale,* had insisted on the important role of reason in ethics. A Kantian, he nevertheless retained the French stress on psychology as a basis for ethics. Victor Cousin, *Cours d'histoire de la philosophie au dix-huitième siècle* (Paris: 1841).

6. *L'Avenir* (May 13, 1855), 1:9-10.

7. See Lenient, *Hommage à M. Delacour* (Paris: 1847).

8. Gerbod, op. cit., pp. 350-52.

9. *l'Avenir* (May 13, 1855), 1:9-10.

10. Ibid., (September 16–30, 1855), 1:145-46, 169-71.

11. Etienne Vacherot, *La Démocratie* (Paris: 1860), pp. 42, 60, 65, 66.

12. Ibid., pp. 70, 281, 185-86. This book caused judicial proceedings to be brought against Vacherot, and a jail sentence of one year, later reduced to three months.

13. Etienne Vacherot, *La Religion* (Paris: 1869), pp. 436, 467.

14. Etienne Vacherot, *Science et Conscience* (Paris: 1870), passim. See also his article in the RDM of June 15, 1868.

15. Barni had been Cousin's secretary in the 1840's. A student of German philosophy, he translated Kant's *Critique of Judgment* and wrote his doctoral thesis on it in 1848. He also wrote on *The Critique of Practical Reason*. His interpretation of Kant was close to Cousin's. See D. Nolen, "Jules Barni," RDM (February 22, 1875).

16. Jules Barni, *Martyres de la libre-pensée* (Paris: 1862).

17. Jules Barni, *La Morale dans la démocratie* (Paris: 1868), pp. 4, 7, 8, 9.

18. Ibid., pp. 10, 111-113, 115, 155, 171-74, v-vi, vii.

19. Vacherot, *La Démocratie* op. cit., p. 63.

20. Barni, *La Morale* op.cit., pp. xi, vii, viii. During the Empire there was much interest in American Unitarianism and the works of Channing.

21. Jules Barni, *L'Instruction républicaine* (Paris: 1872), p. 25.

22. Jules Barni, *Manuel républicain* (Paris: 1872), pp. 9-17.

23. Jules Simon, "Le Devoir," discours à la Réunion littéraire publique, February 20, 1869, p. 12. See also Jules Simon, *Le Devoir* (Paris: 1869), pp. 20-21.

24. See Theodore Zeldin, ed., *Conflicts in French Society* (London: 1970), pp. 13-50.

25. Pierre Leroux, *D'une religion naturelle* (Paris: 1846), pp. iii, iv, 4-5, 113-14.

26. François Huet, *La Révolution religieuse au dix-neuvième siècle* (Paris: 1868),pp. 304-05, 306-07, 308, 309.

27. François Huet, *La Révolution philosophique au dix-neuvième siècle* (Paris: 1871), pp. 254-55, 329-30.

28. Bernard Lavergne, *Curés, pasteurs et philosophes, conclusions d'un laïque* (Castres: 1860), p. 60.

29. M.-L. Boutteville, *La Morale de l'église et la morale naturelle* (Paris: 1866), p. 257; Patrice Larroque, *Examen critique des doctrines de la religion chrétienne* (Brussels: 1859).

30. Patrice Larroque, *Rénovation religieuse* (Paris: 1866), pp. 7, 9-10, 15, 297, appendix.

31. Lazare Caubet, *Souvenirs* (Paris: 1893), pp. 21, 8. *La Solidarité* (December 1, 1866), pp. 2-5, 6-7; (April 1, 1867), p. 55; (November 1, 1867), pp. 145-47; (December 1, 1866), p. 8.

32. Henri Carle, *Vues sur la situation morale actuelle* (Paris: 1866), pp. 3-6.

33. *La Libre Conscience*, October 17, 1868.

34. Ibid., November 24, 1866; February 16, 1870.

35. Ibid., August 15, 1868.

36. Ibid., April 28, 1869; October 2, 1869.

37. Ibid., January 29, 1870.

38. Ibid., February 26, 1870.

39. Organisation communale et centrale de la République, *Projet présenté à la nation par les citoyens* . . . (Paris: 1851), pp. 137, 139.

40. Charles Renouvier, *Manuel républicain de l'homme et du citoyen* (Paris: 1848), pp. 3, 4-5, 11, 14, 19, 25, 27, 6, 8, 32.

41. Oscar Hamelin, *Le Système de Renouvier* (Paris: 1927), pp. 23-25.

42. P. Mony, *L'Idée de progrès dans la philosophie de Renouvier* (Paris: 1927), p. 56. Mony traces successive influences on Renouvier's thought from Saint-Simon through Cousin, Kant and Proudhon.

43. Charles Renouvier, *Introduction à la philosophie analytique de l'histoire* (Paris: 1858), pp. 4, 13, 15-16, 21, 80.

44. Charles Renouvier, *Essais de la critique générale,* deuxième essai, (Paris: 1859) pp. 363-64.

45. Renouvier, *Introduction,* op. cit., pp. 82-83.

46. Ibid., p. 109.

47. Renouvier, *Essais,* op. cit., p. 365.

48. Charles Renouvier, *Science de la morale* (Paris: 1869), pp. 5-8.

49. Elizabeth Waelti, *La Morale kantienne de Charles Renouvier et son influence sur la constitution de la morale laïque dans la deuxième moitié du dix-neuvième siècle en France* (Geneva: 1947), pp. 52-53.

50. Jean Grenu, *La Philosophie de Jules Léquier* (Paris: 1936), p. 68.

51. Renouvier, *Essais,* op. cit., pp. 530, 534, 547-48, 549, 556, 557, 565ff., 671-72.

52. Renouvier, *Science,* op. cit., pp. v-vii, 2-4, 13-15.

53. Ibid., pp. 16, 74-76, 77-79, 79-81.

54. Ibid, pp. 169, 189, 483–84.

55. Ibid., pp. 525, 531, 11.

CHAPTER 5

1. Pierre-Joseph Proudhon, *Lettre de candidature à la Pension Suard* (Paris: 1926), pp. 11-12, 15, 16.

2. Pierre-Joseph Proudhon, Lettre à Pauthier, *Correspondance* (Paris: 1875), 1:161.

3. Pierre-Joseph Proudhon, *De la célébration du dimanche* (Paris: 1926), pp. 50-51, 53-57, 58, 59. Proudhon considered the eighth commandment a ban, not only on stealing, but on "any kind of gain obtained of others without their full acquiescence."

4. Ibid., pp. 61, 89.

5. Ibid., p. 42.

6. Ibid., p. 41.

7. Ibid., pp. 90-91, 93-94.

8. Lettre à Bergmann, *Correspondance*, 1:71.

9. Lettre à Muiron, *Correspondance*, 1:14.

10. Pierre-Joseph Proudhon, *De la création de l'ordre dans l'humanité* (Paris: 1927), pp. 37, 44, 121-22.

11. Lettres à Bergmann, *Correspondance*, 2:36-37, 169.

12. Pierre-Joseph Proudhon, *Contradictions économiques*, 2 vols. (Paris: 1923), 1:34-37, 41, 385, 389.

13. See *Le Peuple*, September 2, October 17, 1848; March 19, May 6, 1849.

14. *Voix du peuple*, November 4, 1849.

15. Pierre-Joseph Proudhon, *Philosophie du progrès*, (Paris: 1946), p. 83.

16. Proudhon, *Contradictions*, op. cit., 1:44.

17. Proudhon, *Création* op. cit., pp. 246-49.

18. Proudhon, *Contradictions*, op. cit., 1:367.

19. Pierre-Joseph Proudhon, *Justice dans la révolution et dans l'église*, 4 vols. (Paris: 1930), 3:432, 501. Proudhon was familiar with Kant from reading his works in translation during the early 1840s, a reading he admitted to be only superficial. However, he was impressed by them to the extent of planning to dedicate a portion of *Création de l'ordre* to the translator, Tissot; and he used Kantian terms in his works. *Création*, op. cit., 2:281; Lettre à Bergmann, November 10, 1840; Lettre à Tissot, July 31, 1842.

20. Proudhon, *Contradictions*, op. cit., 1:178, 387-88.

21. Pierre-Joseph Proudhon, *Qu'est-ce que la propriété?* (Paris: 1926), pp. 303, 303-306, 311-12, 134, 144.

22. Lettre à Cournot, *Correspondance*, 8:370.

23. Proudhon, *Philosophie*, op. cit., p. 13.

24. Proudhon, *Justice*, op. cit., 1:304, 299-300.

25. Ibid., 1:316-26, 323, 413-15, 422-24.

26. Ibid., 1:410-20, 415, 416, 424.

27. Ibid., 1:426, 328.

28. Ibid., 3:513, 517-18, 620-26, 246; 4:363.

29. Ibid., 3:360-62, 2:75-76, 149-151.

30. Ibid., 4:433; 1:314, 415, 434, 226, 217, 221, 223-24, 227-28.

31. J. A. Faucher and A. Ricker, *Histoire de la francmaçonnerie en France* (Paris: 1967), pp. 302-04, 307, 310-13, 315, 283, 193. The main effect of these pronouncements was to reduce the number of Catholic Masons. However, while not anti-Catholic, the Order became anti-clerical as soon as it was safe under the Empire to manifest such a tendency. In 1862 the Paris lodge France maçonnique was preparing to counter the influence of the Church by founding schools and libraries to extend the moral and intellectual ideas of Freemasonry. In October of that year a school for working class women was founded in the Rue de la Perle by Mme Charles Lemonnier and other women. *Monde maçonnique* 5:321ff.

32. Ibid., 5:164.

33. Proudhon, *Justice*, op. cit., 3:63ff.

34. Tchernoff, op. cit., pp. 308-09; Vapereau 4th ed., p. 122-26.

35. *Monde maçonnique*, 6:706-21.

36. Ibid., 7:161 -72, 181. Jules Favre, the editor, commented that the idea of God, like that of the republic in 1848, seemed to be "the idea that divides us most."

37. It was to take place finally in 1876. Faucher and Ricker, op. cit., p. 358.

38. *Monde maçonnique*, 8:147-57.

39. The vote was 120-80. *Annuaire philosophique,* 2:327. *Monde maçonnique*, 8:147-57.

40. *Morale Indépendante*, (August 6, 1865). Morin was a liberal Catholic, follower of Ozanam. He had written for *L'Avenir*, the *Revue de Paris* and the *Revue de l'instruction publique*. He had lost his position as a professor of philosophy by refusing to take the oath to the emperor, and taught in private schools.

41. Ibid.

42. *Morale Indépendante*, (October 8, 1865).

43. François Pillon, "La morale indépendante," *l'Année philosophique*, (1867-

68), pp. 261-362.

44. *Morale Indépendante*, (October 29, 1865). Mme. Coignet, née Gauthier, was active in women's education, and may have taught at Mme. Lemonnier's school for working women. Active in educational reform in the Third Republic, she wrote books on *morale* and other topics. As a collaborator on the *Revue bleue* she defended feminism. She also published works on French Protestantism, philosophy, and Victor Considérant.

45. *Cours de morale à l'usage des écoles laïques* (Paris: 1874); *De l'education dans la démocratie* (Paris: 1881); *La Morale dans l'education* (Paris: 1883).

46. Clarisse Coignet, *La Morale indépendante* (Paris: 1869), pp. 6, 8, 29, 62, 97-97, 102-3, 118-124, 151-54, 155, 170-73, 177-78.

47. *Morale Indépendante,* August 20, 1865.

48. Ibid., August 27, 1865.

49. Ibid., November 12, 1865.

50. Ibid., October 29, 1865. Theologically radical aspects of this first sermon had been omitted from reports in Catholic newspapers. *Monde maçonnique*, 8:470-78; *Morale Indépendante*, December 17, 24, 31, 1865. *Le Siècle* was quoted in the latter as reporting a split among Catholics on the sermons; some felt that Père Hyacinthe conceded too much to Protestants and deists. *Le Monde* failed to cover the sermons at all.

51. In 1868 the Lenten lectures of Père Félix at Notre Dame included in the lexicon of sins to be avoided atheism, materialism and *morale indépendante*. *Morale Indépendante*, March 29, 1868.

52. Ibid., April 1, 1866.

53. *Journal des débats,* April 23, 1866. Deschanel, professor of rhetoric at Louis-le-Grand and lecturer at the Ecole Normale, also defended *morale indépendante* at the dedication of a statue to Voltaire, raised through a subscription drive conducted by *Le Siècle (Morale Indépendante,* March 3, 1867). In the Third Republic, as deputy of the Seine, he continued to campaign for a secular morality. *Discours par M. Emile Deschanel, La Question des femmes et la morale laïque* (Paris: 1876). See also *Morale Indépendante,* April 1, June 17, November 18, December 23, 1866; January 20, 1867.

54. See critique of courses in *Annuaire philosophique*, vol. 4, 1867.

55. The collected works of Proudhon were published in 1868 and Masonic lodges were encouraged to subscribe to them. *Action maçonnique,* October 1, 1868, p. 351; *Monde maçonnique* October-December, 1866.

56. *Monde maçonnique,* May 1869, 12:19ff.; *Morale Indépendante* April 24, 1870. F. V. Raspail donated 5,000 francs to a Société coopérative de l'enseignement libre et laïque to found this school without religion, on the condition that *morale*, that is, rights and duties, be taught daily. *Action maçonnique*, November 1, 1869, pp. 357ff.

57. *Monde maçonnique,* pp. 148-49.

CHAPTER 6

1. *l'Opinion nationale,* November 15, 1866.

2. A. Dessoye, *Jean Macé et la fondation de la Ligue de l'enseignement* (Paris: 1882) pp. 48, 52.

3. Ibid., p. 64.

4. Ibid., pp. 68, 72-73.

5. Jean Macé, *Petit catéchisme républicain* (Paris: 1848).

6. Dessoye, op. cit., pp. 80-83, 85.

7. Ibid., pp. 90-95, 99-106, 117, vi-viii.

8. Ibid., p. 79

9. Jean Maitron, *Dictionnaire biographique du mouvement ouvrier francais* (Paris: 1965), 2:300.

10. Jean-Louis Greppo, *Catéchisme social* (Paris: s.d.), pp. 5-6, 15-16.

11. Proudhon, *Justice,* op. cit., 2:332ff.; 3:83-85, 90-99. *Capacité politique des classes ouvrières* (Paris: 1924) pp. 338-345.

12. Maitron, op. cit., 2:475-76.

13. Gustave Lefrançais, Pauline Roland, et al., *Programme d'éducation, Association fraternelle des instituteurs, institutrices et professeurs socialistes* (Paris: 1849), p. 1.

14. Lefrançais, op. cit., pp. 7-11.

15. George Duveau, *La Penseé ouvrière sur l'éducation pendant la deuxième république et le second empire* (Paris: 1948), pp. 326-29.

16. Ibid., p. 147.

17. See Christopher H. Johnson, *Utopian Communism in France* (Ithaca: 1974).

18. Maitron, op. cit., 2:403.

19. H. Leneveux, *La Propagande de l'instruction* (Paris: 1861), pp. 104-05.

20. I. Tchernoff, *Le Parti républicain au coup d'état et sous le second empire* (Paris: 1906), p. 67.

21. Auguste Vermorel, *Les Hommes de 1848* (Paris: 1869), p. 403.

22. *Courrier français,* May 20, 1863.

23. *La Jeune France* April 7, 1861, p. 89.

24. Duveau, op. cit., pp. 184-87, 194-95.

25. Tchernoff, op. cit., p. 316.

26. Ibid., p. 311.

27. Maitron, op. cit.

28. Duveau, op. cit., p. 115

29. Tchernoff, op. cit., 318, 323.

30. Duveau, op. cit., 163-65, 187.

31. Tchernoff, op. cit., 308-09.

32. Duveau, op. cit., 314-15.

33. Gustave Lefrançais, *Souvenirs d'un révolutionnaire* (Bruxelles: 1902), pp. 333-35.

34. Tchernoff, op. cit., p. 316.

35. Maxime Leroy, *Histoire des idées sociales en France* (Paris: 1950), 2:187; Georges Weill, op. cit., pp. 192–93.

36. Tchernoff, op. cit., pp. 323, 326-27.

37. Auguste Vitu, *Les Réunions publiques à Paris, 1868-1896* (Paris: 1869), pp. 10-11.

38. Duveau, op. cit., p. 314; Tchernoff, op. cit., p. 495.

39. Vitu, op. cit., pp. 16-17.

40. Ibid., pp. 18, 85.

41. *Journal Officiel de la Commune* (Paris: 1878), p. 129.

42. Duveau, op. cit., p. 45.

43. *Journal Officiel de la Commune*, op. cit., p. 253.

CHAPTER 7

1. Waelti, *La Morale kantienne* op.cit., pp. 81-82.

2. *Critique philosophique* (February 8, 1872), 1:3ff.

3. Ibid. (April 11, 1872), 1:155-56, 273, 278-280.

4. Ibid. (October 17, 1872), 2:1-2, 2-4, 6-10, 16.

5. Ibid., pp.161-62.

6. Michel Bréal, *Quelques mots sur l'instruction publique* (Paris: 1872).

7. *Critique philosophique* (May 1, 1873), 3:197-98.

8. Ibid. (July 17, 1873), 369-72.

9. L. Maury, *Le Réveil religieux dans l'église réformée* (Paris, 1891), p. 510.

10. Ferdinand Buisson, Charles Wagner, *Libre-pensée et protestantisme libéral* (Paris: 1903).

11. Evelyn M. Acomb, *The French Laic Laws* (N.Y.: 1941), p. 51.

12. Georges Goyau, *l'Ecole d'aujourd'hui* (Paris: 1889), p.72.

13. Edgar Quinet, *Histoire de mes idées* (Paris: n.d.), pp. 19, 31-33.

14. Edgar Quinet, *Révolution religieuse au dix-neuvième siècle* (Paris: 1870), p. 172.

15. Ibid., pp. 193-95, 212-14, 316.

16. Ferdinand Busson, *De l'enseignement de l'histoire sainte dans les écoles primaires* (Geneva: 1865), pp. 1-65 passim.

17. Edgar Quinet, *Lettres d'exil* op. cit., IV, 125.

18. This was the title he chose for a collection of his articles published in 1911.

19. Quinet, *Lettres d'exil* op. cit., p. 49.

20. Félix Pécaut, *Le Christ et la conscience* (Paris: 1859), pp. 430-31.

21. Félix Pécaut, *Pages choisies* (Paris: 1906), p. 30.

22. E. Paris, *Libres-penseurs religieux* (Paris: 1905), p. 51.

23. Félix Pécaut, *De l'Avenir du protestantisme en France* (Paris: 1865), pp. 44-45.

24. *Nouveau dictionnaire pédagogique*, ed. F. Buisson (Paris: 1911), p. 1536.

25. Jules Steeg, *Le Procès de la Fête-Dieu* (Paris: 1878) records the trial.

26. Jules Steeg *De la Mission du protestantisme dans l'état actuel des esprits* (Paris: 1867), pp. 26, 35.

27. Goyau, op. cit., p. 69.

28. Ibid., p. 270.

29. Buisson, Wagner, op. cit., p. 77.

30. Félix Pécaut, *Etudes au jour le jour sur l'éducation nationale* (Paris: 1879), p. ix (dated 23 mai, 1871).

31. Ibid., p. 2 (8 janvier, 1873).

32. Ibid., pp. 15-21 (2 avril, 1872).

33. Ibid., pp. 7-8.

34. *Félix Pécaut et son systéme d'éducation* ed. J.B. (Seez: 1905), pp. 12–13.

35. *Dictionnaire pédagogique* op. cit., p. 1536.

36. Goyau, op. cit., p. 270.

37. Ferdinand Buisson, *La Religion, la morale et la science* (Paris: 1900), pp. 86–87, 100–101.

38. *Ferdinand Buisson, un moraliste laïque, pages choisies* (Paris: 1933), pp. 159ff., 11.

39. Buisson, *La Religion* op. cit., p. 181.

40. Ferdinand Buisson, *Souvenirs, 1866–1916* (Paris: 1917).

41. Auguste Comte, *Announcement de la fondation de l'Association pour l'instruction positive du peuple dans tout l'occident européen* (Paris: 1848), p. 112.

42. Littré had studied medicine and linguistics, had fought as a republican in 1830, had served as editor of *Le National*. He embraced positivism in the early forties and became its chief propagandist.

43. Emile Littré, *Conservation, révolution et positivisme* (Paris: 1852), pp. 102ff., 110, 131–32.

44. Louis Navez, *Education et instruction, les idées de M. Littré* (Paris: 1880), pp. 30–33.

45. Littré, *Conservation*, op. cit., p. 131.

46. Navez, op. cit., pp. 39–41, 44–45, 47–49, 51.

47. Emile Littré, "Culture morale, scientifique, esthétique" (1849) in Jabeley, *La Religion de Littré d'après lui-même* (Paris: 1894), pp. 21, 24.

48. Gabriel Hanotaux, *Histoire de la France contemporaine* (Paris: 1903), 4:582. See also Legrand, *L'Influence du positivisme dans l'oeuvre scolaire de Jules Ferry* (Paris: 1961).

49. As early as 1870, Ferry praised Condorcet's educational plan in a speech to the Société pour l'instruction élémentaire. Jules Ferry, *Discours et opinions* (Paris: 1893–96) 1:281ff. He also referred to it in his speeches before the Chamber. Ibid., 4:127.

50. Comte esteemed highly the works of Destutt de Tracy. Emile Caillet, *La Tradition littéraire des idéologues* (Philidelphia: 1943), p. 125.

51. Ferry and Quinet corresponded during the late Second Empire, and Quinet urged Ferry to engage in politics because the Empire was nearing its end. Quinet, *Lettres d'exil* op. cit., 3:43f; 4:20–21, 46–47, 80, 95, 115, 118, 188–89.

52. Evelyn Acomb, *The French Laic Laws* (New York: 1941), p. 119.

53. Emile Littré, *Fragments de philosophie positive* (Paris: 1876), pp. 599–602.

54. *Féte anniversaire de la réception du Fr. E. Littré* (Paris: 1876), pp. 9, 14-15, 20, 91.

55. Auguste Comte, *A General View of Positivism* trans. J. H. Bridges (New York: 1957), p. 359.

56. Emile Littré, *Par quelle conduite le République française peut-elle consolider le succès qu'elle a obtenu?* (Paris: 1879), pp. 13-15. See also John A. Scott, *Republican Ideas and the Liberal Tradition in France, 1870–1914* (New York: 1966), pp. 89–194.

57. Auguste Comte, *Discours sur l'esprit positif* (Paris: 1898), pp. 20-22.

58. Ibid., pp. 118- 19.

59. Legrand, op. cit., pp. 22- 28.

CHAPTER 8

1. *Journal Officiel,* Chambre (November 15, 1878), p. 10597.

2. Acomb, op. cit., p. 122.

3. *Dix-neuvième siècle,*February 6, 1879.

4. When Ferry first used the word in the public instruction debate in 1870, there were shouts from the Right: *Barbara res, barbara vox!* Ferry insisted that the word was already part of the French language. Ferry, *Discours* op. cit., 3:243. It had been used by Quinet.

5. Ibid., 4:116, 124, 125.

6. Ibid., 3:224.

7. Ibid., 4:472.

8. See his "Discours au congrès pédagogique" on April 2, 1880, where he spoke of a long process, taking place one step at a time. The primary concentration on *obligation* and *gratuité* did not mean, he emphasized, that he was uninterested in changing the educational programs. But, first things first. Ibid., 3:513.

9. Ibid., 4:19, 21–23, 25, 29–31, 127.

10. Ibid., 4:136-39, 142, 158, 175-76, 177-78, 182, 183, 131.

11. Ibid., 4:176.

12. He had objected also in the debate on female secondary education. Who, he asked, would be capable of teaching it? Ferry had replied: you have been teaching it all your life. Ibid., p. 16.

13. Ibid., pp. 191- 93. This argument is the opposite of the one he used concerning *morale.* The point might be made that if there is only one morality, there is surely only one God.

14. Ibid., pp. 195, 197, 202, 203.

15. Ibid., pp. 208-15, 228.

16. Ibid., p. 192.

17. AN F17 12980, 1882, Section permanente du Conseil supérieur de l'instruction publique, séance du 5 juin.

18. Ibid., séance du 12 juin.

19 Ibid., séance du 21 juin.

20. Ibid., séance du 23 juin.

21. Ibid., séance du 24 juin.

22. Ibid., séance du 26 juin.

23. Ibid., séance du 28 jun.

24 Waelti, op. cit., p. 103.

25. *Critique philosophique* (August 12, 1882, Année 11, No. 28) p. 21.

26. Ferry, *Discours,* op. cit., 4:16.

27. "Rapport par Paul Janet au Conseil supérieur sur la programme des cours de morale dans les écoles normales," *Revue pédagogique,* [1881 (1), Année 4], pp. 206–09, 213.

28. France, Ministère de l'Instruction et des Beaux Arts, *Résolutions adoptées par le personnel enseignant des écoles normales primaires sur les questions soumises au congrès pédagogique, 1882-83* (Paris: 1882), 1:68, 83, 131.

29. Ibid., pp. 74, 195, 202, 265, 331, 346, 419, 431, 446, 453.

30. Ibid., pp. 167, 195, 258, 306, 479.

31. Ferry, *Discours*, op. cit., 4:360.

32. See report of first Congrès pédagogique in Paris in *Revue pèdagogique* [1881 (1) Année 4], p. 538.

33. Jules Ferry, "Instructions aux instituteurs, July 27, 1886" quoted in Senate 31 mai, 1883, *Discours*, 4:354.

34. Henri Marion, *L'Enseignement morale dans l'école primaire et dans les écoles normales* (Paris: 1882), pp. 6-8, 9-11, 12-15.

35. Louis Capéran, *Histoire de la laïcité républicaine* (Paris: 1961), 3:26-30.

36. RDM March 1, April 1, 1883, pp. 237, 710; Capéran, op. cit., p. 41.

37. Ferry, *Discours*, op. cit., 4:351, 361, 379.

38. AN F17 12980, op. cit., séance du 12 juillet, 1883.

39. Ibid., séance du 21 juillet.

40. Ferry, *Discours,* op. cit., 4:259, 261, 264–65.

41. Ibid., pp. 19–20, 14.

42. Emile Boutroux, "Les récents manuels de morale," *Revue pédagogique* (April 15, 1883), p. 296.

43. *Critique philosophique* [June 9, 1883, Année 12, No. 1], pp. 297ff. The manual, published in 1882, is not the best example of Renouvier's work; it is inferior to the 1848 one.

44. *Critique philosophique* (March 24, 1883), pp. 124ff.

45. *Critique philosophique* (February 24, 1883), pp. 55ff.

46. *Critique philosophique* (February 3, 1883), p. 29 (Année 12, no. 1).

47. *Critique philosophique* (April 14, 1883), pp. 167ff.

48. *Journal Officiel,* Chambre 1886, pp. 1577-78, 1668-69.

49. F. Lichtenberger, "l'Education morale dans les écoles à l'occasion de l'exposition universelle de 1889," *Recueil des monographies pédagogiques publiées à l'occasion de l'exposition universelle de 1889* (Paris: 1889), 2:79-80, 81, 103, 89-90, 123, 199ff., 133.

CHAPTER 9

1. For a discussion of the development of organic theories of society, see Frank E. Manuel, *The Prophets of Paris* (Cambridge, Mass.: 1962) and *The New World of Henri Saint-Simon* (Cambridge: 1956).

2. Pierre Leroux, *De l'humanité* (Paris: 1840), 1:196, 207, 217-19, 264, 256, 270.

3. Auguste Comte, *Discours,* op. cit., pp. 154ff., 118.

4. Comte, *A General View,* op. cit., p. 403.

5. Auguste Comte, *Positive Philosophy,* trans. Harriet Martineau (London: 1893), 2:460.

6. Renouvier, *Introduction,* op. cit., pp. 16, 19, 20.

7. Ibid., pp. 77, 53-57, 84, 109.

8. Renouvier, *Essais,* op. cit., pp. 547, 548, 550, 555–56.

9. Henri Marion, *De la solidarité morale* (Paris: 1880), pp. 3-5, 51-52, 5-10, 20-21, 47, 300ff.

10. For biographical details on Fouillée, see Augustin Guyau, *La Philosophie et la sociologie d'Alfred Fouillée* (Paris: 1913), Introduction.

11. Scott, op. cit., pp. 160-69.

12. Alfred Fouilée, *Critique des systèmes de morale contemporaine* (Paris: 1893),

pp. ix-x, xii-xiv, x-xi, xv.

13. Alfred Fouillée. *Morale des idées-forces* (Paris: 1908), pp. iii-iv, 11.

14. Alfred Fouillée, *La Science sociale contemporaine* (Paris: 1885), pp. 112–115, 129, 247, 256. The translation of *conscience* as the English conscience seems to be indicated once the individual consciousness is linked with others in a moral union.

15. Ibid., pp. 280, 358, 325ff., 349, 357, 360.

16. Ibid., pp. 361-62, 369, 374.

17. Alfred Fouillée, *La Propriété sociale et la démocratie* (Paris: 1884), pp. 12, 14, 18ff.

18. Fouillée, *La Science sociale*, op. cit., p. 421. Of course, the term *solidarité* had been in use in socialist circles for a long time, but it was not confined to them. Jean Macé had formed a committee of democrats in 1849 called La Solidarité républicaine.

19. For biographical details on Bourgeois, see Maurice Halbwachs, *Léon Bourgeois, 1851-1925* (Paris: 1932).

20. "Discours prononcé par M. Léon Bourgeois," *Revue pédagogique*, nouvelle série XXVII (2), Oct. 15, 1895, p. 308.

21. *Léon Bourgeois, Solidarité* (Paris: 1912), pp. 4, 6, 10, 11, 15, 16.

22. In *Science Sociale*, op. cit.

23. Bourgeois, *Solidarité*, op. cit., pp. 17ff., 23-29, 33-34, 36-37.

24. Taine's idea on *morale* as science was stated in the introduction to his *History of English Literature*, trans. H. Van Laun (New York: 1875), p. 20: "Let us seek the simple phenomena for moral qualities as we seek them for physical qualities."

25. Walter Simon, *European Positivism in the Nineteenth Century* (Ithaca: 1963), p. 76.

26. Ernest Renan, *l'Avenir de la science* (Paris: 1923), pp. 17, 31, 37, 108.

27. Charles Péguy wrote in *Cahiers de la quinzaine*, 2:74-75: "Il devint le bréviaire de toute une génération. . . . En ce livre elle reconnut ses plus secrètes aspirations. On ne peut pas imaginer l'enthousiasme avec quoi ce livre fut invoqué." Henri Massis, a student at the time of its publication, wrote to this author on Jan. 20, 1964: "*l'Avenir de la science*, ce fut la loi et les prophètes pour les jeunes universitaires de la fin du xixe siècle."

28. Bourgeois, *Solidarité*, op cit., pp. 40–42, 43–45.

29. Ibid., pp. 46–48, 70, 70–72.

30. Ferdinand Buisson, *Leçon d'ouverture du cours de science de l'éducation, Dec. 3, 1896* (Paris: 1896), p. 25.

31. Bourgeois, *Solidarité*, op. cit., pp. 73-75, 76-77, 80-81, 85- 90, 93-96, 97-99, 102.

32 Ibid., pp. 108-09, 111-14. It is clear that a basis for a radical-socialist welfare

program, including a progressive income tax, was being elaborated. The convention adopted resolutions which stopped short of that point, but they advocated, as action to insure social solidarity, education to the limit of each person's individual capacities, as well as various types of social insurance. Ibid, pp. 125-26.

33, Ibid., pp 106 ff., 119-20.

34. Alfred Croiset, *l'Education morale dans l'université, conférences et discours* (Paris: 1901), pp. 35-40, 42-44, 76, 81, 86, 92, 93, 96-98. Belot was a proponent of *morale positive*. See chapter 11.

35. Founded in 1900, the Ecole des hautes études sociales was specifically organized to work out educational programs in the social sciences, including *morale*. It gave courses and organized discussions. See *l'Ecole des hautes études sociales, 1900-1910* (Paris: 1911).

36. Bourgeois, *Solidarité*, op. cit., pp. 168-170, 179-80, 190-91, 193, 195, 197, 198, 249.

37. Alfred Croiset, *Essai d'une philosophie de la solidarité* (Paris: 1907), p. 194. This book contains the lectures and discussions on *solidarité*, other than that of Bourgeois, which took place at the Ecole des hautes etudes sociales from 1901-03.

38. Ibid., pp. 195-98, 122-24, 127-28, 123-33, 135-36.

39. Ibid., pp. 275, 277-78, 280, 281, 283- 84.

40. See Eugène d'Eichthal, *La Solidarité, ses nouvelles formules* (Paris: 1903), a series of lectures at the Adadémie des sciences morales et politiques in 1902-03, pp. 6, 13, 21, 96.

41. Ibid., pp. 27, 37.

42. Ibid., pp. 124-27. On December 5, 1902, a parliamentary *commission d'assurance et de prévoyance* formulated resolutions to serve as a basis for their work, recognizing social solidarity as a fact.

43. Alfred Croiset, *Essai*, op. cit., pp. vii-x.

44. There is a collection of these textbooks in the Musée pédagogique in Paris.

45. (Paris: 1894) p. 63.

46. Pp. 34, 37, 43. The test is tentatively dated 1900 by the Musée.

47. Underlining in the original, where the last five words are doubly underlined.

48. (Paris: 1902), pp. 12, 20ff., 28ff., 37ff., 42ff.

49. (Paris: 1905), pp. 48-50, 59-61.

50. J. Ancell and L. Douglas, *Leçons de morale théorique et notions historiques* (Paris: 1913). Marion's *Leçons de morale*, op. cit., was still used in 1914.

51. V. Martell and W. Morisse, *Cours de morale* (Paris: 1910).

52. "What would be required," declared Radical deputy Charles Couyba in the debate on the secondary education law in 1902, "in pedagogy as in politics, would be to cease resistance to the two great forces that sustain and direct the evolution of the modern world, that is, democracy and science." *Journal Officiel* Chambre, 1902, p. 615.

53. Commission de l'Enseignement, Chambre des Deputés, session de 1899, *Enquête sur l'enseignement secondaire* (Paris: 1899), 1:293, 386, 489; 2:41.

54. *l'Education et la démocratie, conférences à l'Ecole des hautes études sociales, 1902-03* (Paris: 1903), p. 78.

PART IV INTRODUCTION

1. See R. F. Betts, *Assimilation and Association in French Colonial Policy, 1890-1914* (New York: 1961).

2. Ernest Renan, *La Réforme intellectuelle et morale* (Paris: 1870), pp. 55, 47, 49, 43.

3. See Claude Digeon, *La Crise allemande de la pensée française, 1870–1914* (Paris: 1959).

CHAPTER 10

1. For Durkheim biography see Harry Alpert, *Emile Durkheim and his Sociology* (New York: 1939); Célestin Bouglé et al., "l'Oeuvre sociologique d'Emile Durkheim," *Europe* XXIII, 1930; Dominick La Capra, *Émile Durkheim, Sociologist and Philosopher* (Ithaca: 1972); Jean Duvignaud, *Durkheim, his Life and Work* (New York: 1972). On Durkheim's moral philosophy, see Ernest Wallwork, *Durkheim, Morality and Milieu* (Cambridge, Mass: 1972); also, Kurt Wolff, ed., *Emile Durkheim, 1858-1917* (Columbus, Ohio: 1960).

2. *Revue philosophique* XIX (1885), p. 99.

3. Célestin Bouglé, *The French Conception of "Culture Générale" and its Influence upon Instruction* (New York: 1938), p. 18; Lenoir, *Europe*, op. cit., p. 294; Alpert, op. cit., p. 38.

4. Ibid., p. 27. Célestin Bouglé. "Le 'Spiritualisme' d'Emile Durkheim," *Revue bleue* LXXII (1924), p. 552.

5. Emile Durkheim, "La Science positive de la morale en Allemagne," *Revue philosophique* XXIV (1887), pp. 37- 38, 43, 21, 65, 130, 179.

6. Emile Durkheim, "La Philosophie dans les universités allemands," *Revue internationale de l'enseignement* XII (1887), pp. 331, 440, 333-34.

7. Ibid., pp. 427, 437, 440.

8. Duvignaud, op. cit., p. 6; Lenoir, loc. cit.

9. Paul Lacroze, "Emile Durkheim à Bordeaux (1887-1902)," *Annales de*

l'Université de Paris Année 30 1 (1960), pp. 26, 29, 30-31.

10. Emile Durkheim, *Quid secundatus politicae scientiae institutendae contulerit* (Bordeaux: 1892); translation by Armand Cuvillier in *Montesquieu et Rousseau* (Paris: 1953).

11. Emile Durkheim, *De la division du travail social* (Paris: 1893), pp. ii-iii.

12. Ibid., pp. 39-40, 84, 86, 115.

13. Ibid, pp. 140, 181, 183.

14. Ibid., pp. 248, 367-68, 388, 389.

15. Ibid., pp. 448-49, 459-60, vi.

16. Ibid., pp. 395-434.

17. Hubert Bourgin, *Le Solidarisme universitaire* (Paris: 1942), p. viii; Scott, op. cit., p. 180; Alpert, op. cit., p. 138.

18. Emile Durkheim, *Les Règles de la méthode sociologique* (Paris: 1895), p. viii.

19. Ibid. pp. 20–35, 54.

20. A. Lucien Lévy-Bruhl, *La Morale et la science,* 7th ed., (Paris: 1902), pp. 35, 42, 67, 135.

21. Ibid., pp. 256-57, 283.

23. Albert Bayet, *La Morale scientifique* (Paris: 1905), pp. 7-8.

24. Ibid., pp. 48, 56, 59-60, 63-64.

25. Lévy-Bruhl, op. cit., pp. iii, xxix, xxiv.

26. Durkheim, *Les Règles,* op. cit., pp. 80, 93.

27. Alpert, op. cit., p. 45.

28. Lucien Herr, review of *Les Règles* in *Revue universitaire* III (2) (1894), pp. 488-89.

29. Durkheim, "La Science positive," op. cit., p. 37.

30. Durkheim, *Les Règles*, op. cit., p. 14.

31. Emile Durkheim, "Individual and Collective Representations," *Sociology and Philosophy* (Glenco, Ill: 1953), pp. 1–34. Appeared originally in *Revue de métaphysique et de morale* (May, 1898).

32. Emile Benoit-Smullyan, "The Development of French Sociologistic Theory and its Critics in France" (Ph.D. thesis, Harvard University, 1937), p. 510.

33. *Bulletin de la Société française de philosophie* VI (1906), pp. 128-29, 192.

34. Emile Durkheim, "Value Judgment and Judgments of Reality," *Sociology and Philosophy,* op. cit., p. 97.

35. For representation of Durkheim as a conservative, see Lewis C. Coser in Kurt Wolff, op. cit., pp. 211-32.

36. Indeed, his enemies claimed that it was this, and not the value of his sociology, which recommended him to the university. See Pierre Lasserre, "La Sociologie de Sorbonne ou l'école du totem," *Action française XXXII* (1), pp. 412–14.

37. Emile Durkheim, "L'Individualisme et les intellectuels," *Revue bleue* X (1898), p. 11.

38. Durkheim, *Les Règles,* op. cit., pp. 1-3; *Le Socialisme* (Paris: 1928). pp. 148ff.

39. Durkheim, "L'Individualisme," op. cit., pp. 8, 10.

40. Emile Durkheim, *Leçons de sociologie: physique des moeurs et du droit* (Paris: 1950), p. 82.

41. Emile Durkheim, *Pragmatisme et sociologie,* cours inédit prononcé à la Sorbonne en 1913-14 et restitué par Armand Cuvillier d'après des notes d'étudiants (Paris: 1955), p. 196.

42. Emile Durkheim, "The Dualism of Human Nature," Wolff, op. cit., pp. 335-38. It was originally published in *Scientia* (1914).

43. *Bulletin de la Société française de philosophie* VI (1906), pp. 116, 137.

44. See Phyllis H. Stock, *New Quarrel of Ancients and Moderns: the French University and its Opponents, 1899-1914* (Ph.D. dissertation: Yale University, 1965).

45. Raymond Lenoir, "Sur un texte inédit d'Emile Durkheim," *Annales de l'Université de Paris,* op. cit., pp. 53-56.

46. Emile Durkheim, "l'Enseignement philosophique et l'agrégation de philosophie," *Revue philosophique* XXXXIX (1895),p. 142.

47. Emile Durkheim, "Leçon d'ouverture, 1902," *Education et sociologie* (Paris: 1922), pp. 105, 111, 119, 128, 131, 132-33.

48. Emile Durkheim, *L'Education morale* (Paris: 1934), pp. 4, 5–6, 7–10, 12–13.

49. Ibid., pp. 20-29, 38, 49, 68, 73, 98- 99, 104-05, 116-17, 118.

50. Ibid., pp. 120-24, 126-32, 134-35, 138.

51. Ibid., pp. 137, 287-95, 297-98, 300-03.

52. Ibid., pp. 315-316, 318.

53. Durkheim, *Education et sociologie,* op. cit., pp. 143, 145-46, 151- 54.

54. Emile Durkheim, *L'Evolution pédagogique en France* (Paris: 1938), 1:190-93, 194-95.

55. Ibid., pp. 199, 201, 203, 211-12, 218.

56. Durkheim, *l'Education morale* op. cit., pp. 93-95.

57. Emile Durkheim, "Introduction à la morale," *Revue philosophique* CXXXIX (1920), p. 95. According to Alpert, op. cit., p. 28, Durkheim had intended to devote this work largely to a critique of Kant.

CHAPTER 11

1. *La Revue*, December 1, 1905, Anneé 2, XVI, p. 308.

2. Hubert Bourgin, *De Jaurès à Léon Blum, l'Ecole Normale et la politique* (Paris: 1938), p. 24.

3. Albert Bayet, *La Morale Laïque et ses adversaires* (Paris: 1926), pp. 34, 36, 20, 21, 24-26.

4. Among those forbidden were texts by Bayet and Payot (q.v.), as well as certain civics and history texts. Joseph Vaujany, *L'Ecole primaire en France sous la troisième république* (Paris: 1912), pp. 266–290.

5. *Journal Officiel*, Chambre, January, 1910, pp. 98. 193-95.

6. Ibid., pp. 112ff., 143-47, 161, 190, 211-23.

7. Barrès was not so much a Catholic as a nationalist who viewed the Church as a necessary element of French tradition. Stock, op. cit., 111-17.

8. *Journal Officiel*, op. cit., pp. 155ff. The invocation was provided by the University for private schools. It was published in the *Annales de la Jeunesse Laïque* (March 10, 1910), p. 295.

9. *Journal Officiel*, op. cit., p. 228.

10. Pierre Lasserre, "La Sociologie de la Sorbonne," *Action Française*, Vol.43 (1910), pp. 407, 410, 414–18.

11. *Action Française*, Vol.44 (1910), pp. 42, 46, 54–55, 63, 66.

12. Simon Deploige, *Le Conflit de la morale et de la sociologie* (Paris: 1927), p. 116.

13. *Année sociologique*, Vol. 12 (1913), pp. 326-28. In a letter (*revue scolastique*, Vol. 14, pp. 606ff.) Durkheim spoke of his debt to Comte and Boutroux.

14. Deploige, op. cit., pp. 141- 43.

15. Georges Sorel, *Reflections on Violence*, trans. T. E. Hulme and J. Roth (Glencoe, Ill: 1950), pp. 167-69.

16. See Pierre Andreu, *Notre Maître, M. Sorel* (Paris: 1953) and Daniel Halé *Péguy et les Cahiers de la quinzaine* (Paris: 1941).

17. Charles Péguy, *Oeuvres complètes* (Paris: 1916-1935), 3:409.

18. Péguy, *Oeuvres complètes* 11:278,299.

19. Henri Massis & Alfred Tarde, *L'Esprit de la nouvelle sorbonne* (Paris: 1911),

pp. 26–27, 33, 92–94. The original articles appeared in *l'Opinion* during the summer of 1910. The book includes responses to them.

20. Ibid., pp. 8, 161–8, 173–75, 70–71, 80, 120–26, 158–59, 166–67.

21. *La Revue,* Vol. 24 (August 1, 1913), pp. 351-54, 358, 363, 357, 364.

22. See G. Vincent, "Les Professeurs de l'enseignement secondaire dans la société de la belle époque," *Revue d'Histoire moderne et contemporaine* (Jan. Mar, 1966), pp. 49-86.

23. Gustave Belot, *Etudes de morale positive* (Paris: 1907), pp. 11, 111.

24. Alphonse Darlu, "La morale scientifique," *Revue pédagogique* Vol. XLVI (1905), pp. 436ff. Darlu was a lycée professor.

25. Belot, op. cit., pp. vi, 67, 35, 146, 153, 171-72, 178-79.

26. Ibid., pp. 184-87, 486-87, 503-05, 508.

27. *Bulletin de la Société française de philosophie,* Vol. VII (1908), pp. 190-91, 193-95.

28. Ibid., pp. 195-96.

29. Gustave Belot, *Les Fondements de l'éducation morale pour un libre penseur* (Paris: 1926), p. 47.

30. Dominique Parodi, *Le Problème morale et la pensée contemporaine* (Paris: 1910), pp. 42, 55, 60. He used the example of a capitalist's recognition that socialism was inevitable. Would he therefore aid its progress?

31. Ibid., pp. 62, 44, 75, 81.

32. Célestin Bouglé, "Sociologie et action sociale," *Morale générale II,* Bibliothèque du Congrès internationale de philosophie (Paris: 1905), pp. 93-94, 96-97, 101-103.

33. Célestin Bouglé, *Qu' est-ce que la sociologie?* (Paris: 1914), pp. 143, 160-61.

34. Jules Payot, *Cours de morale* (Paris: 1904), pp. 1-35, 98ff., 193-98, 208ff.

35. Arthur Bauer, *La Culture moral sux diverses degrés de l'enseignement publique* (Paris: 1913), pp. 233-34, 237-38.

36. J. Boucher, *Principes généraux de la science et de la morale* (Paris: 1920), pp. 295, 298-300, 320-321, 338- 340, 324ff, 363ff.

37. Bayet, *La Morale scientifique,* op. cit., p. 3.

38. Albert Bayet, *Précis de morale* (Paris: 1902), pp. 31, 53, 55.

39. Bayet, *La Morale scientifique,* op. cit., pp. 7, 9, 48, 56, 81, 85.

40. Emile Durkheim, *Le Suicide* (Paris: 1898), pp. 427-28, 118, 170.

41. Albert Bayet, *L'Idée du bien* (Paris: 1908), p. 2.

42. Ibid., pp. 25, 41, 46-47, 50. What Bayet meant by "better" can only be guessed. More useful, perhaps.

43. Ibid., pp. 66-67, 77, 75, 85-89, 107-109, 129-30.

44. Ibid., pp. 196-197.

45. Albert Bayet, *La Science des faits moraux* (Paris: 1925), pp. 3-4. One might ask what kind of judgments Bayet would use in making the distinction. His answer would be clear—political and social judgments.

46. Ibid., p. 13. Durkheim would have agreed here.

47. Ibid., pp. 16, 19.

48. Albert Bayet, review of Durkheim's *L'Education morale* in the *Revue philosophique,* vol. CII (1926), pp. 308-09.

49. Albert Bayet, *La Morale de la science* (Paris: 1931), pp. 22–23, 38, 54–55, 60, 69, 81.

50. Bayet in *Revue philosophique* op. cit., p. 309.

51. See Albert Bayet, *Notre morale* (Paris: 1926) and *Le Livre moral des écoles primaires* (Paris: 1928).

52. Célestin Bouglé, *Leçons de sociologie sur l'évolution de valeurs* (Paris: 1922), pp. 15-16, 34-40, 45-48, 50-51, 76, 81ff., 235, 238-39.

53. Ibid., pp. 273, 281, 184-86.

54. Célestin Bouglé, "Le 'spiritualisme' d'Emile Durkheim," op. cit., p. 551.

55. Paul Lapie, *Morale et science,* conférences faites à la Sorbonne (Paris: 1924) Avant propos p.v.

56. Paul Lapie, *La Justice par l'état* (Paris: 1899).

57. Paul Lapie, *Du Sage antique au citoyen moderne, études sur la culture morale* (Paris: 1921), pp. x-xi.

58. Paul Fauconnet, "l'Oeuvre pédagogique de Durkheim," *Revue philosophique* vol. XCIII (1922), pp. 195, 196, 200.

59. Dominique Parodi, "l'Idée de responsabilité morale," in *Morale et Science,* ibid., pp. 48–49, 52–53, 53–55.

60. Félix Pécaut, "La philosophie de la morale," ibid., pp. 48-49, 52-53, 53-55.

61. Célestin Bouglé, "La Matérialisme en sociologie," *Science morale et education,* conférences faites à la Sorbonne (Paris: 1925), p. 16.

62. Paul Lapie, *Morale et science* op. cit., pp. 11, 15, 19.

63. R. Thamin and P. Lapie, *Lectures morales* (Paris: 1931), pp. 1-39, 41, 44–45.

64. Célestin Bouglé, "Quelques souvenirs," *Europe,* vol. 33 (1930), pp. 283-84.

65. Georges Davy, "Sur Durkheim," ibid., p. 286.

66. René Maublanc, "Durkheim professeur de philosophie," ibid., pp. 289-300, 305.

CHAPTER 12

1. Henri Marion, "L'Enseignement moral dans l'école primaire et dans les écoles normales," Leçon de clôture, Ecole Normale des institutrices, Fontenay-aux-Roses, Juin, 1882, pp. 6-12.

2. Henri Marion, Leçons de morale (Paris: 1882).

3. Georges Goyau, L'Ecole d'aujourd' hui (Paris: 1910), pp. 99, 199. Perhaps its official abandonment could be dated to 1890, when Buisson attacked it in the Revue pédagogique XVII:493.

4. Georges Compayré, Organisation pédagogique et législation des écoles primaires (Paris: 1900), p. 71.

5. Ibid., pp. 62–65.

6. Henri Marion, "L'Enseignement morale dans l'école primaire et dans les écoles normales," Revue Pédagogique nouvelle série I, 5–15.

7. Pierre Giolito, Histoire de l'enseignement primaire au xixe siècle, 2 vols. (Paris: 1983), pp. 258-260.

8. Dictionnaire 1911 II, 1543-45.

9. Ernest Lavisse, A Propos de nos écoles (Paris: 1895), pp. 8-10.

10. Harrold Johnson, in M. E. Sadler, ed., Moral Instruction and Training in Schools, Report of an International Inquiry 2 vols. (London: 1908), II, 15.

11. Ibid., p. 15.

12. Ibid. p. 33.

13. Sadler, op. cit., pp. 10-11.

14. AN 71AJ¹⁹ 4, 32, 43, 47.

15. Eugene Weber, Peasants into Frenchmen (Stanford: 1976) pp. 54, 167-69, 245.

16. Edward C. Banfield, The Moral Basis of a Backward Society (Chicago: 1958), pp. 167, 48, 143.

17. François Furet & Jacques Ozouf, Reading and Writing: Literacy in France from Calvin to Jules Ferry (Cambridge, England: 1982), pp. 175-195.

18. AN 71AJ⁴⁹

19. Correspondance générale de l'instruction primaire, June 15, 1893.

20. Ibid., Nov. 1, 1892.

21. Ibid., Dec. 1, 1892.

22. Eugene Weber, Peasants into Frenchmen op. cit., pp. 23-26.

23. Barnett Singer, *Village Notables in Nineteenth-Century France: Priests, Mayors, Schoolmasters* (Albany: 1983), Chapter 6.

24. Auguste Aignan, *Notes et documents sur l'enseignement de la morale, écoles laïques de Morbihan 1895–1900* (Vannes: 1900), p. 5.

25. Robert Gildea, *Education in Provincial France* (Oxford: 1983), p. 110.

26. Ida Berger, *Lettres d'institutrices rurales d'autrefois* (Paris: n.d.)

27. Jaques Ozouf, *Nous, les maîtres d'école* (Paris: 1967) pp. 39-40.

28. Auguste Aignan, *Notes et Documents* op. cit., pp. 11-14.

29. Ibid., pp. 44, 95, 47-48, 128-31.

30. Ibid., 129-31.

31. E. Pierre, "A l'Ecole maternelle et l'école primaire de l'Exposition," *Revue pédagogique* 1900, 2 pp. 44-47.

32. AN F¹⁷ 11630 1-114.

33. AN 71AJ⁷⁸ 1346.

34. AN 71AJ⁷⁸

35. AN 71 AJ¹⁹, 43.

36. AN 71AJ¹⁹, 48; F¹⁷ 11630: 167; F. Evellin, "Rapport sur l'enseignement de la morale," *Revue pédagogique*, Nouvelle série XXXIV, 1899 p. 301; *Correspondance générale primaire*, Jan. 1, 1893, p. 65.

37. AN F¹⁷ 11630: 156 Evellin, op. cit., p. 303: *Correspondance*, Nov. 15 1894, p. 29.

38. AN F¹⁷ 11630: 120, 134, 142, 156.

39. AN 71AJ¹⁹, 43, 45, 80, 50.

40. E. Sadler, *Moral Instruction*, op. cit., p. 36.

41. *Revue pédagogique* 1887 1, nouvelle série 10, p. 64.

42. Roger Thabaut, *Mon Village 1848–1914* (Paris: 1944), pp. 233–236.

43. AN 71AJ¹⁹, 44.

44. For information about the gender- specific moral education given to girls in the Third Republic, see Linda L. Clark, *Schooling the Daughters of Marianne* (Albany: 1984).

45. C. Chabot, "Une Enquête pédagogique dans les écoles primaires de Lyon," *Revue pédagogique* XXIV 1889 1, pp. 329-330.

46. Georges Duveau, *Les Instituteurs* (Bourges: 1957), p. 124.

47. See Sally T. Gershman, "Good Workers and Good Soldiers: Attitude Forma-

tion in the Primary Schools of the French Third Republic, 1880-1914," *Proceedings and Papers of the Georgia Association of Historians*, 1986, pp. 32–42.

48. Cahier de morale, found in the Musée Pédagogique.

49. See Danielle Delhome, Nicole Gault, Josiane Gonthier, *Les premières institutrices laïques* (Paris: 1980).

50. George Duveau, *Les Instituteurs* (Paris: n. d.), pp. 145–52.

51. John E. Talbott, *The Politics of Educational Reform in France, 1918-1940* (Princeton: 1969), p. 13c-37.

52. For example, L. Emery, *Devant la vie* (Paris: 1936).

53. See G. Imbert, *Leçons de morale* (Paris: 1935).

54. See Jean Piaget, *The Moral Judgment of the Child*, trans. Marjorie Gabain (N.Y.: 1965).

55. *Correspondance* April 1, 1893 p. 166.

56. Lawrence Kohlberg, *The Philosophy of Moral Development: Moral Stages and the Idea of Justice* (San Francisco: 1981), also Kohlberg chapters in *Moral Education, a First Generation of Research and Development*, ed. Ralph L. Mosher (N. Y.: 1980).

57. Ralph Mosher in *Evaluating Moral Development*, ed. Lisa Kuhmerker, Marcia Montowski, V. Lois Erikson, (Schenectady: 1980).

58. John Rawls, *A Theory of Justice* (Cambridge, Mass: 1971), pp. 565–66, 454, 462–72, 490–91.

Bibliography

Place of publication is Paris, except where otherwise indicated.

Abadie, E. *Manuel d'instruction morale et civique à l'usage des écoles primaires.* 1894.

Acomb, Evelyn. *The French Laic Laws.* 1875-1889. New York, 1941.

Aignan, Auguste. *Notes et documents sur l'enseignement de la morale, écoles laïques de Morbihan, 1895–1900,* Vannes. 1900.

Alaux, J. E. *Manuel d'instruction morale et civique.* 1884.

Alexandre, Israel. *L'Ecole de la république, la grande oeuvre de Jules Ferry.* 1931.

Allain, E. *L'Oeuvre scolaire de la révolution.* 1891.

Alpert, Harry. *Emile Durkheim and his sociology.* New York, 1939.

Anderson, R. D. *Education in France, 1848-1870.* Oxford, 1975.

Andreu, Pierre. *Notre maître, M. Sorel.* 1953.

Ansell, J. and L. Douglas. *Leçons de morale théorique et notions historiques.* 1913.

Aulard, A. *Christianity and the French Revolution,* trans. Lady Frazer. New York, 1966.

Auspitz, Katherine. *The Radical Bourgeoisie: The Ligue de l'enseignement and the Origins of the Third Republic 1866-1885.* Cambridge, Eng. and N.Y., 1982.

Baker, Donald & Patrick J. Harrigan, eds. *The Making of Frenchmen: Current Directions in the History of Education in France.* Ontario, 1980.

Bancal, A. *Nouveau carnet de morale.* 1908.

Banfield, Edward C. *The Moral Basis of a Backward Society.* N.Y., 1967.

Barni, Jules. *Martyres de la libre-pensée.* 1862.

———. Histoire des idées morales et politiques en France au dix-huitième siècle. 2 vols. 1867.

———. *La Morale dans la démocratie.* 1868.

———. *L'Instruction républicaine.* 1872.

———. *Manuel républicaine.* 1872.

Barthelemy Saint Hilaire, J. *Victor Cousin, sa vie et sa correspondance.* 3 vols. 1895.

Batisse, L. *Régénération de la France par l'éducation.* Clermont- Ferrand, 1870.

Bauer, Arthur. *La Culture morale aux divers degrés de l'enseignement public.* 1913.

Bayet, Albert. *Leçons de morale.* 1902.

———. *Précis de morale.* 1902.

———. & Alphonse Aulard. *Instruction morale et civique.* 1902.

———. *La Morale scientifique.* 1905.

————. *L'Idée du bien.* 1908.

————. *La Morale laïque et ses adversaires.* 1925.

————. *La Science des faits moraux.* 1925.

————. *Notre morale.* 1926.

————. *Le Livre moral des écoles primaires.* 1928.

————. *La Morale de la science.* 1931.

Bayle, Pierre. *Pensées diverses sur la comète.* 1939.

Beaussire, Emile. *La Liberté de l'enseignement et de l'université sous la troisième république.* 1884.

Belot, Gustave. *Etudes de morale positive.* 1907.

————. *Les Fondements de l'éducation morale pour un libre-penseur.* 1926.

Benoit-Smullyan, Emile. *The Development of French Sociologistic Theory and Its Critics in France.* Ph.D. thesis, Harvard University, 1937.

Berger, Ida, ed. *Lettres d'institutrices rurales d'autrefois.* 1964.

————, & Roger Benjamin. *L'Univers des instituteurs.* 1969.

Bert, Paul. *Rapport au nom de la commission chargée d'examiner la proposition de loi de M. Barodet sur l'instruction primaire.* Chambre des Députés. 1879.

————. *Le Cléricalisme.* 1900.

Berthelot, M. *Science et morale.* 1897.

Betts, R. F. *Assimilation and Association in French Colonial Policy, 1890-1914.* N. Y., 1961.

Boisdé, Victor. *L'Enseignement primaire sous la Révolution.* 1908.

Boucher, J. *Principes généraux de la science et de la morale.* 1920.

Bouglé, Célestine. *Qu'est-ce que la sociologie?* 1914.

————. et al. *Du Sage antique au citoyen moderne, études sur la culture morale.* 1921.

————. *Leçons de sociologie sur l'évolution des valeurs.* 1922.

Bourgeois, Léon. *Discours d'ouverture,* deuxième congrès national d'Education sociale. Oct. 24, 1908. Bordeaux, 1908.

————. *Solidarité.* 1912.

Bourgin, Hubert. *De Jaurès à Léon Blum, l'Ecole Normale et la politique.* 1938.

————. *Proudhon.* 1901.

————. *Le Solidarisme universitaire.* 1942.

Boutteville, M.-L. *De la nécessité d'un nouveau culte en France.* 1930.

————. *La Morale de l'église et la morale naturelle.* 1866.

Bremond, E. et D. Moustier. *L'Education morale et civique à l'école.* 1929.

Brunetiére, Ferdinand. *Cinq lettres sur Ernest Renan.* 1910.

Buisson, Ferdinand *De l'Enseignement de l'histoire sainte dans les écoles primaires.* 1869.

————. ed., *Dictionnaire de pédagogie et d'instruction primaire.* 1882.

————. *Leçon d'ouverture du cours de science de l'éducation.* 1896.

————. *La Religion, la morale, et la science.* 1900.

———— & Charles Wagner. *Libre-Pensée et protestantisme libéral.* 1903.

————. ed., *Nouveau dictionnaire pédagogique.* 1911.

————. *La Foi laïque.* 1911.

————. *Souvenirs 1866 - 1916.* Neuchâtel, 1916.

————. *Leçons de morale.* 1926.

————. *Un Moraliste laïque, pages choisies.* 1933.

Bureau, Paul. *Quinze années de séparation.* 1921.

Burnichon, Joseph. *Les Manuels d'éducation civique et morale.* Marseille, 1883.

Caillet, Emile. *La Tradition littéraire des idéologues.* Philadelphia, 1943.

Capéran, Louis. *Histoire de la laïcité républicaine.* 3 vols, 1957, 1960, 1961.

————. *Histoire contemporaine de la laïcité française.* 1957.

————. *La Laïcité en marche.* 1961.

Carle, Henri. *Vues sur la situation morale actuelle.* 1866.

Carnot, Hippolyte. *Le Ministère de l'Instruction publique et des cultes depuis le 24 février jusqu'au 5 juillet 1848.* 1848.

Carnot, Paul. *Hippolyte Carnot et le Ministère de l'Instruction publique de la Deuxième République.* 1948.

Cassirer, Ernst. *Rousseau, Kant et Goethe.* New York, 1965.

Caubet, Lazare. *Souvenirs.* 1893.

Chevallier, Pierre. *Histoire de la franc-maçonnerie française* 2 vols. 1976.

Chisick, H. *The Limits of Reform in the Enlightenment: Attitudes Toward the Education of the Lower Classes in Eighteenth-Century France.* Princeton, 1981.

Clark, Linda L. *Schooling the Daughters of Marianne.* Albany, 1984.

Clifford-Vaughan, M. & M. Archer. *Social Conflict and Educational Change in France and England, 1789-1848.* Cambridge, Mass. 1971.

Cogniot, Georges. *La Question scolaire en 1848 et la loi Falloux.* 1948.

Coignet, Clarisse. *De Kant à Bergson.* 1911.

————. *De l'Education dans la démocratie.* 1881.

————. *La Morale dans l'éducation.* 1883. (First ed. under name *Cours de morale à l'usage des écoles laïques.*)

————. *La Morale indépendante.* 1869.

Commission de l'Enseignement, Chambre des Députés, Session de 1899. ·*Enquête sur l'enseignement secondaire.* 7 vols. 1899.

Compayré, Gabriel. *Histoire critique des doctrines de l'éducation.* 2 vols. 1879.

————. *Elements d'éducation civique et morale.* 1881.

————. *Organisation pédagogique et législation des écoles primaires.* 1900.

————. *Jean Macé et l'instruction obligatoire.* 1902.

————. *Félix Pécaut et l'éducation de la conscience.* 1904.

————. *Etudes sur l'enseignement et sur l'éducation.* 1907.

Comte, Auguste. *Cours de philosophie positive.* 6 vols. 1830-42.

————. *Catéchisme positiviste.* 1874.

————. *Discours sur l'esprit positif.* 1898.

————. *A General View of Positivism.* trans. J.H. Bridges, New York, 1957.

————. *Positive Philosophy.* 2 vols. trans. Harriet Martineau, London, 1893.

Condorcet, Nicolas. *Oeuvres choisies* 1893.

Cotereau, Jean. *Idéal laïque . . . concorde du monde, anthologie des grands textes laïques.* 1963.

Cousin, Victor. *Cours de philosophie professé à la Faculté des Lettres pendant l'année 1818 sur le fondement des idées absolues du vrai, du beau et du bien.* 1836.

————. *Cours d'histoire de la philosophie morale au dix-huitième siècle.* 1841.

————. *Défense de l'université.* 1845.

————. *Les Pensées de Pascal.* 1843.

————. *Fragments de philosophie cartésienne.* 1845.

————. *Oeuvres de Platon.* 1846.

————. *Justice et charité.* 1848.

————. *Philosophie populaire.* 1848.

————. *Du bien.* 1895. 3rd part of *Du vrai, du beau et du bien.*

Cresson, André, *Le Problème moral et les philosophes.* 1933.

Crocker, Lester G. *The Embattled Philosopher.* Michigan State College Press, 1954.

————. *Nature and Culture: Ethical Thought in the French Enlightenment.* Baltimore, 1963.

Croiset, Alfred. ed. *L'Education morale dans l'université, conférences et discussions.* 1901.

————. ed. *Essai d'une philosophie de la solidarité.* 1907.

Dansette, Adrien. *Religious History of Modern France.* N.Y., 1961.

Decaumes, L. et L. Cavalier. *Réformes et projets de réforme de l'enseignement français de la Révolution à nos jours.* 1962.

Delhome, Danielle, Nicole Gault, Josiane Gonthier. *Les premières institutrices laïques.* Mayenne, 1980.

Deploige, Simon. *Le Conflit de la morale et de la sociologie.* 1927.

Deschanel, Emile. *A batons rompus.* 1868.

————. *La Question des femmes et la morale laïque.* 1876.

Desjardins, Paul. *Le Devoir présent.* 1892.

Desprey, Adrian. *Massol.* 1865.

Dessoye, A. *Jean Macé et la fondation de la Ligue de l'Enseignement.* 1882.

Destutt de Tracy. *Quels sont les moyens de fonder la morale d'un peuple.* 1798.

————. *A Commentary and Review of Montesquieu's Spirit of the Laws.* Philadelphia, 1811.

————. *Rapports du physique et de la morale de l'homme, extrait raisonné servant de table analytique de l'oeuvre de P. J. Cabanis.* 1815.

————. *A Treatise on Political Economy.* Georgetown, 1817.

————. *Elémens d'idéologie.* 1827.

————. *De l'Amour,* ed. Gilbert Chinard. 1926.

Dictionnaire des sciences philosophiques. 1849.

Diderot, Denis. *Oeuvres.* 1821.

Digeon, Claude. *La Crise allemande de la pensée française, 1870-1914.* 1959.

Dreyfus-Brisac, Edmond. *L'Education nouvelle.* 1897.

Dreyfus, Ferdinand. *L'Ecole en 1848 et le ministère d'Hippolyte Carnot.* 1908.

Duprat, Jeanne. *Proudhon, sociologue et moraliste.* 1929.

Dupuy, Charles. *Livre de Morale.* 1891.

Durkheim, Emile. ''La Philosophie dans les universités allemandes,'' *Revue internationale de l'enseignement* XIII (1887).

————. ''La Science positive de la morale en Allemagne,'' Ibid., XXIV 1887.

————. *Montesquieu et Rousseau,* trans. Armand Cuvillier. 1953.

————. *Le Suicide.* 1898.

————. *De la division du travail social.* 1893.

————. *Les Règles de la méthode sociologique.* 1895.

————. ''L'Individualisme et les intellectuels.'' *Revue bleue* X, 1898.

————. *Sociology and Philosophy.* Glencoe, Ill., 1953.

————. *Pragmatisme et sociologie,cours inédit prononcé à la Sorbonne en 1913-14 et restitué par Armand Cuvillier d'après des notes d'étudiants*. 1955.

————. "Introduction à la morale," *Revue philosophique* 89 & 90. 1920.

————. *Education et sociologie*. 1922.

————. *Les Formes élémentaires de la vie religieuse*. 1925.

————. *L'Education morale*. 1934.

————. "Morale professionelle," *Revue de Métaphysique et de Morale*. XLIV (1937) pp. 527-44, 711-38.

————. *L'Evolution pédagogique en France*. 2 vols. 1938.

————. *Leçons de sociologie: physique des moeurs et du droit*. 1950.

————. *Emile Durkheim 1858-1917*, ed. Kurt Wolff. Columbus, Ohio, 1960.

Duveau, Georges. *Les Instituteurs*. Bourges, 1957.

————. *La Pensée ouvrière sur l'éducation pendant la deuxième république et le second empire*. 1948.

Duvergier, J.- B. *Collection complète des lois, decrets, ordonnances, règlements et avis du Conseil d'Etat publiées en France depuis 1789*. 1824.

Duvignaud, Jean. *Durkheim, sa vie, son oeuvre*. 1965.

d'Eichthal, Eugène. *La Solidarité sociale, ses nouvelles formules*. 1903.

Eisenstein, Hester. *Victor Cousin and the War on the University of France*. Ph.D. dissertation, Yale University, 1967.

Elwitt, Sanford. *The Making of the Third Republic: Class and Politics in France, 1868-1884*. Baton Rouge, 1975.

Emery, L. *Devant la vie*. 1936.

Faguet, Emile. *L'Anticléricalisme*. 1906.

————. *Politiques et moralistes du dix-neuvième siècle*. 1900.

Falcucci, Clément. *L'Humanisme dans l'enseignement secondaire en France au dix-neuvième siècle*. 1939.

Farrington, Frederic Ernest, *The Public Primary School System of France*. N.Y., 1906.

Faucher, J.- A. et A. Ricker. *Histoire de la franc-maçonnerie en France*. 1967.

Fauvety, Charles. *Catéchisme philosophique de la religion universelle*. 1874.

————. *Critique de la morale indépendante*. 1865.

Fédération française de libres-penseurs. *Principes de morale et d'éducation laïque*. n.d.

Ferrari, Joseph. *Les Philosophes salariés*. 1849.

Ferry, Jules. *De l'Egalité d'éducation*. 1870.

————. *L'Ecole gratuite, obligatoire et laïque*. 1881.

————. *Discours et opinions*. 4 vols. 1893-96.

Fête anniversaire de la réception du Fr. Littré. 1876.

de la Fontainerie, F. ed. and trans. *French Liberalism and Education in the 18th century*. New York, 1932.

Fortier, L. et A. B. Vistorky. *L'Education morale au cours préparatoire et au cours élémentaire*. 1964.

Fouillée, Alfred. *La Propriété sociale et la démocratie*. 1884.

————. *La Science sociale contemporaine*. 1885.

————. *Critique des systèmes de morale contemporains*. 1893.

————. *Les Eléments sociologiques de la morale*. 1905.

————. *La France au point de vue moral*. 1900.

————. *Morale des idées-forces*, 1908.

France, Chambre des Députés, Commission de l'Enseignement, Session de 1899, *Enquête sur l'enseignement secondaire*. 7 vols. 1899.

————. Ministère de l'Instruction des Beaux-Arts. *Résolutions adoptées par le personnel enseignant des écoles normales primaires sur les questions soumises au congrès pédagogique 1882-1883.*

Furet, François & Jacques Ozouf. *Lire et Ecrire*. 2 vols. 1977.

Gérard, J. *Morale*. 1898.

Gerbod, Paul. *La Condition universitaire au dix-neuvième siècle*. 1965.

Gildea, Robert. *Education in Provincial France 1880-1914*. Oxford, 1983.

Giolito, Pierre. *Histoire de l'enseignement primaire au dix-neuvième siècle*. 2 vols. 1983.

Giraud, Victor. *Essai sur Taine, son oeuvre et son influence*. 1902.

Gontard, Maurice. *L'Enseignement primaire en France de la révolution à la loi Guizot*. Lyon, 1959.

————. *La Question des écoles normales*. Toulouse, 1962.

————. *Les Ecoles primaires de la France bourgeoise*. 1964.

————. *l'Oeuvre scolaire de la troisième république*. 1967.

Goyau, Georges. *L'Ecole d'aujourd'hui*. 1910.

Gréard. Octave. *La Législation de l'instruction primaire en France depuis 1789 jusqu'à nos jours*. 7 vols. 1898-1900.

Grenier, Jean. *La Philosophie de Jules Léquier*. 1936.

Guillaume, J., ed. *Procès-verbaux de l'assemblée constituante*. 1889.

————. *Procès-verbaux du comité d'instruction publique de l'assemblée législative. 1889.*

————. *Procès-verbaux du comité d'instruction publique de la convention nationale.* 1889.

Gurvitch, Georges. *Essais de sociologie*. 1939.

Guyau, Augustin. *La Philosophie et la sociologie d'Alfred Fouillée*. 1913.

————. *Esquisse d'une morale sans obligation ni sanction*. 1885.

Guy-Grand, Georges. *La Pensée de Proudhon*. 1947.

Hippeau, C. *L'Instruction publique en France pendant la révolution*. 1883.

Habert, O. *L'Ecole sociologique et les origines de la morale*. 1923.

Halbwachs, Maurice. *Sources of Religious Sentiment*, trans. John A. Spaulding. New York, 1962.

Halévy, Daniel. *Péguy et les Cahiers de la Quinzaine*. 1941.

Hamburger, Maurice. *Léon Bourgeois 1857-1925*. 1932.

Hamelin, O. *Le Système de Renouvier*. 1927.

Hanotaux, Emile. *Doctrine religieuse et philosophique, fondée sur le témoignage de la conscience*. 1842.

Headings, Mildred J. *French Freemasonry under the Third Republic*. Baltimore, 1949.

Helvetius, Claude Adrien. *De l'esprit*. 1909.

————. *De l'homme*. 1909.

Hermand, Pierre. *Les Idées morales de Diderot*. 1923.

Horvath-Peterson. *Victor Duruy and French Education*. Baton Rouge, 1984.

Hubert, René. *Traité de pédagogie générale*. 16th ed. 1965.

Huet, François, *La Révolution religieuse au dix-neuvième siècle*. 1868.

————. *La Révolution philosophique au dix-neuvième siècle*. 1871.

———. *L'Idée de solidarité et ses conséquences sociales,* conférences, 1901-1903 Ecoles des Hautes Etudes sociales. 1903.

Imbert, G. *Leçons de morale.* 1935.

Jacob, B. *Pour l'école laïque.* s.d.

Janet, Paul. *La Crise philosophique.* 1865.

———. *Victor Cousin et son oeuvre.* 1885.

Jaurès, Jean. *Oeuvres.* 1931.

Jeannot, Camille. *La Nature et l'homme.* 1900.

Journal officiel de la Commune, 4th ed. 1878.

Kant, Immanuel. *The Metaphysical Elements of Justice.* Indianapolis & New York, 1965.

———. *Religion within the Limits of Reason alone,* trans. Theodore M. Greene and Hoyt N. Hudson. Chicago, 1934.

Kohlberg, Lawrence. *The Philosophy of Moral Development: Moral Stages and the Idea of Justice.* San Francisco, 1981.

Kuhmerker, Lisa, Marcia Mentowski, V. Louis Erickson, eds. *Evaluating Moral Development.* Schenectady, 1980.

La Capra, Dominick. *Emile Durkheim, Sociologist and Philosopher.* Ithaca, 1972.

Laloi, Pierre (Ernest Lavisse). *La première année d'instruction morale et civique.* 1891.

Lapie, Paul. *La Justice par l'Etat.* 1899.

———. *Du sage antique au citoyen moderne, études sur la culture morale.* 1921.

———. *Morale et science, conférences faites à la Sorbonne.* 1924.

———. et R. Thamin. *Lectures morales.* 1931.

———. *Morale et pédagogie.* 1927.

Larroque, Patrice. *Examen critique des doctrines de la religion chrétienne.* Brussels, 1859.

———. *Rénovation religieuse.* 1868.

Lasserre, Pierre. *Faust en France.* 1929.

Lavergne, Bernard. *Curés, pasteurs et philosophes, conclusion d'un laïque.* Castres, 1860.

———. *L'Evolution sociale.* 1893.

Lavisse, E. *A propos de nos écoles.* 1895.

———, Alfred Croiset, Charles Seignobos, P. Malapert, G. Lanson, J. Hadamard. *L'Education de la démocratie.* 1907.

Launez, H., J. Launez, L. Rascol. *Morale.* 1920.

Lefrançais, Gustave. *Souvenirs d'un révolutionnaire.* Bruxelles, 1902.

———, & Pauline Roland, etc., *Programme d'education.* Association fraternelle des instituteurs, institutrices et professeurs socialistes. 1849.

Legrand, Louis. *L'Influence du positivisme dans l'oeuvre scolaire de Jules Ferry, les origines de la laïcité.* 1961.

Leguay, Pierre. *La Sorbonne.* 1910.

———. *Universitaires d'aujourd'hui.* 1912.

Lemonnier, Charles. *Elisa Lemonnier, fondatrice.* 1866.

Leneveux, H. *La Propagande de l'instruction.* 1861.

Lenient, C., E. Vacherot, B. Saint-Marc Girardin. *Hommage à la mémoire de M. Delacour.* 1877.

Lépine, F. *Receuil de maximes et pensées morales.* 1894.

Leroux, Pierre. *De l'humanité.* 1840.

————. *D'une religion naturelle.* 1846.

Leroy, Maxime. *Histoire des idées sociales en France.* 2 vols. 1954.

Lévy-Bruhl, Lucien. *La Morale et la science des moeurs.* n.d.

Levasseur, E. *L'Instruction primaire et professionelle en France sous la troisième république.* 1906.

Liard, Louis. *Principes de morale.* 1883.

Lichtenberger, R. *Recueil des monographies pédagogiques publiées à l'occasion de l'exposition universelle de 1889.* 6 vols.

Ligue de l'enseignement, Cercle parisien de la. *Compte-rendu* 1. 1877.

————, Cercle parisien de la. *Bulletin* no. 1. 1881.

————, Congrès internationale de la. *Premier Bulletin.* 1889.

Littré, Emile. *Conservation, révolution et positivisme.* 1852.

————. *Fragments de philosophie positive.* 1876.

————. *Par quelle conduite la republique française peut-elle consolider le succès qu'elle a obtenu.* 1879.

————. *La Religion de Littré, d'après lui-même.* 1894.

Lukes, Steven. *Emile Durkheim, His Life and Work.* New York, 1972.

Macé, Jean. *Petit catéchisme républicain.* 1848.

————. *Les Vertus du républicain.* 1848.

Manuel, Frank E. *The New World of Henri Saint-Simon.* Cambridge, Mass. 1956.

————. *The Prophets of Paris.* Cambridge, Mass. 1962.

Manuel général de l'instruction primaire. Jan. 22, 1898.

Maret, Henri et al. *Le Catholicisme et le rationalisme en France.* Louvain, 1845.

Marion, Henri. *De la solidarité morale.* 1890.

————. *Leçons de morale.* 10th ed. 1899.

————. *L'Enseignement moral dans l'école primaire et dans les écoles normales.* Leçon d'ouverture, Fontenay-aux-Roses. 1882.

————. *Leçons de morale.* 1899.

Martell, V. et W. Marisse. *Cours de morale.* 1910.

Massis, Henri et Alfred Tarde. *L'Esprit de la nouvelle Sorbonne.* 1911.

Massol, Alexandre. *Morale indépendante.* Nancy, 1872.

Mayeur, Françoise. *L'Education des filles en France au dix-neuvième siècle.* 1979.

Maynes, Mary Jo. *Schooling for the People: Comparative Local Studies of Schooling History in France and Germany, 1750-1850.* N. Y., 1985.

————. *Schooling in Western Europe.* Albany, 1985.

McManners, John. *The French Revolution and the Church.* 1969.

Michel, Henri. *Notes sur l'enseignement secondaire.* 1902.

————. *Propos de morale.* 1905.

Michelet, Jules. *Cours professé au Collège de France 1847-48.* 1848.

————. *Nos fils.* 1870.

Montesquieu, Charles-Louis Secondat. *Lettres persanes.* Amsterdam, 1724.

Moody, Joseph N. *French Education Since Napoleon.* Syracuse, 1978.

————. *The Church as Enemy: Anticlericalism in Nineteenth Century French Literature,* Washington, 1968.

La Morale à l'école primaire, compte-rendu des journées franco-belges les 28, 29, 30 avril et 1 mai, 1936. 1936.

Morale générale, 2 vols., Bibliothèque du congrès internationale de philosophie. 1905.

Morale et Science, conférences faites à la Sorbonne, deuxième série, 1924.

Mony, P. *L'Idée de progrès dans la philosophie de Renouvier*. 1927.

Morin, Frédéric. *Les Idées du temps présent*. 1863.

Mosher, Ralph, ed. *Moral Education, a First Generation of Research and Development*. N. Y., 1980.

Musée pédagogique, *Programmes révisés des écoles normales primaires*. Fascicule 81. 1888.

Organisation communale et centrale de la République. *Projet présenté à la nation* par H. Belonard, Benoît du Rhône, F. Charrassin, A. Chouippe, C. Fauvety, C. Renouvier, et al. 1851.

Ozouf, Jacques. *Nous, les maîtres d'école*. 1967.

Ozouf, Mona. *L'Ecole l'église et la république*. 1963.

Palmer, Parker J. *Religion, Political Modernization and Secularization*. Dissertation, University of California, Berkeley, 1970.

Palmer, Robert R. *Catholics and Unbelievers in Eighteenth-Century France*. Princeton, 1939.

Paris, E. *Libres-Penseurs religieux*. 1905.

Parodi, Daniel. *Le Problème moral et la pensée contemporaine*. 1910.

Payot, Jules. *L'Education de la démocratie*. 1895.

———. *Avant d'entrer dans la vie, aux instituteurs et institutrices, conseils et directions pratiques*. 1897.

———. *Cours de morale destiné pour les instituteurs*. 1904.

———. *La Morale à l'école, opuscule du maître.*1907.

———. *La morale à l'école*. 1908.

Pécaut, Félix. *Le Christ et la conscience*. 1859.

———. *De l'avenir du protestantisme en France*. 1866.

———. *Etudes au jour le jour sur l'éducation nationale*. 1881.

———. *Quinze ans d'éducation*. 1902.

———. *Félix Pécaut et son système d'éducation*. Séez, 1905.

———. *Pages choisies*. 1906.

Pécaut, Pierre-Félix. *Petit traité de morale sociale*. 1902.

Péguy, Charles. *Oeuvres complètes*. 1916-35.

Pelissier, M. *Lectures morales à l'usage des écoles de filles*. 1902.

La Philosophie morale au dix-neuvième siècle, conférences à l'Ecole des Hautes Etudes sociales 1902-03. 1904.

Piaget, Jean. *The Moral Judgment of the Child*, trans. Marjorie Gabain. N. Y., 1965.

Picavet, François. *Les Idéologues*. 1891.

Poirons, Charles. *Manuel élémentaire de morale*. 1873.

Ponteil, Félix. *Histoire de l'enseignement en France: les grandes étapes, 1789-1965*. 1966.

Primaire, E. *Manuel d'éducation morale, civique et sociale*. 1901.

Prost, Antoine. *Histoire de l'enseignement en France, 1800-1967*. 1968.

Proudhon, Pierre-Joseph. *Qu'est-ce le gouvernement? Qu'est-ce que Dieu? Programme de Voix du Peuple*. 1849.

———. *Correspondance*. 1875.

———. *Contradictions économiques*. 1923.

———. *Lettre de candidature à la pension Suard.* 1926.

———. *De la célébration du dimanche.* 1926.

———. *Qu'est-ce que la propriété?.* 1926.

———. *De la création de l'ordre dans l'humanité.* 1927.

———. *De la justice dans la révolution et dans l'èglise.* 1930.

———. *Philosophie du progrès.* 1946,

———. *Ecrits sur la religion.* 1959.

Quinet, Edgar. *Oeuvres.* 1870.

———. *Histoire de mes idées.* n.d.

———. *Le Livre d'exil.* 1880.

Rawls, John. *A Theory of Justice.* Cambridge, Mass. 1971.

Renan, Ernest. *La Réforme intellectuelle et morale.* n.d.

———. *Essais de morale et de critique.* 1859.

———. *Questions contemporaines.* 1868.

———. *De la part de la famille et de l'état dans l'éducation.* 1869.

———. *Feuilles détachées.* 1892.

———. *Dialogues philosophiques.* 1895.

———. *L'Avenir de la science.* 1923.

———. *Correspondance 1846-1871.* 1926.

Renouvier, Charles. *Manuel républicain de l'homme et du citoyen.* 1848.

———. *Essais de critique générale 2.* 1859.

———. *Science de la morale.* 1869.

———. *Petit traité de morale à l'usage des écoles primaires laïques.* 1882.

———. *Introduction à la philosophie analytique de l'histoire.* 1896.

———. *Le Personnalisme.* 1903.

Ribot, Alexandre. *La Réforme de l'enseignement secondaire.* 1900.

Richer, Léon. *Lettres d'un libre-penseur.* 1869.

Ringer, Fritz. *Education and Society in Modern Europe.* Bloomington, Ind.,

Rousseau, Jean-Jacques. *Oeuvres complètes.* 2 vols. 1873.

———. *The Political Writings,* C. E. Vaughan, ed. 1962.

Rouvier, Gaston. *L'Enseignement publique en France.* Stockholm, 1905.

Sadler, M. E., ed. *Moral Instruction and Training in Schools, Report of an International Inquiry.* 2 vols. London, 1908.

Science morale et éducation, conférences faites à la Sorbonne. 1925.

Scott, John A. *Republican Ideas and the Liberal Tradition in France.* N. Y., 1966.

Séailles, Gabriel. *Les Affirmations de la conscience moderne.* 1909.

———. *Education ou révolution.* 1914.

Simon, Jules. *La Religion naturelle.* 1856.

———. *L'Ecole.* 1865.

———. *Le Devoir.* 1869.

———. *Le Livre du petit citoyen.* 1880.

Simon, Walter M. *European Positivism in the Nineteenth Century.* Ithaca, 1963.

Singer, Barnett. *Village Notables in Nineteenth Century France.* Albany, 1983.

Sorel, Georges. *Reflections on Violence.* trans. T. E. Hulme and Jack Roth. Glencoe, Ill., 1950.

Souché. A. *Le second livre de morale du jeune français.* 1936.

Spuller, Eugène. *Au Ministère de l'instruction publique.* 1894.

Steeg, Jules. *De la Mission du protestantisme dans l'état actuel des esprits.*1867.

———. *Le Procés de la fête-dieu.*1878.

———. *Instruction morale et civique.* 1882.

———. *La Vie morale.* 1892.

Stock, Phyllis H. *New Quarrel of Ancients and Moderns: The French University and Its Opponents, 1899-1914.* Ph.D. dissertation, Yale University. 1965.

Strumingher, Laura S. *What Were Good Little Boys and Girls Made Of? Primary Education in Provincial France, 1880-1914.* Albany, 1983.

Sue, Eugène. *Lettres sur la question religieuse,* preface by Edgar Quinet. Bruxelles, 1857.

Taine, Hippolyte. *History of English Literature,* trans, H. Van Laun. N. Y. 1879.

Talbott, John E. *The Politics of Educational Reform in France, 1918-1940.* Princeton, 1969.

Tchernoff, J. *Le Parti républicain au coup d'état et sous le Second Empire.* 1906.

Thabault, Roger. *Mon Village, 1848-1914.* 1944.

Thalamas, A. *Rapport sur l'enseignement de la morale laïque.* 1904.

Thibaudet, Albert. *La République des professeurs.* 1927.

Thomas, Jules. *Principes de philosophie morale.* 1890.

Thureau-Dangin, Paul. *Histoire de la monarchie de juillet.* 7 vols. 1880-1900.

Tissot, Claude-Joseph. *Principes de morale.* 1866.

Turgot, Anne-Robert Jacques. *Oeuvres.* 1884.

Vacherot, Etienne. *La Démocratie.* 1860.

———. *La Religion.* 1869.

———. *La Science et la conscience.* 1870.

Vaujany, Joseph. *L'Ecole primaire en France sous la troisième république.* 1912.

Vermorel, A. *Les Hommes de 1848.* 1869.

Vignery, Robert J. *The French Revolution and the Schools.* Madison, 1965.

Vitu, Auguste, *Les Réunions publiques à Paris 1868-1869.* 1869.

Vial, Francisque. *L'Enseignement secondaire et la démocratie.* 1901.

Vincent, Gérard. *Les Professeurs du second degré.* 1967.

Waelti, Elizabeth. *La Morale kantienne de Charles Renouvier et son influence sur la constitution de la morale laïque dans la deuxième moitié du dix-neuvième siècle en France.* Geneva, 1947.

Wallwork, Ernest. *Durkheim, Morality and Milieu.* Cambridge, Mass, 1960.

Weber, Eugene. *Peasants into Frenchmen.* Stanford, 1976.

Weill, Georges. *L'Enseignement secondaire en France.* 1921.

———. *Histoire de l'idée laïque au dix-neuvième siècle.* 1925.

Wolff, Kurt, ed. *Emile Durkheim, 1858-1917.* Columbus, Ohio, 1960.

Wylie, Laurence. *Village in the Vaucluse.* N.Y., 1964.

Zeldin, Theodore, ed. *Conflicts in French Society.* London, 1970.

PERIODICALS

Action français
L'Action maçonnique
L'Avenir
Annales de la jeunesse laïque
L'Année philosophique
Année sociologique
Annuaire philosophique
Archives de sociologie européenne
L'Avant-Garde
Bulletin du Grand Orient
Bulletin de la Société française de philosophie
Cahiers de la quinzaine
Critique philosophique
Correspondance générale de l'instruction primaire
L'Ecole nouvelle
L'Education morale, cahiers de pédagogie moderne
L'Education républicaine
La Liberté de Penser
La Libre Conscience
La Jeune France
Journal des débats
Journal des écoles
Journal générale de l'instruction publique
Journal officiel de la Troisième République, Chambre.
La Libre-Pensée/La Pensée nouvelle
Le Mercure de France
Le Monde maçonnique
La Morale indépendante
L'Opinion
Le Peuple/Voix du peuple
La Solidarité
Revue bleue
Revue philosophique
Revue des deux mondes
Revue française de sociologie
Revue d'histoire moderne et contemporaine
Revue internationale de l'enseignement
Revue de métaphysique et de morale
Revue pédagogique
Revue philosophique
Revue universitaire

Index